INDOOR GARDENING
WITH THE
AID OF ARTIFICIAL LIGHT

The cover picture of this book is that of The Royal Borough of Kensington &
Chelsea's, Chelsea Flower Show Exhibit of 1989. This entry was entitled: 'The
Garden of T.. Medal.

034533

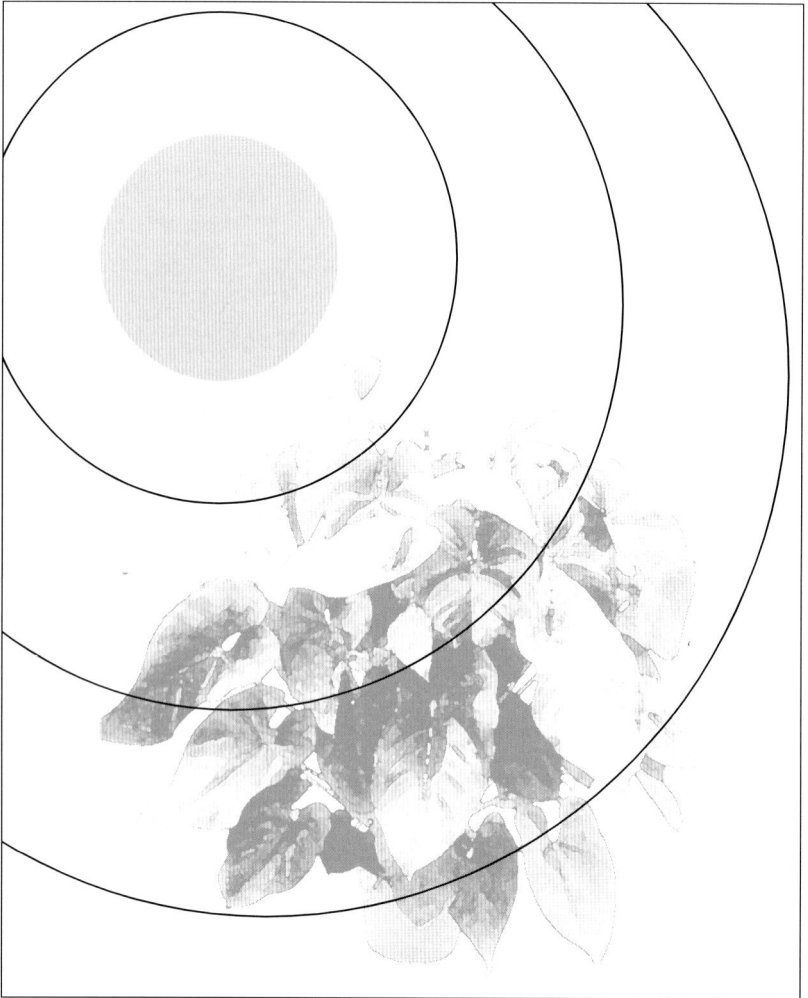

THIS DRAWING SERVES TO ILLUSTRATE THE IMPORTANCE OF LIGHT TO PLANT LIFE.

Light is a form of energy, and the light source at the top left is providing the *Anthurium* (Flamingo Plant) with a pool of light energy.

Some of this light energy is absorbed by the leaves, and plays an essential role in its life processes.

Some of the light is reflected by the plant, thus giving it its characteristic colours, whilst any that remains and serves neither of these two purposes passes straight through.

It is not simply the intensity of the light which is important, but also its spectral composition and duration, and this book serves to provide the reader with a clear understanding of all that needs to be known about gardening indoors with the aid of artificial light.

This is the most exciting and innovative new book on indoor gardening for many years.

It contains a great deal of fresh information on this fascinating subject and moves the art of indoor gardening into an entirely new era.

"John must be congratulated on his persistence in getting this book published. His shear enthusiasm for his subject and his endeavour to give even the "armchair" gardener the opportunity to sow seeds and watch them grow has to be admired"

Terry Felstead

Indoor Gardening
with the
aid of artificial light

By

John C Dale
FILAM, MIAM, FLS

William Sessions Limited
York, England

DEDICATION
To my dear wife, Ann Margaret Dale,
without whose encouragement, help, and forbearance
this book and its predecessors could not have been written.

Printed in 10 point Times New Roman
from Author's Disk
by Sessions of York
The Ebor Press
York, England

CONTENTS

AUTHOR INFORMATION

John C. Dale, F.I.L.A.M., M.I.A.M., F.L.S., is an author, novelist, plant photographer, and lecturer, who has devoted the whole of his life to his chosen profession. His early experience was gained in commercial horticulture, before moving on into local government. This is his fourth book.

For some twenty years he served The Royal Borough of Kensington and Chelsea, and during his time there held the posts of Parks and Cemeteries Manager, and Amenities Officer Technical, and he was, for many years, regularly to be seen at the Chelsea Flower Show, and The Royal Horticultural Society's late autumn show, creating magnificent award winning exotic plantscape exhibits, with superb specimens of indoor plants.

At the 1986 Chelsea Flower Show he had the honour of being introduced to Her Majesty The Queen, when she visited the exhibit entitled, 'Treasure Island'. The Royal Borough has long been renowned for its horticultural excellence and won an impressive collection of The Royal Horticultural Society's* medals, including the much coveted, Gold Medals.

John is fascinated by the miracle of the green leaf, as photosynthesis is the basis of all life on Earth**, and he says that the cultivation of plants is an affirmation of one's faith. That this is true in his case is witnessed by his devotion to plant cultivation and the considerable expertise he has exercised in the compilation of this remarkable book on gardening indoors with the aid of artificial light. This is the first <u>English</u> book to cover this subject in such detail, and it has been written especially for the benefit of all the millions of amateur indoor gardeners everywhere.

* The Royal Horticultural Society is the world's leading horticultural organisation.

** **The Miracle of the Green Leaf** (See Page 187).

PREFACE

A knowledge of the benefits which artificial light can bestow on ornamental indoor plants, will permit indoor gardeners to improve their cultural skills and extend the range of plants which they can grow successfully.

What artificial light cannot do is enable them to grow all their indoor plants entirely independent of natural light. Some of the plants can be grown completely independent of natural daylight, others become more floriferous with its assistance. There are also other flowering plant species, which need some summer sunlight, before they will bloom.

Light, is one of the most important single factors which affects the growth and development of plants indoors, and it has been the lack of this in the past which has restricted what could be grown, or maintained indoors.

Special growth lamps are not necessary for this form of indoor gardening. Ordinary domestic fluorescent tubes of the 'Cool White and 'Warm White' types serve the purpose quite adequately and provide good colour rendering to plants. And with the introduction of the newer energy efficient more compact fluorescent lamps there is the added potential for energy saving while at the same time creating pools of high intensity illumination for one's choice plants.

INTRODUCTION

With the aid of artificial lighting the indoor gardener is able to grow a larger selection of plant species than previously, providing their other general cultural requirement can be met.

This method of cultivation however does have its limitations. For while it is feasible to grow almost anything indoors, with the application of sufficient artificial lighting, (and here I am talking of light levels in the region of 60,000 lux to 80,000 lux), the light intensity under the lamps recommended in this guide does not exceed the 15,000 lux level, attainable with the use of the ordinary readily available domestic type fluorescent lamps.

These lamps provide the amateur indoor gardener with the most cost effective means of providing plants with light. A single compact energy efficient lamp of 38W rating for example will provide a light level of some 13,000 lux and is very cheap to operate. The reader need possess nothing more than a desk lamp, fitted with a fluorescent tube in order to start with this type of indoor gardening in the first instance.

See Slide C26. A Gold Medal winning display of exotic foliage plants on the grand scale at the Chelsea Flower Show 1988. The exhibitor – Anmore Exotics.

The range of exotic foliage plants, which can be grown and maintained indoors, is quite extensive, and their life expectancy may be anything from one to four or more years, depending on the plant species concerned.

Flowering plants by comparison need higher light levels than do the foliage plants, if they are to sustain themselves and remain floriferous for any length of time. The appropriate intensity of light, which they will require, may be found in the Indoor Light-Garden. Here some flowering pot-plants will be entirely at home throughout their life cycle. Other plants however, may need the full brilliance of natural summer sunlight, or a lightly shaded spot outdoors, before they will produce their flower buds and bloom indoors later in the year. Acacia, Azalea, Chrysanthemum, Cyclamen, Cytisus, Hydrangea, Kalanchoe, and Schlumbergera, are examples of such plants. So the indoor gardener should take full advantage of this, by putting these and other sun-loving plants outdoors during the summer months.

Even so, sun-loving plants can still benefit from the provision of some additional artificial lighting when they are returned indoors. This serves not only for their better illumination whilst on display, but also as a means of maintaining and promoting their well-being. Light is as essential to indoor plants as oxygen is to our selves, and without an adequate supply of this, they will soon deteriorate and perish.

I must also stress here that some of our indoor plants are not purely orna-mental in character, they are positively beneficial to our own health and well-being! This is because they improve the quality of the air we breathe by their action in consuming the chemical pollutants that lurk in our homes, so this is a further good reason for their cultivation indoors. (See The Importance of Indoor Plants as Air-filters pages 112-113.)

Artificial Light Applications

Artificial light, may be applied by the indoor gardener in various ways*:

1. To supplement the amount of natural light entering the room where plants are grown. This is especially effective where foliage plants are concerned, as this can be achieved at little expense.

2. As decorative plant lighting for house plants and flowers in the home, and in the office situation. Here the light serves not only as an additional deco-rative element, in that it highlights the colours of the foliage, or flowers it illuminates; it also assists in maintaining the plants.

3. It may completely replace daylight in rooms where the daylight would oth-erwise be too poor to support plant life on its own.

    The needs of ornamental foliage plants would be the easiest to satisfy in this direction, but flowering plants would need a much higher light intensity, if flowering was to be induced. Even so, it would not be possible to meet the needs of all the indoor pot-plants as some require a high degree of bright summer sunlight before flower bud initiation takes place. Such plants are normally bought and brought indoors when their flower buds are showing colour, and then discarded with once flowering ceases. Nevertheless, the indoor light gardens described within these pages provide a high enough intensity of light, to enable the indoor gardener to achieve far more than was possible previously.

4. Artificial light may be used as a substitute for natural daylight, not only for the cultivation of a range of ornamental plants, but also for propagating plants from seeds and cuttings. This has been done commercially for many years past, and amateur gardeners may now use the same techniques for their own benefit.

    These methods are not limited simply to ornamental species indoors, but also extend to some outdoor plants in due season e.g., summer bedding plants, and garden vegetables. A limited range of edible crops may also be produced indoors with the aid of artificial light. In short, with the introduc-tion of artificial light, the future could not be brighter for the indoor garden!

*But one needs to possess nothing more than an ordinary desk lamp fitted with a fluorescent tube to begin trying out this type of indoor gardening, in the first instance.

A New Approach To Indoor-Gardening

Cultivating plants indoors has become an increasingly popular pastime in recent years. Seasonal plants bloom on sunny windowsills, and permanent arrays of foliage decorate every niche with tolerable growing conditions. Indoor gardening is, however, undergoing a revolution: Previously unforeseen opportunities are now available to all those who love to live with plants. If you have patiently coaxed your plants to survive through the winter, and wondered at the lush displays that seem to flourish without daylight in hotel foyers and large office blocks, the key to your own year around success is now available-a simple, efficient, attractive, and inexpensive way of using electric lighting to stimulate the full development of plants.

This kind of indoor light gardening is adapted from methods used by commercial plant growers and plantscape designers. There is no need for special plant lamps. The "secret" lies in the measured use of ordinary domestic fluorescent lighting. All the equipment is readily available and easily installed, and no structural alterations are required to bring the pleasure of a full-scale garden into your home. Space need not be a limiting factor, either, as you will find a number of new ideas for small-scale garden features. Your indoor garden can be designed to correspond perfectly to the conditions in which you live, and the amount of time you wish to spend with your plants.

The practice of growing plants indoors has a long history. The Romans are known to have grown tender plants out of season during their occupation of Britain two thousand years ago. Glass structures for plant cultivation go back to the seventeenth century, but did not become really efficient until two centuries later, when huge metal and glass conservatories were erected for exotic and flowering plants. Interest in growing plants at home led to the building of attached conservatories for year-round foliage species and for flowering plants, which were moved into the house once they were in bloom. Within the rooms, however, plant cultivation was limited to the most tolerant foliage species-the enduring aspidistras, rubber plants, and ferns that could adapt to lower light levels.

Light is a vital factor in plant growth. The small amount of natural light that enters an enclosed space has always been the main disadvantage of indoor gardening. With the superior insulation and improved heating systems of modern houses, it has become possible to control room temperature and humidity. Even with large window areas, however, the relatively low levels of illumination provided by standard electric lighting and seasonal daylight variations have restricted the variety, quality, and healthy development of indoor plants.

Our new method of measured electric lighting will allow you to gain complete control over all aspects of your indoor garden. Every day becomes a good day for plant cultivation. By simply adjusting the time of starting your plants and understanding their light requirements at all stages, they can be made to produce foliage and flowers at the preferred time, independent of their natural cycles.

A remarkable interior plantscape can be created if you have a whole room available for your garden. In modern homes, there may be a spare bedroom, family room, attic, or entrance hallway that can be transformed into a garden area. If there is not a full room to spare, your indoor garden can be incorporated into a room used for other purposes. Even if you are restricted to a tiny apartment or only one room, suitable lighting can be installed in the most unpromising places, and a shelved alcove, or room divider, can spring into life as an attractive environment for plants. If none of these suggestions seem plausible, then you can make a start with the cultivation of a few plants that are illuminated by a desk lamp equipped with a fluorescent tube. You will be surprised what a difference the application of some additional light can make to just a few Saintpaulias (African Violets) for example, for they will very quickly become much more floriferous than those which have previously been cultivated without the benefit of improved illumination. Indeed, at the opposite end of the scale of indoor gardening, if you have always wanted to have your own special feature indoor ornamental tree, in the lounge or dining room, by improving the lighting in the immediate vicinity of this special room feature, this can be achieved, assuming always that its other cultural requirements can also be satisfied.

A shelved alcove.

All indoor spaces are far better insulated than greenhouses, and benefit from the heating supplied to the rest of the home. In colder months, if the house is warm enough for your own needs, you can enjoy your plants at little or no extra heating cost.

Indoor gardening is a delightful and absorbing pastime for people of any age. It is of particular value for the elderly and disabled, as the scale of the garden can

4

be tailored to suit one's abilities. Within a compact and well-organized area, it is possible to enjoy the growth of established plants, to propagate new ones, and even to develop small-scale edible crops, which give a special satisfaction. An indoor garden provides a simply achieved opportunity to use your gardening talents in comfortable and controlled surroundings.

There are three general types of indoor garden-the garden room, the light garden, and the working garden, which can all occupy the same room, or be located separately. Between them, they offer a complete range of activities that may be pursued together, or selectively, as space and leisure permit.

The garden room

A garden room is a plant display area-a whole or part of a room for cultivating and exhibiting a wide range of foliage and flowering species. Fluorescent lights are spaced evenly across the ceiling for a much higher level of illumination than is usually provided indoors. Both the quality and intensity of the light encourage the plants to grow and flourish. The garden room can be devoted solely to plant display, or it may include a living space, with chairs, tables, and perhaps a music system to create a complete sanctuary.

If you cannot spare a full room for an indoor garden, you can apply the same principles to one section of a room to create a growing wall, alcove or corner plantscape, leaving the rest of the room for day to day living, with the usual furnishings. You can also make use of hanging baskets, window boxes, and self-watering planters for special displays (See Watering Systems.)

Garden room – wall garden.

5

The light garden

A number of flowering plants, including Begonias, Bromeliads, Gloxinias, Orchids, Saintpaulias, and others, grow more vigorously with a higher light intensity than can be achieved in a garden room. To provide sufficient light to cultivate these plants, you can create a light garden-a relatively small area where the plants are placed close to the fluorescent lighting. Here they bathe in a pool of intensely bright light.

You can build a light garden in a small, specially constructed open box-like unit, or install lights in existing shelves, a bookcase, or even in an adapted piece of furniture, such as a sideboard. Even if you live in one small, dark room you can still have a flourishing light garden offering fresh foliage and flowers for your pleasure year round. If you have more space, you can set up a variety of light garden features in different parts of your home. Alternatively, the light garden can be a specialized display unit within a garden room, providing ideal conditions for propagating plants from seed or cuttings. While a single fluorescent tube is enough to start a light garden beautifully massed with flowering plants, a progressive increase in the lighting power and intensity will put all forms of indoor cultivation within your reach.

A coffee table light garden.

The working garden

An extension of the light garden principle, a working garden can be installed in a converted pantry, or coalhouse, where there is no natural light at all, or so very little that it is of no significance. In the working garden you can cultivate plants for display in your garden room, light garden, or elsewhere in your home. A working garden enables you to develop a special interest in particular species, to increase your stock of plants by propagation, or to grow foods, such as herbs and salad crops, which otherwise are not available to the indoor gardener.

See Slide D9. A light garden with two propagation units and some recently rooted plants.

The working garden functions like a potting shed or a greenhouse, except that all the light is electric. The plants in a working garden are not intended to be on show, so they can be massed in ranks to fill the space. All that is required is a convenient arrangement, that allows you to move and handle the plants as necessary, the special value of the working garden is that it can be maintained in a secluded, otherwise dark place, but if you have no obvious space for it, you can design it as part of the full garden room or as a single, small light garden area.

Designing your plantscape

Once you have fitted your garden area with lights and any necessary furnishings, you are ready to introduce the plants you want to grow into their new home. Within the chapters on the garden room and light garden are suggestions for designing attractive plantscapes.

Understanding plant names

Horticultural writers are sometimes criticised by their readers for giving plants their scientific names when it is thought their common names would do just as well. However it has to be appreciated that not all plants have common names, and a number of plants often share the same common name, or have different common names in different regions, moreover a common name in one language is not understood in others, and is therefore useless in plant identification. Hence the need for an acceptable system of plant classification, which provides every plant with a name which is understood and accepted throughout the world.

Over the centuries there were many attempts to establish a generally acceptable system of plant classification, and while some gained favour for a time they were later discarded. But this chaotic state of affairs was finally resolved by an eighteenth century Swedish physician named Carl von Linne (now affectionately remembered by the Latinised version of his name, Linnaeus). He devised a binominal or two word name for systematically categorizing plants, and used a simplified form of Latin for naming and describing them, so that botanists and plants people everywhere would know exactly which plants were being discussed. The system gained universal acceptance and it is the 'one,' which remains the basis of all plant classification today.

See Slide F15. *Neoregelia* 'Madam Van Durme'.

While the scientific names may first seem long and sometimes difficult to pronounce, they are built up quite logically of two words. The first part is the genus (surname), and it includes those plants that have a similar structure. The second part of the name is the species (first name), and is given to only one plant within the genus (although a specific species name can be used again in other genera). Both the species and genus are always in Latin. The name of the genus always begins with a capital letter and the name of the species with a small letter, and both names are written in italics. For example *Ficus deltoidea* (Mistletoe fig), *Ficus benjamina* (Weeping fig), *Ficus pumila* (Climbing fig, Creeping fig) are Latin names describing three different species within the genus *Ficus*.

When natural variations in species occur in the wild, these variations, which are known as varieties, are given names that begin with a small letter, usually in italics. These may or may not be in Latin. For example, the species *Aechmea fulgens* has stiff green leaves which are dusted grey, while its variation, *Aechmea fulgens* var. *discolor*, has stiff leaves which are deep green on their upper surface and purplish on their lower surface.

We have also improved wild plant species by hybridisation (making crosses between two species), and the resulting variation is known as a cultivar. The name of a cultivar is set within single quotations, is capitalized, and is not in italics. Examples are *Anthurium crystallinum* 'Illustre' and *Nephrolepis exaltata* 'Fluffy Ruffles'.

The symbol X before a plant name indicates that it is a hybrid of species from different genera. An example is X*Fatshedera lizei*, a cross between *Fatsia japonica* 'Moseri' and *Hedera* 'Hibernica'.

The genera are grouped together in larger plant families that have certain characteristics in common. For example, the BROMELIACEAE family, which is mostly epiphytic, includes *Aechmea, Ananas, Billbergia, Cryptanthus, Fascicularia, Guzmania, Neoregelia, Nidularium, Tillandsia*, and *Vriesea*, almost all of which have stiff leaves forming a rosette capable of holding water, and an inflorescence (flower cluster), often with pretty coloured bracts.

Another is the MARANTACEAE family, including *Calathea, Ctenanthe, Maranta*, and *Stromanthe*, which are all fancy foliage plants whose leaves are patterned in feathery, attractive designs, with generally inconspicuous flowers.

The Latin plant names used in this book generally conform to those listed in **The New Royal Horticultural Society DICTIONARY OF GARDENING** published in the United Kingdom by THE MACMILLAN PRESS LIMITED, 1992 and published in the United States of America and Canada by THE STOCKTON PRESS, 1992. Where some names of long horticultural usage have changed synonyms have been provided to assist the reader. (See pages 179-180 **Plant Nomenclature**) (See also pages 181-186, **SOME COMMON NAMES OF EXOTIC PLANTS**.)

PLANTS AND LIGHT: SOLAR RADIATION

See Slide D25. This slide serves to illustrate that all light energy is one.

Some facts about the Earths's source of light – the Sun.

Without the presence of the light energy of the Sun, Earth would be a very dark, cold, lifeless planet

Earth: diameter 25,000 miles

The Sun: diameter 865,000 miles

The distance from the Sun to Earth is 92,000,000 miles

It is estimated that the Sun's mass is being converted into energy at the rate of approximately 120 million tons every minute. This awesome mass of energy is released as the result of a thermo-nuclear reaction, which converts hydrogen atoms into helium atoms and it is then projected into space in all directions in the form of electromagnetic radiation.

This electromagnetic energy is more generally referred to as solar radiation and it is composed of a whole mass of different things such as cosmic rays, gamma rays, X-rays, Ultra-violet rays, visible light (the visible spectrum), infra-red rays, heat radiation and subsequently leads on into that area of radiation related to radar, television and radio frequencies.

The light of day is the light of all life, not solely of plant life. Although our sun is a star of quite tiny proportions in relation to most of the myriad other stars in the universe, it is vastly larger than the earth: its diameter is 865,000 miles, while the earth's is only 25,000 miles. The sun sends forth in all directions a tremendous stream of light and heat that could quite easily supply 2,000 million planets like the earth with all their requirements for warmth and illumination.

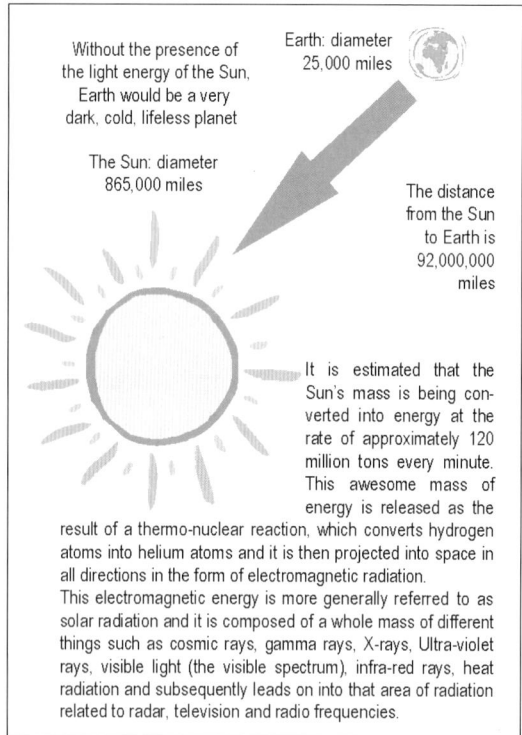

This stream of energy from the sun (solar radiation) is composed of many different elements. Cosmic rays, gamma rays, x-rays, and ultraviolet rays are followed in the electromagnetic spectrum by the range of visible light, which is followed by infrared rays, and finally by those related to radio frequencies. The visible light, which concerns us here, represents a very, very, small fraction of the sun's total emission.

Although sunlight appears to be white or colourless to the human eye, the visible light spectrum is composed of the seven colours of the rainbow: violet, indigo, blue, green, yellow, orange, and red, collectively referred to as the solar spectrum. The colour of light is properly described by its wavelength, that is, the space between complete cycles of vibrational energy for that colour. Wavelength is usually measured in nanometers (nm) or billionths of a meter.

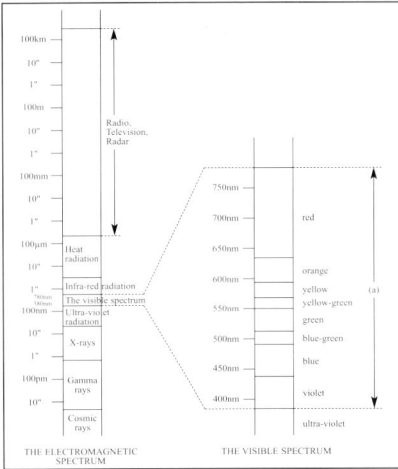

THE ELECTROMAGNETIC SPECTRUM

THE VISIBLE SPECTRUM

The electromagnetic spectrum, the visible light spectrum.

In sunlight, plants are able to use those parts of the solar spectrum which best meet their needs at the various stages of their life cycles: germination, growth, flowering, and dormancy. They make most use of red light (610-700nm), and also use violet/blue light (400-510nm), but to a lesser extent. Plants make little use of the light in the green and yellow parts of the visible spectrum.

The graph shows the various types of electromagnetic radiation in sunlight, arranged according to wavelength. Wave-length is measured in meters; km = kilometer; m = meter; mn = millimetre (one thousand of a meter); um = micrometer (one millionth of a meter); nm = (one billionth of a meter), pm = picometer (one trillionth of a meter. Visible light is a tiny part of the total spectrum-from 380nm to 780nm-only 400nm in total.

The top graph indicates the absorption characteristics of chlorophyll that has been extracted from leaves. Note the double peaks in the blue and red wavebands. Chlorophyll within plants has a far less pronounced pattern of absorption due to the presence of other pigments, leaf age*, leaf thickness, leaf temperature, and the light scattering properties of the leaf cells. This more general utilisation of light for photosynthesis does not extend to the other physiological responses as these are far more closely linked to the spectral quality of light. (See the general response of plants to the visible light spectrum on page 16).*Young leaves are more efficient than older ones.

The bottom graph illustrates the more general utilization of the visible light spectrum for photosynthesis in leaves of various thickness.

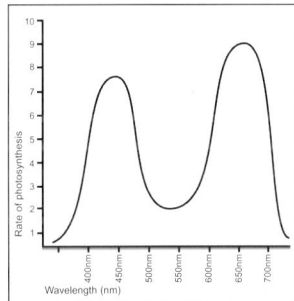

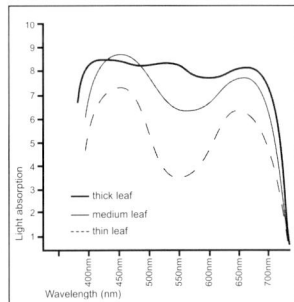

11

Photosynthesis

The light energy of the sun stimulates a process that is unique to plant life but is vital to every form of life on earth: the process of photosynthesis. Photosynthesis means the building up of food substances within the leaves, in the presence of light. It occurs through the action of light on the green pigment chlorophyll, which is present in all plants in the leaves and some green stemmed plants. (In some variegated plants there is little or no green colouring in the leaves, but chlorophyll is still an essential component, overlaid by other pigmentation.)

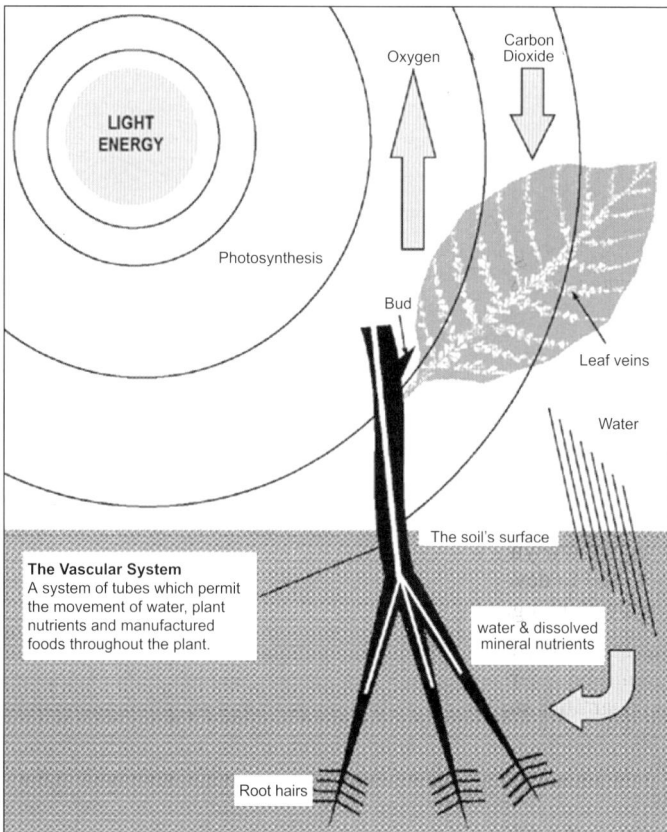

Under the influence of light energy, chlorophyll manufactures food substances from carbon dioxide that has to be absorbed from the air and combined with water obtained through the plant's roots. During this process a sugar, the

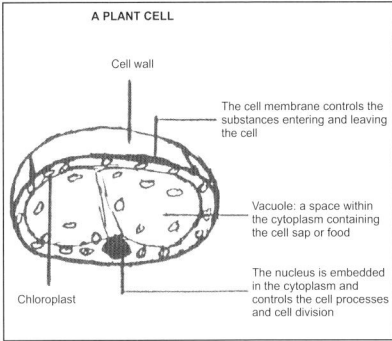

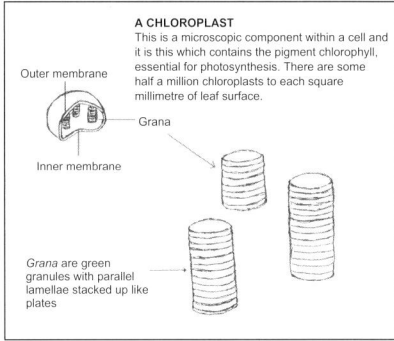

Chloroplasts are responsible for photosynthesis in leaves and some green stemmed plants.

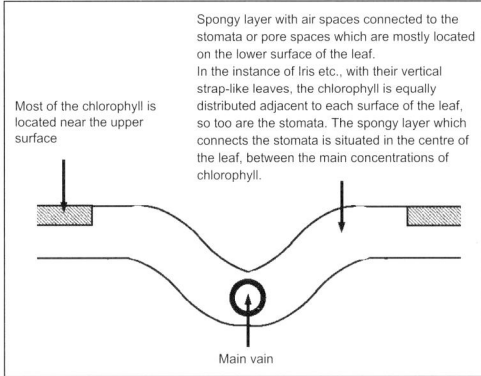

carbohydrate glucose, is produced, and oxygen is released into the atmosphere. In this way, plants maintain the oxygen level essential to human and animal existence.

Through photosynthesis, every leaf provides itself with a form of chemical energy used to develop other substances, including proteins, and fats, necessary for the plant's growth.

When supplied with adequate light and moisture, a suitable temperature, and useful mineral nutrients from the soil, the plant is able to produce these substances in quantities sufficient to satisfy its immediate needs and to store them for such future needs as seed production, or the development of tuberous roots. Plants are virtually the only forms of life capable of converting chemical elements into essential nourishment.

During photosynthesis, more glucose is manufactured than can be moved away from the leaves immediately; the rest is turned into starch and stored within the leaf cells. When darkness falls, photosynthesis stops, and the starch is converted back to glucose and transferred in the plant's sap to other areas where it is needed. This process is called translocation.

During the course of its evolution, every plant species has adapted to the particular quality and quantity of light found in its natural outdoor habitat. While plants can acclimatize, within limits, to lower light intensity, they still require relatively high levels of available light to maintain primary functions. Without this light the plant will weaken and die.

Understanding light levels

Light levels are measured by the standard metric unit-of lumens per square meter, or lux. One lux equals one lumen per square meter. (Light levels can also be measured in foot-candles, the amount of light produced by a standard candle at a distance of 30cm (1 foot) from any surface. One foot-candle is equal to one lumen per square foot.) Lux can be measured precisely with a lux meter, so that it is possible to know the level of light under any condition. Our eyes alone cannot judge light levels accurately, since they adjust quite rapidly to changes in order to achieve comfortable vision.

On a bright summers day in England, the light intensity out doors may well exceed 60,000 lux, while on a dull, overcast day in the same season it may be only 5,000 lux. On a winters day by comparison, the light intensity out doors may only be about 5,000 to 10,000 lux.

The natural light varies in respect to both its intensity and continuity. This is not simply the seasonal variation in intensity, but a constant variation, which can, when there is broken cloud cover, result in quite noticeable changes in the light intensity from minute to minute. During a plant's growing season, this variability in intensity does not interfere with the normal growth processes if the other vital factors, such as temperature and moisture, are adequate. Plants do not need all the sunlight available on a bright summer's day, in order to carry out their normal functions. Only a small fraction of the light radiation that plants receive during high summer is utilized and is actually necessary. The light that filters through on a cloudy day in summer is not only adequate, but meets all the plants' requirements.

The opposite is true indoors. Light readings from daylight only taken indoors just 90cm (3 feet) from a window, will likely be around 25 percent of outdoor levels (depending on window size and exposure). Further back in the room, the lux readings will drop quite dramatically, in some areas to less than 5 percent of outdoor illumination. Even in mid summer, indoor readings are likely to be less than 200 lux, and in winter no more than 60 to 90 lux during the middle of the day, diminishing quickly as the days grow shorter. The standard lux levels for the living room and stairwell, for example, are only 100 lux. To read easily we need only 200 lux, and 600 lux is enough for doing even close or detailed work. Plants, however, need a much higher level of light than is usually available indoors. Few plants will survive at levels as low as 300 lux and most require upwards of 800 or 900 lux, just to stay alive.

below 5%

50% | 25% | 15% | 5%

below 5%

below 5%

50% | 25% | 15% | 5%

below 5%

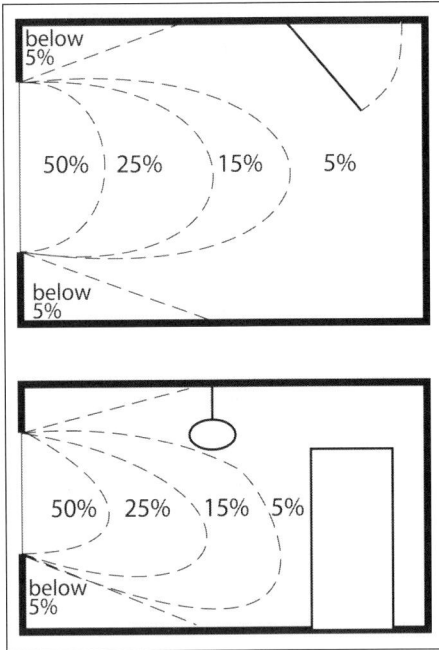

The distribution of the available light entering a room.

Everyone who grows plants indoors knows that they tend to decline in the darker months of the year; even when other indoor conditions are sympathetic and they are placed near the windows to take up all the available light. Some survive better than others, but in general they lose their lustre and clarity. Their colouring becomes pale, growth is elongated and spindly, leaves appear more sparsely at intervals along the stems. An entire plant may become noticeably distorted as it leans towards the light. Further back in the room, all species except the most tolerant of foliage plants stop growing and may simply die. These are all signs of inward disturbance due to the lack of light. These symptoms may appear even during longer, brighter days among plants placed away from windows.

In an indoor light garden, however, your plants will not merely survive indoors they will positively flourish even in winter, and extend the seasons of active growth and flowering. Your plants will show inward and outward vigour, improved colour and texture, and will produce lush foliage and lots of flowers.

Replacing the Sun
Sunlight versus Lamp Light

The successful cultivation of plants under electric lights does not require a spectral energy distribution comparable with that of the sun. As discussed earlier, plants do not make equal use of all parts of the visible spectrum. Light in green and yellow range (510-610nm) has little influence on plant growth or photoperiodism (control of flowering), but has some influence on photosynthesis. Light in the violet/blue range (400-510nm) has a strong influence on photosynthesis; a slight influence on photoperiodism, and strong influence on growth, red light (610-700nm) has a very strong influence on photosynthesis, a strong influence on photperiodism, and strong influence on growth. If plants are to thrive indoors, they must receive light that is composed of the colours they can use for growth, photosynthesis, and photoperiodism.

Like sunlight, electric light appears white to the human eye, it too is made up of the colours of the rainbow, as well as ultraviolet, and infrared rays. The different kinds of electric light available (incandescent, cool white fluorescent, warm white fluorescent, compact fluorescent, and grow lamps) produce differing amounts of the colours in the visible light spectrum, as shown in the following graphs.

Providing plants with the right kind of light

The graph below illustrates the colour of light that plants typically utilize best. It is followed by graphs that show the typical colour composition of sunlight and several different lamp types.

The general response of plants to the visible light spectrum:-

Wavelength NM	Colour	Growth	Photosynthesis	Photoperiodism
400/510	Violet Blue	Extension growth Restricted	Strong influence	Slight influence
510/560	Green	Little influence	Moderate influence	Little influence
560/610	Yellow	Little influence	Strong influence	Little influence
610/700	Red	Stimulates etiolated growth	Very strong influence	Strong influence involving photoperiodic response e.g., control of flowering.

1. Sunlight contains the full range of colours, including those that plants can use most effectively and those they cannot use.

2. Incandescent lamps produce light mainly in the red/orange/yellow range and very little, in the violet/blue range.

3. Cool white fluorescent lamps produce a high percentage of violet/blue light that plants can use effectively, but less of the red light plants prefer. They also provide a high percentage of green/yellow light which plants do not use for growth

4. <u>Warm white fluorescent lamps</u> produce <u>slightly less violet/blue</u> light than cool white lamps. They produce <u>more of the desired red</u> than cool white, and slightly less yellow/green light.

5. Grow lamps, also known as wide spectrum lamps, produce the most complete spectrum of colours that plants can utilize. However they are costly, and conventional lamps, will provide appropriate lighting, particularly when warm and cool white lamps are used in combination.

6. <u>Compact fluorescent lamps</u> produce less violet/blue light than do the cool white lamps, but <u>more of the most effective red</u> light. They produce less of the ineffective yellow/green light.

The sun's visible spectrum. The typical colour composition of sunlight 380nm-700nm

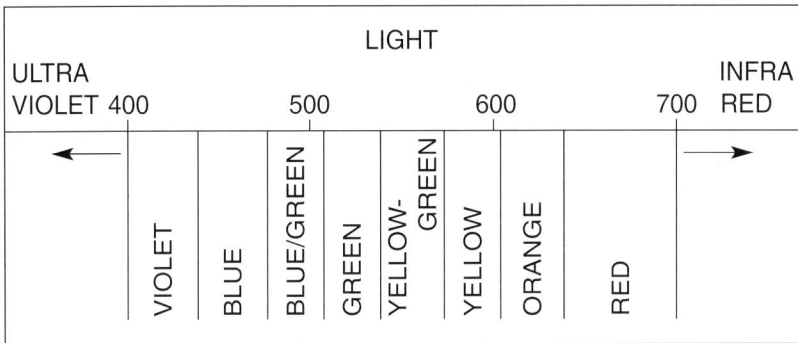

The spectral energy distribution of three different types of fluorescent tubes and an incandescent lamp.

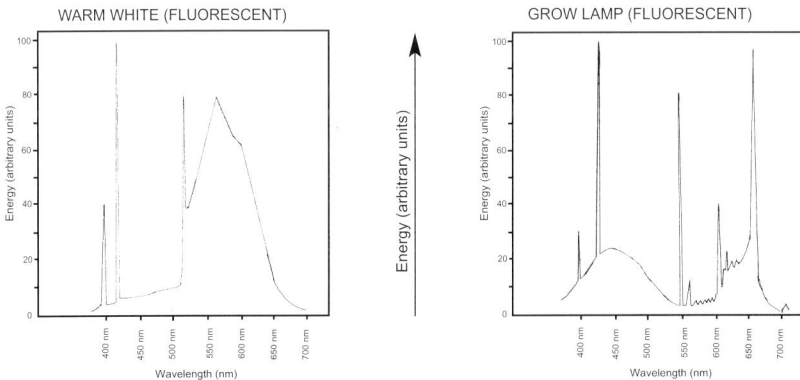

COOL WHITE (FLUORESCENT)

Energy (arbitrary units)

100

80

60

40

20

0

400 nm 450 nm 500 nm 550 nm 600 nm 650 nm 700 nm

Wavelength (nm)

Energy (arbitrary units)

INCANDESCENT LAMP

Energy (arbitrary units)

100

80

60

40

20

0

Ultra-violet radiation

Visible radiation (LIGHT)

Infra-red

400 nm 450 nm 500 nm 550 nm 600 nm 650 nm 700 nm

Wavelength (nm)

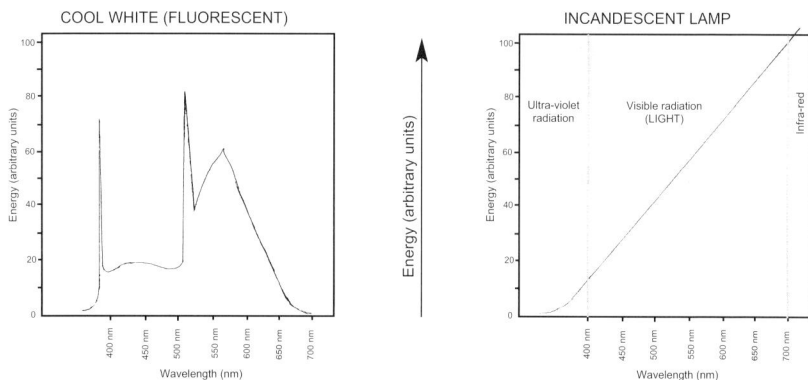

Incandescent Lamps

Incandescent lamps, sometimes known as domestic tungsten filament or GLS (general lighting service) lamps, are the most common form of household lighting but are not suitable for indoor plant cultivation. They are not an efficient lighting source in relation to the amount of electricity they consume, and a large amount of their output is produced in the form of heat and infrared radiation. Even for accent lighting, compact fluorescent lamps are a far better choice because they are more efficient, cooler and their light is suitable for plant growth.

The light from an incandescent lamp comes from one central spot within the lamp, and radiates in a circular pattern, declining rapidly the farther it is from this central source. The light is only adequate within a small radius, and if plants are placed close enough to take advantage of the light they will suffer from its heat. Fluorescent tubes provide a far more even light distribution within a correspondingly larger area, without the production of a high degree of heat.

Fluorescent Tubes

As can be seen from the graphs, the light composition of cool white and warm white fluorescent tubes does not exactly match natural sunlight, but is quite adequate to meet a plant's needs. A fluorescent tube provides a steady, unobstructed stream of light energy for as long as it is lit. What may be lacking in quality and intensity is largely compensated for by the overall consistency of fluorescent lighting. Plants raised in commercial growing rooms under both cool white and warm white tubes, have shown consistently excellent results in their growth rate and plant shape.

Unlike incandescent lamps, fluorescent tubes do not generate a great amount of heat. You can grow plants very close to a fluorescent tube without fear of the plants becoming dried out or even singed. They are long lasting, economical to use, and range in size from 225mm (9 inches) to 2400mm (8 feet), and from 6-watts to 125-watts. (See page 34 for calculating running costs.)

A fluorescent light cannot operate, without a ballast. This is an electrical device that regulates the flow of electricity to the fluorescent tube, and supplies the necessary starting and operating current to the lamp. The ballast does generate some heat, although the amount given off is too slight to be significant in an indoor light garden. The ballast is usually housed in the light fixture or in the lamp base.

Grow Lamps

Grow lamps are specially designed fluorescent lamps that produce a complete spectrum of colours that plants can utilize. They also generate heat, which benefits some but not all plants. Grow lamps are quite costly, and the spectral differences between them and other fluorescent lamps are not actually very significant to plant growth. In addition, they produce less light per watt and require replacement sooner than other types of fluorescents. Many indoor gardens rely on combinations of conventional fluorescents lamps with no loss of plant vigour or growth.

Compact Fluorescent Lamps

Recent developments in the lighting industry have resulted in a new generation of super-efficient, miniature lamps. These are modified forms of the standard fluorescent tube. The tube has been folded to form a convenient, compact unit. The folded tube is often attached to an adaptor that allows it to screw into a standard light bulb socket. (Some compact fluorescent tubes do not come with adaptors, and must be used with fluorescent tube fitting.) Like the standard tube, a compact fluorescent light requires a ballast, which can be housed inside the adaptor casing, elsewhere in the fixture, or even at a distant location in order to maintain an attractive design. (See the chapter on Light Garden Design, page 90 for suggested ballast locations.)

Some models are manufactured as single units, with the lamp, the adaptor and ballast, and sometimes a reflector or globe, sealed together. When the lamp is spent, the whole unit must be replaced. Other models have reusable adaptors, ballasts and reflectors; you replace only the lamp when it is spent. It is more economical and less wasteful to use the models with reusable ballasts and adaptors, as a ballast will outlive several lamps.

Compact fluorescent lamps have all the advantages of standard fluorescent tubes-they burn for 5,000 to 10,000 hours, depending on the model (5 to 10 times as long as an incandescent lamp), and they are very energy efficient. (A 13-watt compact fluorescent lamp will provide the same lux as a 75-watt incandescent lamp but will use about 25% of the electrical energy.) Because compact fluorescent tubes are small, they light a smaller area than the longer tubes, but they allow greater flexibility in use and are simpler to install. Compact fluorescent lamps can be used in spotlights, in small track lighting, in table and floor lamps and in hanging light fittings. As their light is well suited to plant growth, they have considerable potential for small-scale light gardens and for lighting individual plants and small groups of plants. (Some ideas for using compact fluorescent lamps effectively in your indoor light garden are discussed in Light Garden Designs, pages 89-93.)

Compact fluorescent lamps may seem expensive compared to incandescent lamps, but the price usually includes the adaptor and ballast, and in more expensive models it will probably also include a reflector or globe. Since you will only need to replace the lamp and occasionally the ballast, if you purchase a model with reusable ballast and adaptor, the cost is not as high as it may seem at first. In addition the greatly reduced energy consumption and the long life of the lamps make these very economical over time, particularly in areas with high electricity charges.

Compact fluorescent lamps are manufactured in a number of shapes and sizes. The fluorescent tube can be folded into a D shape, a double D, an S shape, a double S, or a ring shape. Some models come with a spotlight reflector; others come inside glass globes, and look very much like incandescent lamps. These lamps are fitted with adaptors that screw into standard light fittings.

Providing plants with the right amount of light

While the right kind of light is crucial to a plant's healthy development, the right amount of light is equally important. It would be a mistake to assume that all plants can benefit equally from a particular intensity and duration of light. The needs of plants vary, but in general, foliage plants have the lower light requirements than flowering plants. It is also important to note that a daily period of darkness is necessary to plants and that they would become exhausted if exposed continuously to light, just as their health is impaired by an inadequate light supply.

When introducing new plants into your indoor garden, it will take them a few weeks to acclimatize to their new environment. Acclimatization is possible within certain limits, as the chlorophyll in plant leaves can adapt to allow more absorption of the available light. The acclimatization of older leaves is slight however, so the process is not complete until all the older leaves, have been replaced by new ones.

If no new leaves are produced within six to ten weeks, but all the existing leaves remain healthy, the light level is at the minimum. The existing leaves can merely produce sufficient food to maintain the plant. Under these conditions, the plant will remain attractive for quite some time, but as the leaves grow old and are shed, no new leaves will be produced and the plant will die.

When the light level is below the minimum necessary for a particular species, the leaves will not be able to meet the plant's immediate requirements. Its food resources will soon be exhausted, and an obvious deterioration in general appearance will follow, with rapid defoliation. If more light is not provided, the plant will die.

When the light level is above the minimum needed for your plant's immediate requirements, it will have food reserves available to produce new leaves, and will be a source of pleasure to you for a long time.

The specific light recommendations given in the Plant Light Tables are based on the experience of professional plant growers, but you must remain alert to the behaviour of the different species under various conditions and be prepared to make adjustments. It is quite possible, though, to calculate light levels that are suitable for particular plants or groupings of plants. And of course, it is better to provide a generous level of light, leaving the plants to absorb what they need, than to err with too little.

Special light needs of flowering plants

Every plant species has a kind of built-in clock mechanism that is sensitive to the length of the light and the dark period in each 24-hour day. While foliage species will flourish with a consistent intensity and duration of light year round most flowering plants require a seasonal variation to induce them to flower. This is an important factor in both when and how profusely a plant will bloom. Sensitivity to day length is known as photoperiodism, and it can be divided into three general categories, as follows.

Short-day plants

See Slide H25. *Euphorbia pulcherrima* 'Marble Queen' (Poinsettia). A short term indoor plant.

Among the short-day flowering plants are the winter flowering *Begonia* 'Lorraine' F1 hybrids, *Chrysanthemum*, *Euphorbia pulcherrima* (Poinsettia), *Kalanchoe blossfeldiana*, and *Schlumbergera* x*buckleyi* (Christmas cactus).

The year-round production of chrysanthemums is a good example of how commercial growers take advantage of the photoperiodic response when it is profitable to induce flowering at times other than the natural period. For bud initiation in these short-day plants, the period of darkness should be more than 12 hours, in any 24-hour period. To induce flowering in plants being grown during the lighter months of the year, the chrysanthemums are blacked out at 6.30 pm and their covering is not removed until 7.30 am the next day. This procedure is continued until the flower buds begin to show colour, otherwise the plants may fail to flower. Conversely, as natural daylight shortens flowering can be delayed by providing additional electric lighting to extend the vegetative growth period and prevent bud initiation.

Long-day plants

Campanula, Fuchsia, and the flowering tuberous-rooted *Begonias* are examples of popular houseplants that require a long day to flower. Some *Fuchsia* hybrids will flower throughout the year, but their flowers are much more profuse during the longer days. Begonias develop their tubers during short-day months, so while continuous long-day treatment will enable them to flower over a much longer period, it will be at the expense of root development.

With the correct light intensity, and a day length of 16 to 18 hours, you will see the most astonishing results in your long-day plants. They will show a noticeable longer flowering period, and will bear larger more heavily massed, and more colourful flowers.

Day-neutral plants

These plants are unaffected by day length, and there are many examples among commonly cultivated house plants, including *Anthurium, Aphelandra, Browallia, Exacum, Impatiens*, and *Saintpaulia*. But this does not imply that all will flower equally well at any time of year, and you can experiment with varied intensities of light, and different day lengths, to see which plants responds best under any given set of conditions.

See Slide H8. *Anthurium andraeanum* 'Brazilian Sunrise'.

Day-neutral plants show clearly the rewards of indoor gardening with artificial light *Impatiens* and *Saintpaulia*, for example, can be brought to flower more abundantly and for much longer under artificial light than when simply grown indoors by natural light. However, some plants have to reach a certain stage of maturity before flowering, while others in this category may need a period in specifically cool or warm growing conditions to trigger flower bud initiation.

Light-loving plants

In your light garden, you can provide as much as 15,000 lux for your light loving plants, by placing them close to the light source. Some flowering plants, however, need higher light intensities and are best purchased as potted plants when they are just coming into flower. Examples are *Chrysanthemum, Cyclamen*, and *Rhododendron* (Indoor azalea). Tuberous *Begonias* flower extremely well in a light garden but fail to produce tuber, so you have to obtain fresh tubers once flowering is over. Crocuses, Hyacinths, Narcissus, and Tulips can all be enjoyed in flower in a garden room or a light garden, but after flowering their bulbs will not produce more flowers indoors, so fresh bulbs will be required each year. (Old bulbs can be naturalized in the garden, and in a year or two they will start flowering once more in the open ground.)

While it is true that with sufficient light of the right quality, intensity and duration, any species that grows in the open can be grown indoors (assuming that its other cultural needs are satisfied) a light intensity of some 60,000/80,000 lux would be needed. This intensity would not be practical for an indoor garden, due to the added complexity and cost of installation, and the added cost of energy consumption too!

This is hardly a limitation to the possibilities of your indoor garden though. Within the lux range readily available in your light garden, you will be able to cultivate a wide variety of plants, including cacti, bromeliads, and even orchids.

PLANT SPECIES LUX LEVELS: CALCULATING LIGHT LEVELS

You can devise a basic lighting plan for your garden room or light garden using the following simple calculations. The lux levels given take no account of any additional natural light, and so the calculations are suitable for any area of your house that you choose for an indoor garden.

The recommended minimum light level for indoor gardening under – fluorescent light is 800 lux at a height of 85cm (34 inches) above the floor. This is roughly the height of tables, counters and many plant stands.

In a room given over entirely to growing plants, fluorescent tubes can be spaced out across the ceiling. The important factor is the amount of light falling on the plants' foliage canopy, so that large foliage species placed on the floor, or smaller plants on stands or tables will absorb this basic level of 800 lux. The needs of a wide range of foliage plants will be met if the lights are on for 12 to 14 hours a day all year round.

Closer to the light source the lux level rises to a maximum of approximately 2,000 lux. High shelves, wall brackets, and hanging baskets provide positions where more demanding plants, such as the variegated types and some flowering species, can take advantage of the extra illumination.

The determination of light levels is a complex, specialized subject, but there is no need to become involved in a mass of technical detail: nor is it necessary to buy a lux meter to monitor light levels. The simple and accurate calculations below will determine the number and power of fluorescent tubes you will need for a given space.

The main factors to take into consideration are the floor area, the height of the room, and the condition and wattage of the fluorescent tubes. These technical factors are expressed as area, utilization factor, maintenance factor, and light design lumens. They are all converted to numerical units that are used to calculate the lux level produced by a specific tube. You can then workout quite simply how many of these tubes are needed to give a lux level of 800 or slightly more.

LDL = Light design lumens, which is the amount of light produced by the fluorescent tube over a given area. LDL is based on the average output over approximately the first 6,000 hours of use. During the first 100 hours the light is very bright, but then it settles down, deteriorating slowly with age.

Manufacturers recommend that you replace the lamps after 8,000 hours. In the garden room or light garden, you should replace the lamps after 6,500 hours, that is to say about 15 months use in the garden room, or about 13 months use in the light garden, depending upon the total hours of lamp usage. After this, their power will have declined to the point where they are no longer a satisfactory light source for your indoor garden.

Lux output of warm white and cool white fluorescent tubes

Wattage of lamp	lamp length	LDL* (Warm White)	LDL.* (Cool White)
125	2400mm (8ft.)	9,600	9,600
85	2400mm (8ft.)	7,250	7,250
75	1800mm (6ft.)	6,200	6,050
65	1500mm (5ft.)	4,800	4,700
40	1200mm (4ft.)	2,900	2,800
40	600mm (2ft.)	2,900	2,900
30	900mm (3ft.)	2,250	2,250
20	600mm (2ft.)	1,250	1,200
15	450mm (1ft 6in.)	750	750

*LDL = Light design lumens after 2,000 hours of use.

The wattages of lamps suggested are the standard widely used domestic type lamps.

These figures, provided by a major lamp manufacturer, are the basis for the calculations in this book. LDL values do vary slightly from manufacturer to manufacturer, so you will have to ask your local supplier for information on specific brands.

UF = Utilization factor for the luminaire, the spacing, and the room.

MF = Maintenance factor, calculated as the amount of illumination midway through the cleaning cycle compared to when the lamps have just been cleaned with a dry duster. The maintenance factor will be affected by the age of the fluorescent tubes, the running hours, and the regularity with which they are cleaned. For this calculation, a maintenance factor of 0.9 is used in all cases. You must keep the tubes free of dust to maintain this factor. Turn the lights off and let them cool, before you dust them, and make certain no water comes in to contact at any time.

A= Floor area, in square metres.
Lux readings per tube

$$= \frac{LDL \times UF \times MF}{A}$$

$$\frac{LDL \quad X \quad UF \quad X \quad MF}{\text{Light Design Lumens x Utilisation Factor x Maintenance Factor.}}$$
$$\text{Area}$$

Example;
(Using 65-watt fluorescent tubes 1500mm (5ft.) long)
Floor area = 3M X 3M) = 9 Sq.M
LDL = 4,800
UF = 0.46
MF = 0.9
Lux reading per tube= 4,800 X 0.46 X 0.9 Divide by 9 = 220. X 4 = 883.2 lux

$$\frac{}{9}$$

Thus, to achieve the basic lighting level of 800 lux in this room four 65-watt tubes will be required. In order to simplify the calculations, certain technical factors have been left out which a lighting engineer would take into account. However, if you always exceed your desired lighting level (usually 800 lux) by 5% to 10% you will be certain to provide sufficient light. (Also see the chapters on garden design for more examples of lighting arrangements.

Spacing of fluorescent tubes

The spacing of light fittings should be calculated according to their height above the working plane of 85cm (34 inch). In these pages, a ceiling height of 2.4M (8ft) is assumed. If your room has a higher ceiling, the best solution is to suspend the fluorescent tubes on chains, and set the tubes in reflector units, which direct all the light downwards into the room.

The distribution of artificial light within a room

An essential requirement for any garden room is good lighting. While a centrally positioned ceiling light does satisfy the general domestic need it is merely a point of light and the light intensity falls away rapidly in every direction the further away from this light source one goes. The light pattern is circular as indicated: -

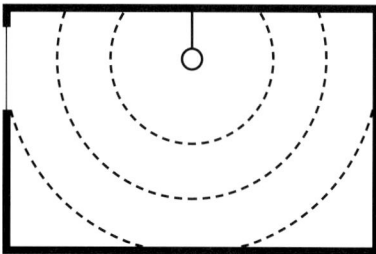

(a) Side elevation of a room.
(Illuminated with a GLS lamp).

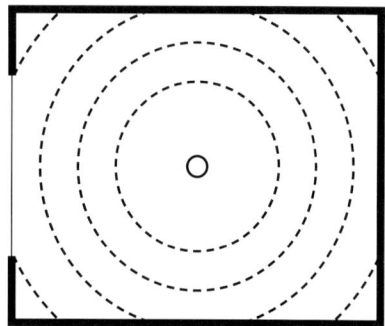

(b) Plan of the same room.
(Illuminated with a GLS lamp).

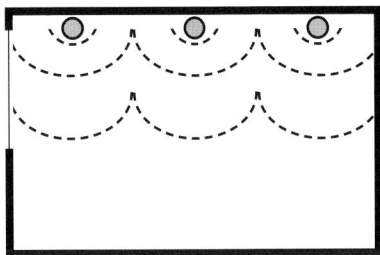

(c) Side elevation of a room. (Illuminated with flourescent lamps).

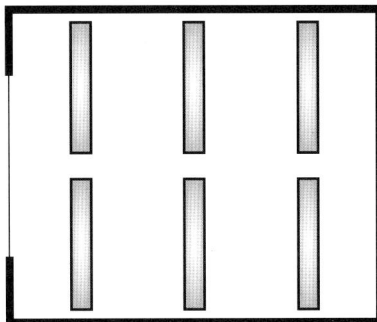

(d) Plan of the same room. (Note the distribution of the flourescent lamps on the ceiling).

Although the light from a fluorescent tube spreads out more evenly than light from a conventional lamp, the strongest light level occurs directly underneath the tube. There is a slight dispersal of intensity on either side. To compensate, the tubes should be spaced evenly so the illumination overlaps as much as possible. Always place plants that need a high level of light directly below the tubes, rather than under the spaces between them, so that they will benefit from maximum illumination.

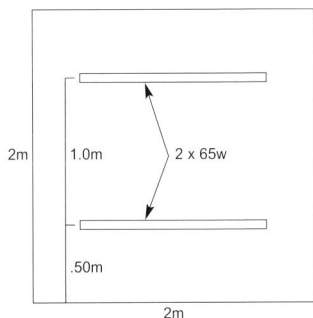

2m | 1.0m | 2 x 65w | .50m | 2m

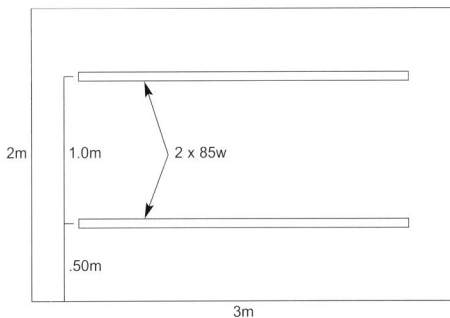

2m | 1.0m | 2 x 85w | .50m | 3m

27

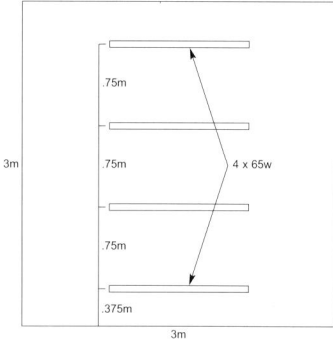

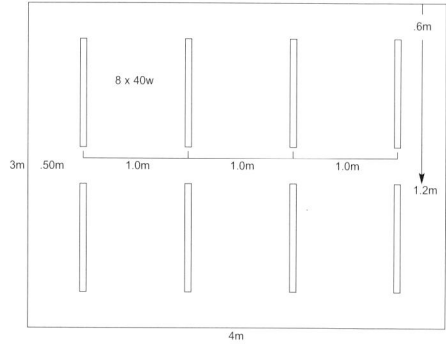

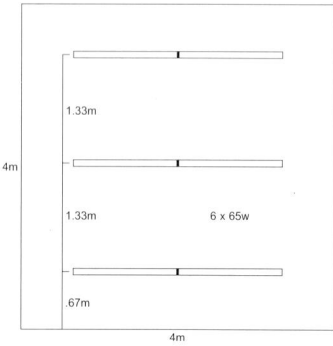

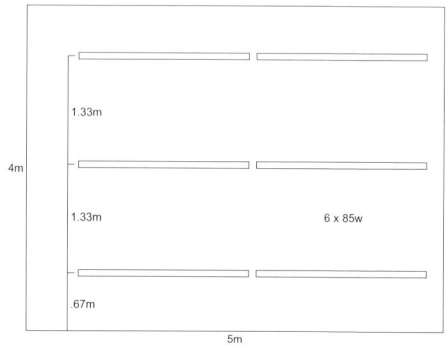

Have the work of wiring the lighting equipment carried out by a professional. It must above all be safely installed, and conform to current electrical wiring regulations, and also must give long term consistently reliable use. Do not attempt to provide additional lighting sockets and switches yourself. While the additional lighting is not a major alteration, it must be carried out expertly and with due care.

THE GARDEN ROOM

A garden room is a whole room or part of a room that you choose for cultivating and displaying your plants. Any room will do, whatever its size and window area. The electric lighting you provide meets all the plants' light requirements for healthy growth. Incoming sunlight may be a bonus, especially for flowering plants, but is not necessary to stimulate and maintain the natural cycles of your plants.

You can create a garden room wherever you have space. A small den or utility room is perfectly adequate for a display of plants that will give much pleasure. You can even convert an attic or basement with no windows at all into a garden room. If these rooms are well insulated, they will benefit from the heating supplied to the rest of the home.

Once the right environment has been established, you have an area that rivals the greenhouse in some respects, in its potential for the cultivation of plants, yet readily accessible, light, warm and clean. Your garden room can become a restful haven for family and friends, offering all the pleasures of an outdoor garden within four walls, untroubled by the weather.

If you are able to develop a large garden room, you can incorporate a living area where you can sit to read, listen to music, watch television, or eat a meal, surrounded by a beautiful plantscape. The scope of the indoor garden is limited only by your ambition. A full-scale garden room will require a serious commitment of time and energy, but the rewards are immense. Long-term foliage plants can be interspersed with temporary, seasonal flowering species. Such a garden keeps attractive throughout the year, with no grey days, bare-stemmed plants, or dull, muddy conditions to interrupt enjoyment.

A spectacular display of plants is possible even if you cannot afford the space to turn over a whole room into an indoor garden. Lighting can be arranged to illuminate a single growing -wall-an attractive feature for a living or dining area. You can enjoy the same range of plants, whatever the size of your indoor garden. You can indulge your personal preferences for green plants or colourful variegated foliage, tall-growing species with elegant shaped leaves, such as monstera, or palms, or bushy, vigorous plants with indoor trees behind them to give height. Many kinds of luxurious flowering plants can be added to the garden room on a seasonal basis, to provide colour and freshness for day-to-day enjoyment, or to brighten your plantscape for a special occasion.

Equipping a garden room with fluorescent lighting and turning it into the right kind of environment for plants is a relatively simple matter. Once the room is freshly decorated and benches or shelves are installed, you have only to start introducing your plant collection. This is where your imagination really comes into play.

If you are preparing a large-scale display, plan it carefully beforehand. You can avoid mistakes if you first draw a simple diagram of your room then illustrate your proposed plant scheme. Remember that bought plants are generally not yet at their full size, so leave space for them to expand both upwards and outwards. Make sure that all the plants will receive adequate lighting and do not obstruct each other. You can add to your plant display over months and years, starting on a small scale and gradually extending the garden area.

If you wish to go in for full range indoor gardening-propagation, growing edible crops, special collections of unusual plants, and so on- you will also need a light garden and working garden, either of which can be incorporated within the garden room, or set out separately in your home (See the following chapters.) Even if you decide to restrict the range of plants, you can include some special features. Hanging baskets, indoor window boxes, and ornamental groupings of plants in large containers can be reserved for your particular favourites among the many indoor plants available.

These individual displays can, not only provide colourful accents, if you choose flowering plants, or brightly variegated foliage, but can also extend the available planting space if your garden room is small.

Creating the right environment

Whatever the size of your garden room, and whether or not it is used as a working garden, as well as a plant display area; there are some general practical guidelines for turning the space into the right kind of environment for plants, and making it comfortable and convenient for the gardener. In an outdoor garden there is invariably at least one particular disadvantage to be overcome, but with indoor gardening the working conditions and plantscape can be well organized right from the start. If you are beginning with a modest arrangement, you can plan it so that additions and expansions can be easily incorporated later on.

The walls must reflect as much light as possible. By far the cheapest and simplest method of achieving good reflections is to coat the walls with brilliant white emulsion, or paint. If you are willing to go to a little more trouble and expense, a hardwearing vinyl-coated wall covering in pure white is a practical investment. Mirrors mounted on the walls will increase light reflection and create the illusion of spaciousness in the garden room. They make a fine background to a special plant display, or feature in you room.

Ceiling

Like the walls, the ceiling should be painted brilliant white to reflect the light towards the plants.

Floor coverings

The contained scale of indoor gardening keeps dirt and mess to a minimum, but there will be the odd problem with spilled water or loose potting mix, especially when you are potting up seedlings or re-potting mature plants. There will also be a small amount of plant debris, both from natural leaf fall or flowers dying off, and from pruning. What you will need therefore, is a floor covering that is easy to clean and safe to walk on.

Bear in mind that non-slip properties are very important; ordinary vinyl floor covering can be dangerously slippery when wet. It is far safer to use rubber flooring with a slightly rough surface that provides a good grip, or to lay solid, flexible vinyl floor tiles. Ceramic tiles with a rough surface are an attractive, though more expensive, solution. Concrete flooring is quite suitable in its original state, or it can be given a coat of floor paint recommended for concrete.

Carpet provides a good foothold and gives the garden room a warm and comfortable atmosphere, but it will require more maintenance than other materials. If you install a new carpet in the garden room, find a type that will resist staining from potting mix and water, such as kitchen carpet. Consider using rubber matting to protect the carpeted areas where you may be likely to spill potting mix or water.

Whatever flooring materials you use, remember that plain, earthy colours complement the foliage and flowers of plants better than bright colours and large patterns.

Windows

Curtains detract from the general appearance of an indoor garden. They tend to blow when the window is open and may damage plants when they are opened and closed. Furthermore, if you intend to grow climbing plants up the garden room walls, you will find that they just do not blend naturally with curtains. The best window covering for the garden room is a simple Venetian blind, preferably equipped with a locking device that prevents the slats from rattling when the window is open. The angle of the slats can be altered to give light or shade as necessary, and the blind will provide a slight degree of insulation on cold nights. An alternative is the plain fabric roller blind, but this is less versatile.

Ventilation

One advantage of having a window in the garden room is that it provides a ready source of ventilation. Without a gentle movement of air, plants can become stifled. Outdoors, air is always moving, and there is only 0.033% carbon dioxide present. If there is no air movement indoors, the leaves of the plants become surrounded by their own exhaled oxygen and begin to suffocate. Some air circulation is not only desirable but also necessary.

Plants will suffer though, if there is any sudden change in the air temperature, and it is important that cold blasts of air do not disturb them. For exotic plants, only ventilate via the door or window when the outside temperature is close to that of your garden room. The more hardy plants are less exacting, but by far the easiest solution is to install a fan.

A tabletop, oscillating fan, is inexpensive and practical. It will provide gentle air movement without creating a cold draft, and can be used in a room with no windows, or in any room when outdoor air temperatures are too cold for the plants. A fan has the added benefit of reducing condensation and maintaining a more even temperature within your garden room. They are surprisingly inexpensive to run, consuming only about 30 watts of electricity per hour.

Another option, if your garden room is too cool, is to purchase a convection heater, which contains a fan. When it is not needed to heat the room, it can be used to simply circulate air. (See Heating, below.)

If you are creating a garden room and live in an area where humidity is a problem, you should equip the room with an exhaust fan, or other suitable means of ventilation. A dehumidifier stood in the stair well of your home will provide you with the best of all worlds, in that you will be able to adjust the humidity setting to enable you to control the level of relative humidity while at the same time causing the air to circulate freely without causing draughts

Water supply

It is very useful to have a water supply in the garden room, but unless your garden room is in your basement, kitchen or laundry area, it is unlikely that you will have water "on tap". There are several devices available that make the task of watering less tiresome, and reduce the need to fetch and carry water constantly from one room to another. Whatever planting system you choose, you will be able to devise a suitable watering system using self-watering planters, capillary matting, or a trickle irrigation system. (See pages 95-100.)

If your garden room is at ground level, it may be possible to use an outdoor tap (faucet in US), which will be more convenient than carrying water through your home from the kitchen or bathroom. Make sure out-door pipes are well wrapped, to prevent frost damage during the winter, and never pour very cold water directly into the potting mix. Let it stand until it reaches room temperature before watering your plants.

Electricity

A garden room must be equipped with an electrical supply, not only for the lighting but to power any other equipment you might use, such as a heated propagator, or a ventilation fan. Individual needs will depend on the size of the room and your particular gardening interest, but safety must always be the prime consideration. *Proper grounding and insulation are essential, so employ a qualified electrician to install any new switch or lighting. Do not allow electrical wires to trail across the floor or workbenches. Keep both permanent and temporary water supplies well away from electrical outlets. Never water plants near electrical sockets or switches.*

Heating

Your garden room will be far better insulated than any greenhouse. It will not be subjected to the sudden, violent fluctuations of temperature that a change in the weather can cause in the greenhouse, and so will not present the same heating demands. Ideally, the temperature range in your indoor garden should be between 16°C and 21°C (60°F and 70°F) during the daytime, with a minimum night temperature of 10°C (50°F). Specific care instructions indicate a plant's tolerance outside this range, but remember that the temperature level must suit all the different species you wish to grow. To avoid having the temperature stray beyond the range on either side, aim for an average of 18°C (65°F), as plants can suffer from being either too cold or too warm.

Any system that can be turned off immediately and that cools quickly, offers greater control over heat regulation. A good source of supply is an electric fan or convector heater specifically designed for greenhouse heating. These reliable heaters have built-in thermostats and non-corrodible parts, and they can double as cooling and air circulating fans in warmer weather.

If your home is centrally heated to a level comfortable for its human occupants, some of the warmth will be transmitted to your garden area. Central heating does tend to dry out the air in a home, so you will have to be particularly careful about keeping the humidity in the garden room at a suitable level for the plants. (See Caring for Plants pages 101-111.)

Electrically operated night storage heaters are not suitable for heating the garden room. Part of their operation is that they absorb heat during the night and automatically radiate the heat during the day, so you have very little control over the temperature in the room.

While it may be tempting to utilize a gas heater, if one is already installed in the room, remember that it will give off fumes unless the flues are cleaned and checked regularly. The same applies to systems that burn coal or oil; equipment of this type is far from ideal, for at best the heat distribution will be uneven.

Lighting the garden room

The aim of the garden room's electric lighting is to provide a quality and intensity of light that will meet the needs of the long-term indoor plants. To achieve this you will need to space Cool White or Warm White fluorescent tubes of equal power across the ceiling. The number required will depend upon the dimensions of your garden room. Chapter Two Plants and Light, provides the information to determine the number of fluorescent tubes you need, the wattages required, and how they should be spaced. Read that information carefully before you buy or install any lighting.

Running costs of the garden rooms lights

You can calculate the cost of lighting your garden room accurately once you have worked out the wattage of the tubes to be installed, checked out the total circuit watts per tube and the number of tubes that will be required

Total Circuit Watts:

125w – 139 watts

85w – 102 watts

75w – 92 watts

70w – 83 watts

65w – 79 watts

58w – 71 watts

40w – 50 watts

30w – 40 watts

20w – 31 watts

15w – 25 watts

In the example of a small room 2M by 2M two 65-watt fluorescent tubes are needed to light this space. Total circuit watts per tube are 79-watts X two = 158-watts (one kilowatt-hour in 6.329 hours). The amount of electricity consumed in one day is therefore a maximum of 14 X 158-watts, 2.212 kilowatt-hours. Multiply this by the unit price of electricity in your locality to calculate the actual cost per day of illuminating your garden room. For example, if the unit cost in your area is 5p per kilowatt-hour, it costs 2.212 X 5p = 11.06p per day to light a 2M by 2M square room. The average monthly cost is £3.364p, and the annual cost £40.369p.

In the example of a room 3M x 3M, the table on page 23 shows that 4 65-watt fluorescent tubes are needed to light this space. Total circuit watts per tube are 79-watts X 4 = 316-watts (one kilowatt hour in 3.164 hours), The amount of electricity consumed in one day is therefore a maximum of 14 X 316-watts, 4.424 kilowatt-hours. Multiply this by the unit price of electricity in your locality to calculate the actual cost per day of illuminating your garden room. For example, if the unit cost in your area is 5p per kilowatt-hour, it costs 4.424 X 5p = 22.12p per day to light a 3M by 3M square room. The average monthly cost is £6.728p, and the annual £80.738p.

In a large room 5M X 4M 6 85 watts fluorescent tubes will provide a suitable level of lighting for the plants. The total circuit watts for each fluorescent tube are 102-watts. So 6 X 102-watts is 612-watts (one kilowatt hour in 1.633 hours) the amount of electricity consumed in one day is therefore a maximum of 14 X 612-watts, 8.568 kilowatt-hours. Multiply this by the unit price of electricity in your locality to calculate the actual cost per day of illuminating your garden room. For example, if the unit cost in your area is 5p per kilowatt-hour, it costs 8.568 X 5p = 42.84p per day to light a 5M by 4M square room. The average monthly cost is £13.03p, and the annual cost £156.366p.

In the room of this size, there is likely to be a fair amount of window area, and in midsummer you may be able to take advantage of natural light during the middle of the day to bring down running costs slightly. (See Combining natural and electric light, below)

A time switch is useful for the operation of lights. Lighting the plants is not usually necessary beyond the 14-hour day, and a regulated switch will ensure that the lights are not left on all night, or while you are away. Plants do need the period of darkness, and if you are not able to maintain a routine of switching on and off the lights, a time switch is the best solution. However, as long as your plants receive the correct amount of light, it does not matter at what time during a 24-hour day period they receive it, or if it is all supplied continuously. The plants will suffer only if the light is inadequate on a daily basis or, at the other extreme, if it is continuous and deprives the plants of any rest.

Combining natural and artificial light

In most garden rooms, some natural light will enter during the daytime through windows or skylights. The value of this light to the plants will depend on the time of day, the local climate, and the season of the year, and whether your room faces north, south, east or west. The fluorescent lighting of the garden room is calculated to meet the plants needs regardless of available natural light, but in a south-facing room with large window area, it may be possible to switch off the lights and make use of the sunlight during the brightest hours of a summer's day. This will save a small amount on your garden room's running costs.

Remember that natural light near the window is much brighter than the natural light further inside the room. If plants are well away from the window they will not benefit much from the natural light, even on a very bright day. In winter natural light within a room is not useful to indoor plants.

You can learn how to take advantage of the incoming natural light by watching the plant's growth very carefully over a period when the lamps are switched off for part of each day. If they seem tired or their foliage becomes yellow or sparse, the combination of natural and fluorescent lighting is not adequate and you should return to a continuous 12 to 14 hours of fluorescent lighting every day.

Some plants will appreciate direct sunshine as well as fluorescent light. Check the needs of the plants you wish to grow, as some do not like to be exposed to direct sun, and make sure they are not pressed close to the window glass where the leaves will be scorched by hot sunlight. There are foliage plants and a few flowering species that do well in a north-facing window that receives bright light but no direct sunlight. As a rule, though, only those plants within 90cm (3 feet) of the windows will obtain much benefit from natural light. The great advantage of fluorescent lighting is that it frees your indoor gardening from dependence on seasonal factors.

Furniture and Fittings

An important part of the garden room concept is that it should be a place where you can relax, and enjoy the setting as well as carry out the work of tending plants. Even in the tiniest room you will want something to sit on and a small table.

In many garden rooms there will be space for some simple, comfortable, and practicable furniture. Chairs should be stain-resistant and lightweight so they can be moved easily. Standard garden furniture fits these requirements perfectly, and so do many kinds of simple kitchen furniture. If you are working on a limited budget, you can buy lightweight furniture-chairs, tables, and storage units-in kit form, or you can buy second-hand furniture.

Where space is limited, foldaway furniture is an excellent solution. There is a wide choice of design, in wood, metal, and plastic, to suit all tastes and settings.

If space is not too tight and you intend to spend a good deal of time with your plants, you might like to install a favourite chair, or look for a special find in an auction or second-hand shop. Wicker and cane furniture have a natural, inviting look that complements an indoor garden. You can use white wicker to create a fresh, summery feeling all year round. Country-style furniture in plain or treated wood is often available second-hand, and looks very much at home in a garden room. Before you buy, check that all the joints are sound and the piece is free of woodworm. Old wood can be cleaned easily, and given a coat of fresh paint or stain before it is installed.

If you want a storage area in your garden room for convenience, or because you have no other space available, it can be achieved simply, and need not take up much room. A kitchen base unit will serve nicely as a worktop, and will generally have a drawer and cupboard below where tools, potting mix, and other equipment can be stored out of sight. Some cabinets are equipped with a pull-out work surface, freeing the top of the unit to serve as a plant stand.

Shelving systems

Many kinds of shelving system for your garden room or light garden are available at building supply stores. If you want shelves attached to the walls, vertical aluminium standards can be screwed securely to the walls. Aluminium shelf brackets to support shelving are available in various sizes. These are slotted into the standards at the spacing you choose. You then simply add acrylic, glass, or plastic laminated shelving in matching widths.

If you do not want your shelves attached to the walls, you can buy easy-to-assemble, free standing shelving systems as kits. These shelves form a very stable structure ideally suited for use in the indoor garden. Acrylic, glass or plastic are the most practical materials for shelving because they are easy to clean and will not become stained. Wood shelves will eventually become discoloured by water; and more importantly-they are a barrier to light.

Containers and supports

There are almost as many different kinds of container for plants-pots, tubs, troughs, planters, decorative baskets, bowls, and stands-as there are different kinds of houseplants. Your choice will be guided by both practical and aesthetic considerations. In a working garden, the appearance of pots and seed trays is unimportant, but in your garden room or for an individual plant display, a harmonious scheme depends upon the balance between the plants themselves, and their containers and supports. As the plants are intended to be the focal point, it is preferable to choose containers of simple design and unobtrusive colouring.

Plastic pots, tubs and troughs are available in a variety of colours. Shades of green and terracotta will not compete with the richness of flowers and foliage. Clay pots are sometimes preferred for their natural quality, but they are heavier, and their porosity allows potting mix to dry out more quickly, so extra care is needed in handling and watering. Self-watering planters (see page 95) are a useful investment, allowing the plants to control their moisture intake.

The larger Kentia Palms and *Schefflera*, will ultimately need sizeable individual containers. Groupings of smaller plants can be planted together in a trough or planter, but you will have more scope to vary your plantscape if you pot them individually, and then group the pots within a large container. You can use decorative baskets, ceramic ware, or metalwork stands, as long as watering and drainage can be arranged efficiently.

Freestanding planters are available that are designed to hold a number of pots, and that display the plants attractively while allowing them to be easily removed or rearranged. A patio wall grill, originally intended for outdoor use, can be used indoors. A typical patio grill stands 1.2M (4ft.) high and 30cm (1ft.) wide, and is equipped with several plant-pot brackets. Floor stands add height to troughs and tubs, and can also be used to assemble a collection of small pots.

Plant stands and platforms are particularly useful to vary the height of the display of particular specimens, and to bring some plants nearer the light source.

When designing or choosing plant stands or platforms, make sure they do not take up space unnecessarily or cast shade on plants at lower levels.

To integrate the plants with their supports, you can include fast-growing trailing species – *Hedera* or *Tradescantia*, for example – which help to disguise the containers and link the different types of foliage. For climbing plants, you will need to supply a trellis or net over the area where you want them to extend.

A broad shelf or narrow table at a comfortable working height is a practical item. While most of the time it can be used for plant display, it will also provide a stable work surface for pruning and re-potting.

You do not have to buy every item brand new or ready-made. Some can be constructed quite simply, or you may come across attractive and unusual second-hand finds. (For example, you can sometimes find used plate glass for shelving in shops. Have it cut to size and the edges smoothed.)

Initially, you need only to ensure that your existing plants have containers of the right size and are placed correctly in relation to the light source. You can then acquire extra stands and planters as your garden room develops, according to the plants' needs and your own creative ideas.

Hanging baskets

The use of hanging baskets in the home has become very popular, and manufacturers of gardening equipment have responded quickly by introducing a range of hanging containers specially designed to meet indoor requirements. The new type is really a hanging pot, made from lightweight plastic and equipped with a built-in reservoir-this is suspended by strong plastic cords or wire. The reservoir ensures that water does not drip on the floor or over the furniture. If you top up the reservoir regularly with water, the plants also benefit from the humid microclimate, and can flourish better than ever before.

You can arrange hanging baskets so that they blend in with the overall plantscape of your garden room and add to the general visual effect, or they can be eye-catching features in their own right. These are particularly attractive when placed near windows, either to complement the view outside, or to soften the impact of an undesirable view.

For the best visual impact and ease of maintenance, a hanging basket should be at eye level, but you will need to choose a place where it is not going to obstruct pedestrian traffic or be knocked around. In the hallway, for example, the best position may be hanging from a point directly above the stair rail, neither forming an obstruction on the stairs, nor dropping into the area where it may receive cold drafts from the main entrance. In a large room, hanging plants are an effective way of dividing the space, in conjunction with a room divider or as a visual feature on their own. You can accent a corner of a room or a recess with a hanging basket-either hang it from a wall bracket or from a hook in the ceiling.

Remember that a hanging basket can be quite heavy, and it is particularly important to hang it where there is a ceiling beam (or stud if you are hanging the basket from a bracket on the wall). To find the beam or stud, tap the ceiling or wall with your fist and listen for where it sounds hard and solid. This is where the beams or studs are, and the areas in between will sound hollow by comparison.

Next check to gauge the precise position of your chosen beam or stud, as it is important that the screw goes into the middle of it. Probe with a fine screwdriver to find the exact location, and then use wall-patching compounds to fill in the holes again before installing the screw. Use at least a number 10 wood screw or screw hook to support the basket.

If you have solid brick walls, use a masonry drill to make holes and insert wood, lead, or plastic anchors prior to using number 8 or 10 screws to secure your basket brackets in position.

Lighting for hanging baskets

The best position for a hanging basket will depend on the plant's light needs. Near a window is an obvious spot for light-loving plants (including most flowering species). In this position, they can serve to integrate the indoor plantscape with the planstcape outside. Plants needing a lot of light can also be suspended from the ceiling almost immediately below a fluorescent lamp, while those needing a moderate amount of light could be hung on wall brackets in corners.

You will find a brief list of suggested plants for hanging baskets at the end of this chapter.

Designing the plantscape

To design a beautiful plantscape, you should look on the plants as living sculpture, and try to gain an appreciation of their different shapes and colours. Some are large and tree-like, needing space to spread and be seen in their full elegance, while others are small and intricately textured, to be viewed at close quarters for their curiosity value.

You can utilize contrast and similarities to create dramatic effects. Large-leaved plants can be contrasted with delicate ferny or grassy types. Compact, bushy species can be placed against the base of taller, upright plants, or those that tend to become leggy as they grow. Climbing and trailing plants will provide a dense ground cover, or may cascade across an entire wall, forming a lush green back ground for the entire room.

If you grow only foliage plants, there need be no lack of colour in your garden room. Beautiful variegated plants are available in all the different categories of size, shape, and growth habit. Against the rich, plain green of some of the more hardy foliage species, you can splash the plantscape with white, cream, pink, red, yellow, orange, or russet, without introducing a single flower. You can mass variegated plants together in groups to form an accented area, or they can be distributed generously throughout the room to create the effect of a riotous jungle. There is such a wide range of plants that will grow readily in a garden room that you are free to choose whether you want yours to be brimful of all manner of plants, or carefully planned to display a few complementary species.

Few people can resist the pleasure of flowering plants, which bring seasonal colour, as well as new elements of shape and texture to the plantscape. You can choose from the tiny, vivid blooms of summer flowering annuals, large and exotic bell-shaped or trumpet-shaped flowers in bright or delicate colours, dense, bushy plants massed with flowers in the autumn, and fresh spring bulbs, long established as indoor favourites.

If you bring plants in flower into your garden room for a single flowering season, their light requirements will be met adequately by the room's overall fluorescent lighting. Some species will need the added illumination of a light garden, either to bring them into flower or to sustain the flowering period at its best, but you can use the plants cultivated there to enliven your garden room from day to day, or season to season.

To achieve a pleasing balance, your garden room will need some variation in the levels of plant display. An outdoor garden often has a natural background of trees and shrubs to provide height. Tall growing or climbing plants indoors will serve the same purpose. You can arrange your other plants on the floor, or on individual stands benches, or shelving. It is important to remember that the life-giving light is coming from above, and that the larger species must not overshadow their smaller neighbours.

The dimensions of your room will naturally affect your choice of plants. If the room is very small, indoor trees will look out of place, but climbing and trailing plants can be trained to form a vertical background to a display of small foliage and flowering plants. A more spacious room will need a foundation of larger plants: palms, ferns, and small trees can create vertical accents, supplemented with your choice of plants of varying heights, and including variegate ones to provide some year-round colour. When flowering plants are brought in, they will benefit from a spot near the windows, if there are any, to take advantage of the natural light. Hanging baskets, high shelves and window boxes can provide additional planting space, and if there is little or no window area, you can use these containers to bring your flowering plants close to the fluorescent tubes.

Be wary of crowding plants into every available space; instead, allow each plant to be seen at its most characteristic, whether it is arching gracefully or creeping across the compost. You can make use of the different heights and shapes of the plants themselves to disguise pots or plant stands. As the plants acclimatize and grow more actively, they will help to take care of the element of disguise, as they spread their leaves and stems to create an integrated pattern of foliage. (See **Garden Room Designs,** pages 47-56 for specific examples of room arrangements and plantscapes.)

Long-term foliage plants for the garden room

Some of the most effective accent plants are the evergreen foliage plants. You can obtain some species as small pot plants that will grow to occupy the intended space, while you may buy others as established plants. To encourage sizeable trees and bushes, re-pot the plants into progressively larger containers as they grow. The height given for each of the plants below represents its full growth potential under this treatment.

Vertical accent plants

Araucaria heterophylla (Norfolk Island pine) Of fine, erect growth and can easily reach 2.1M (7ft).

Caryota mitis (Fishtail palm) Produces erect stems, and a canopy of fine foliage up to 2.1M (7ft) tall.

Coffea arabica (Coffee plant). A well-known bushy indoor plant with dark green shiny, wavy-edged leaves. It will grow to a height of 1.5M (5ft).

Cordyline terminalis (Cabbage palm) With a rosette habit, and will reach 90cm. (3ft) in height.

See Slide A48. *Cyperus alternifolius.*

Cyperus alternifolius (Umbrella plant). An unusual plant, with arching, vertical stems, 60cm (2ft) or more in height.

Dieffenbachia maculata 'Veerie' (Dumb cane). A large vigorous plant, which develops a single trunk, and in time may reach a height of 1.2M (4ft).

Dracaena fragrans 'Massangeana'(Corn plant). A member of a large genus of plants with palm-like, arching leaves. It will grow in time to about 2.1M (7ft) tall. Two other good species are *D. marginata*, of branching habit, up to 2.1M (7ft) tall, and *D. deremensis* 'Warneckii', which has a rosette habit and grows up to 1.2M (4ft) tall.

See Slide A8. *Fatsia japonica* 'Variegata'.

Fatsia japonica (Caster oil plant.) A branching, leafy, robust plant, growing to a height of 1.5M (5ft).

*Ficus benjamina, (*Weeping fig*).* A very attractive, robust, quick growing, tree of weeping habit, which can reach a height of 2.7M (9ft).

41

Ficus elastica 'Decora', (Rubber plant).This familiar plant, will easily attain a height of 2.4M (8ft).

Howea forsteriana, (Kentia palm). This well known erect branching plant, will reach 2.4M (8ft) in height.

Monstera deliciosa, (Swiss Cheese Plant). This popular vine, with elegant, deep cut leaves, will grow to 3M (10ft) in height, if staked.

Philodendron bipinnatifidum, (Tree Philodendron). This slow-growing plant can live to a great age. Shrubby in its early stages, it subsequently develops a trunk and can attain a height of 1.5M (5ft).

Phoenix roebelinii, (Pygmy date palm.) Slow-growing, it will eventually attain a height of 3M (10ft).

Polyscias scutellaria 'Balfourii' (Dinner-plate aralia) An erect plant, it will reach a height of 1.8M (6ft).

Schefflera actinophylla (Queensland umbrella tree). An old favourite that produces a fine canopy of foliage, and reaches an eventual height of 2.7M (9ft).

Schefflera elegantissima (False aralia) this bushy plant may develop a tree-like habit. It grows to a height of 1.8M (6ft).

Syagrus cocoides (Dwarf coconut palm.) A highly suitable palm for a small room. It will grow slowly, eventually reaching a height of 2.1M (7ft).

Yucca aloifolia (Spanish bayonet) A scaly-stemmed plant topped with a spray of sword-like, blue green leaves. It will grow to a height of 1.8M (6ft) or more.

Climbing and trailing plants

Below are some of the best and most tolerant plants that you can use to create a background wall of foliage to set off your other plants.

Cissus antarctica (Kangaroo vine) A robust plant with glossy green leaves.

Cissus discolor (Begonia rex vine) Vigorous, with metallic, marbled foliage.

Cissus rhombifolia. A robust plant with fresh green, serrated leaves divided into leaflets.

Epipremnum aureum (Golden pothos vine) another attractively variegated plant with oval leaves marked in light green, yellow, and white.

Ficus pumila (Climbing fig). The stems of this plant are densely packed with small, heart-shaped green leaves.

Hedera (Ivy). An immense range of variegations providing green, grey, white, and cream colouring.

Philodendron melanochrysum, and *Philodendron scandens.* Vigorous plants, with heart-shaped, rich green leaves.

Syngonium podophyllum (Goosefoot plant) An excellent plant for background cover, with its large, lobed, glossy leaves.

Tradescantia fluminensis (Spiderwort) Fast-growing, offering purple, silver, or creamy marking to add a touch of colour.

The plantscape can be installed without disrupting the room's fixtures and fittings. Indoor gardening does not need to create a mess even at the height of activity, when plants are being re-potted and propagated. The right choice of plant containers and stands, offers a neatly organized garden area within the overall décor of the room.

If, as a beginner, you are uncertain which species of indoor foliage plants you should choose firstly to try growing in your own garden room, this list will be very useful, for it is compiled of foliage plants species I have grown indoors quite happily under fluorescent lamps over many years.

Aglaonema crispum 'Silver Queen'
Ananas bracteatus var. *striatus*
Anthurium scherzerianum

See Slide A9. *Araucaria heterophylla.*

Aspidistra elatior
Asplenium nidus
Chamaedorea elegans 'Bella'
Chamaedorea erumpens
Cissus rhombifolia 'Ellen Danica'
Codiaeum variegatum var. *pictum*

See Slide A42. *Cordyline terminalis* 'Kiwi'.

Cordyline terminalis
Cordyline stricta
Dieffenbachia maculata 'Exotica'
Dieffenbachia maculata 'Tropic Snow'
Dieffenbachia maculata 'Veerie'

See Slide B6. *Dracaena deremensis* 'Lemon And Lime'.

Dracaena deremensis
Dracaena fragrans 'Massangeana'
Dracaena marginata
Epipremnum aureum
X*Fatshedera lizei*

Fatsia japonica,
Ficus benjamina
Ficus elastica 'Decora,'
Ficus elastica 'Schrijveriana'
Ficus lyrata
Ficus pumila
Howea forsteriana
Maranta leuconeura
Monstera deliciosa
Nephrolepis exaltata 'Bostoniensis'
Nidularium innocentii
Pandanus veitchii
Philodendron bipinnatifidum
Philodendron erubescens 'Red Emerald'
Philodendron scandens
Sansevieria trifasciata 'Laurentii'
Schefflera actinophylla

See Slide B50. *Schefflera arboricola* 'Jacqueline'.

Spathiphyllum wallisii 'Clevelandii'
Syagrus cocoides.
Syngonium podophyllum
Trachycarpus fortunei (Fan Palm/Windmill Palm)
Tradescantia species
Vriesea splendens
Yucca elephantipes

* *Araucaria heterophylla* (Norfolk Island Pine) is a fine example of a species of tree, which can acclimatise to lower light levels, and be grown indoors, where it will attain a height of 2.1m (7 feet). It was first discovered by Captain Cook in the 1770s in its natural habitat, where it attains a height of 60m (200 feet).

Plants for hanging baskets

Choosing plants for hanging baskets presents no difficulty, as there is a great variety of suitable species available. Below are listed some of the best plants for hanging containers, but they are merely suggestions and do not imply that other species are unsuitable.

Foliage plants

Asparagus densiflorus 'Sprengeri'
Asparagus setaceus
Begonia rex

Calathea makoyana
Chlorophytum comosum 'Variegatum'
Cissus antarctica
Cissus discolor
Cyanotis kewensis
Cyanotis somaliensis
Epipremnum aureum 'Golden Queen'

See Slide B11. *Epipremnum aureum* 'Marble Queen'.

Epipremnum aureum 'Marble Queen'
Ficus pumila
Ficus sagittata
Gynura procumbens
Hedera helix
Hemigraphis alternata, (Red Ivy)
Oplismenus hirtellus 'Variegatus'
Pelargonium odoratissimum
Pellionia repens
Peperomia serpens, 'Variegata'
Philodendrons scandens

See Slide B41. *Pilea involucrata* 'Moon Valley'.

Pilea involucrata 'Moon Valley'
Pilea nummularifolia
Saxifraga stolonifera
Senecio herreianus
Soleirolia soleirolii syn. *Helxine soleirolii*
Syngonium podophyllum
Tradescantia albiflora 'Albovittata'

Ferns

Adiantum hispidulum
Adiantum raddianum

See Slide F46. *Asplenium nidus*.

Nephrolepis exaltata
Platycerium bifurcatum

Flowering plants

Anthurium scherzerianum

Begonia Semperflorens
Impatiens hybrids
Pelargonium peltatum
Saintpaulia cultivars
Spathiphyllum 'Woozie Woozii'
Streptocarpus X*hybridus*

Cacti and succulents

See Slide F41. *Aporocactus flagelliformis.*

Euphorbia pulcherrima (Poinsettia)
Hatiora gaertneri. (Easter Cactus).
Hylotelephium sieboldii 'Medio-variegatum' (Japanese Stonecrop)
Kalanchoe blossfeldiana
Kalanchoe 'Tessa'
Kalanchoe 'Wendy'
Kalanchoe pumila
Nopalxochia ackermannii. (Orchid Cactus)
Rhipsalis paradoxa
Schlumbergera X*buckleyi* (Christmas Cactus)
Schlumbergera truncata (Thanksgiving Cactus)
Sedum lineare
Sedum morganianum (Burro's Tail)
Senecio herreianus
Senecio rowleyanus

GARDEN ROOM DESIGNS

A home extension garden room

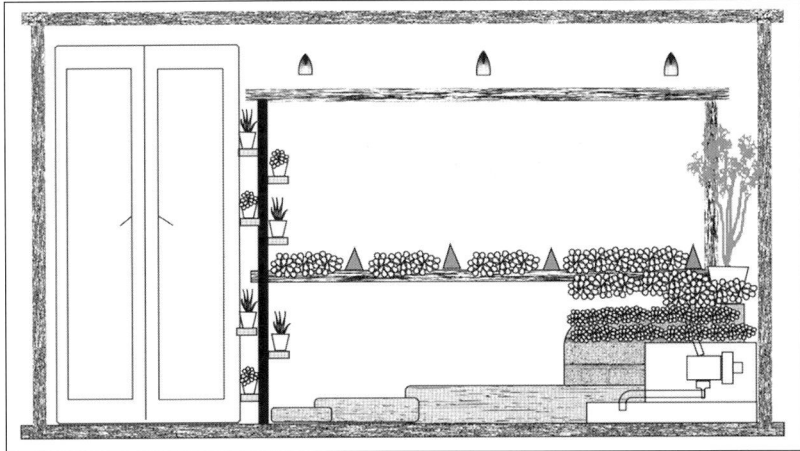

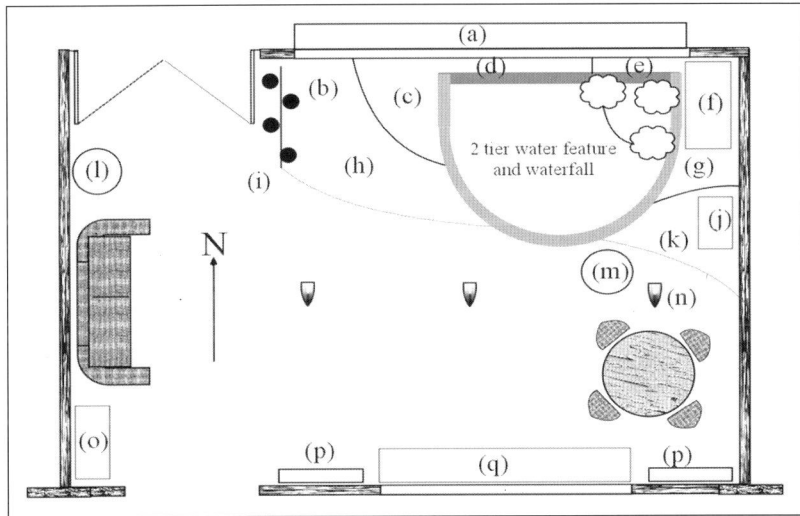

The plantscape design for this indoor garden takes into consideration the view of the garden beyond the window and shows doors of the home extension. The water feature, wall-pots, and a window box, directly outside the window, forge the visual link between the two. During the warmer months of the year both doors can be kept open during much of the day to allow free circulation of air.

47

The Water Feature

This is designed to stand on a solid concrete floor and it consists of a two-tier pool system made of fibreglass edged with either a few loose bricks, or loose stones, to provide the necessary physical support; and at the same time allow the whole fixture to be removed, quickly and easily, if necessary. The larger lower pool is 30cm (12 inches) deep and contains 20cm (8") of water. The second much smaller pool is also 30cm (12 inches) deep, and has a distinctly moulded lip to it to enable the water gathered therein to cascade down into the lower pool again, when the water is pumped up into it. This is set so that the upper lip of this pool is some 70cm (28 inches) above the floor level, and it incorporates three pieces of natural stone, two of these provide the waterfall with a more natural appearance and limit the width of the actual flow of water. The third piece of stone conceals the supply pipe, which delivers the water via a pump connected to the lower pool.

When the ornamental plants are introduced to the low wooden staging surrounding this water feature, the few stones or bricks will be hidden from sight, and the whole feature looks positively delightful; and with the addition of three ceiling mounted floodlights to accentuate the colours of the foliage and flowers, in addtion to the fluorescent ceiling lamps, even more so.

Hiding the plant pots

There are various attractive solutions to the problem of hiding groups of plant pots. You could put those plants, which are in the front, in long plant troughs, avoiding the problem entirely. Another solution would be to make a number of wooden edging boards either unpainted or painted, green or earth colours, so as not to distract the eye from the plants themselves. With time and patience, a do-it-yourself person could make short lengths of rustic edging to stand up at the front of the plant display. Straw matting or woven bamboo cut to suitable width could also create an attractive finish. Pieces of rock, or bricks are another possibility, or lengths of silver birch to lie along the front of the pots, the more natural the finish, the better.

The planting plan

(a) The month is January and the long window-box adjacent to the large picture window is gay with colour provided by a collection of *Erica carnea* (winter flowering heather) consisting of '<u>Ruby Glow</u>', with its deep carmine pink flowers and bronze foliage, '<u>Springwood Pink</u>' with its rose pink flowers, '<u>Springwood White</u>', which displays the finest white flowers against bright green foliage, and '<u>Vivelli</u>', which displays the deepest red of all the winter flowering heathers and has dark bronze foliage. Interspersed among the heathers are a number of dwarf <u>*Chamaecyparis lawsoniana*</u> 'Glauca'.

This is a very slow growing conifer with a rounded conical shape and its tightly packed foliage is sea green. Both the heathers and the conifers are pot grown, and simply plunged in the peat in the window-box, each year. In the spring, these plants are removed and put in an out of the way spot until they are needed once more late the following autumn.

(b) *Philodendron scandens* is trained along a short section of low trellis below the window. This is a quick-growing plant, which will soon cover the lower area of wall.

(c) Coleus 'Buttermilk'.

(d) *Chlorophytum comosum* 'Variegatum'.

(e) *Nephrolepis exaltata*. This will partially spread out over the small pool in a natural way, while at the same time hiding from sight the bottom corner of the large picture window.

(f) *Cyperus papyrus*. This aquatic plant looks very interesting together with the water feature. It will grow quite tall and disguise the edge of the window frame, drawing the viewer's attention through the plantscape and out into the garden beyond.

(g) *Nephrolepis exaltata*. This fern again is useful to hide the planter containing the *Cyperus* while at the same time fanning out over the edge of the small pool. As the fern is placed on two levels it will appear to bring down the height of the plant display, providing a visual link.

(h) This area at floor level is kept permanently for seasonal floral displays throughout the year. In winter the space may be filled with the chrysanthemums or the winter-flowering *Begonia* x*heimalis* 'Love Me' syn. *Begonia* x*elatior* 'Love Me' (Lorraine Begonia.). In summer there is a wealth of flowering plants to choose from. Here and there in this part of the indoor garden *Asparagus setaceus* are interspersed as "dot plants".

(i) This is a double-sided plant-pot stand filled with *cyclamen, poinsettia, primula*, or *kalanchoe*.

(j) This is either a natural stone pedestal planter, or a very good imitation one. Arranged in it are *Dracaena sanderiana, Begonia rex, Philodendron scandens,* and *Hedera helix* 'Green Ripple'.

(k) Creamy white pot grown chrysanthemums 25cm to 35cm (10 inches to 14 inches) tall, edged with a natural looking material.

(l) *Chamaedorea elegans.*

(m) A hanging basket containing, *Ficus sagittata* 'Variegata'.

(n) The three ceiling mounted floodlights.

(o) Here, on a low plant stand, is an arrangement consisting of a group of *Kalanchoe blossfeldiana*, with flowers of white, yellow, and pink which stand out delightfully against the dark green glossy leaves. These *Kalanchoe* are trimmed with <u>*Tradescantia fluminensis*</u> 'Aurea', which helps to hide the pots from view with its cascading bright green, yellow and pale purple coloured leaves.

(p) These are two 2,000 watt, wall mounted convector heaters equipped with thermostats.

(q) The window-box is planted with a mass of *Streptocarpus* X*hybridus* 'Constant Nymph', which produces its blue-purple flowers over most of the year, and they are rotated with others growing in an indoor light garden in the dining room. There are also several *Peperomia serpens* 'Variegata', which trail down from the front of the window box creating a green and cream cascade with their variegated foliage.

An attic garden room

Room Dimensions: 4.95m X 8.4m = 41.58m^2
(16.6" X 29ft = 478.5 sq feet 53.16 Square yards.)

Your attic may well have ceilings with awkward angles and roof beams, which in the past have been much cursed. Nevertheless, when viewed for its potential as an indoor garden, these old problems may well prove to be to the attic's advantage!

There will be spots to place floodlights which are hidden from view yet accentuate the plantscape design.

The spacing of light fittings should be calculated according to their height above the working plane of 85cm (34 inch) and in these pages, a ceiling height of 2.4M (8ft) is assumed. So if your attic has a higher ceiling, the solution is to suspend the fluorescent tubes on chains, and set the tubes in reflector units, which direct all the light downwards into the room. (See also pages 26-28).

If seating is placed at the side where the ceiling is lowest, the room will appear to have added spaciousness. In this attic the main plantscape display would look most attractive if arranged at the right hand side of the room, leaving the left hand side for other uses.

A roof support may prove to be the ideal spot to locate a large plant box, and the beam above just the ideal spot to fix some fluorescent tubing.

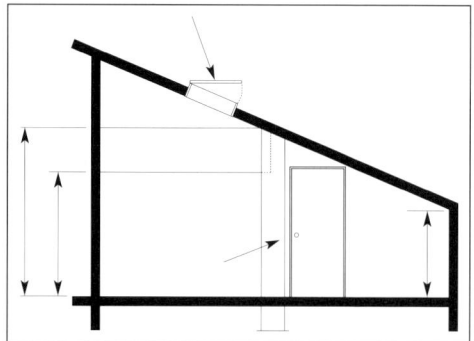

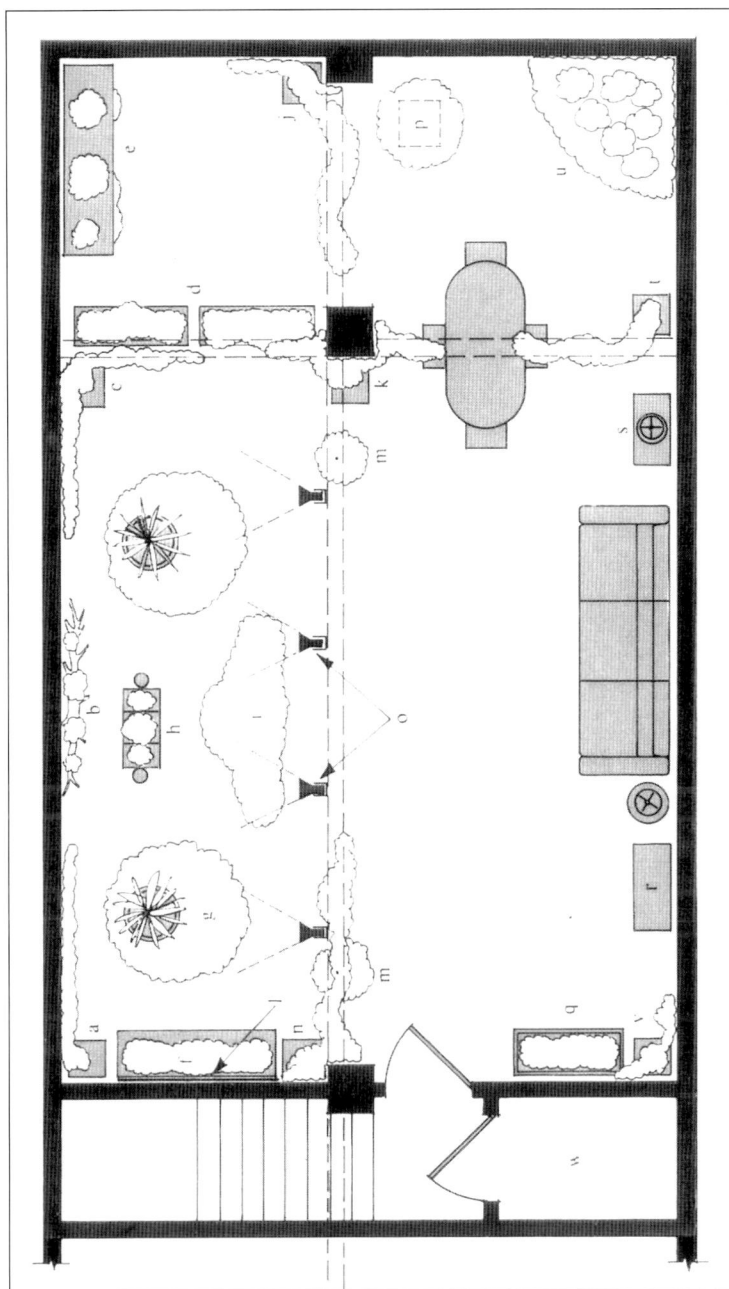

A skylight will let in a good deal of natural daylight. Indeed it will admit at least three times as much light as a similar sized window in the side of the house (if you remember to keep the glass regularly cleaned). But this is not to be taken into consideration when one is calculating the number of fluorescent lamp fittings required to provide the light necessary within the attic nor their distribution across the ceiling.

The plantscape plan

(a) This planter contains *Cissus rhombifolia* 'Ellen Danica.' A robust plant with fresh green serrated leaves divided into leaflets and is furnishing a trellis on the back wall.

(b) This planter contains *Monstera deliciosa* 'Variegata'.

(c) This planter contains the relatively large leaved, usually three lobed, variegated ivy *Hedera algeriensis* 'Gloire de Marengo' and it is climbing a trellis on the back wall and a roof supports beam.

(d) Two boxes displaying *Anthurium scherzerianum, Codieum variegatum* var.*pictum, Ficus elastica* 'Doescheri', *Hedera helix* 'Tricolor,' ideal for trailing over the sides of these boxes, and *Peperomia magnoliaefolia*.

(e) A two tier light garden offers scope for growing plants that may be fussy over their light requirements indoors, and if this light garden is equipped with a propagation unit there is the added potential for the propagation of all kinds of plants.

(f) A single long plant box strategically placed immediately in front of a large mirror and between two self-watering planters containing climbers. This planter creates the impression of being a room divider as a result of the view reflected in the large mirror, and it is planted with this in mind. An attractive display is provided by *Asparagus setaceus, Calathea makoyana, Schefflera elegantissima, Dracaena demerensis* 'Warneckii,' *Ficus pumila,* and *Streptocarpus* x*hybridus*.

(g) Here are two large planters, each containing a single 1.5m (5ft) tall *Ficus benjamina*. Around the base of each are a number of pots of *Syngonium podophyllum* 'Variegatum' its firm green leaves irregularly splashed milky white slowly embracing each one.

(h) This is the site of a Chelsea Planter for the display of a large range of pot plants such as *Anthurium andreanum, Rhododendron simsii* (Azalea indica), *Calceolaria,* Coleus, *Cyclamen persicum, Euphorbia fulgens, Euphorbia pulcherrima* (Poinsettia), Florest's Cinararia, Florest's Chrysanthemum, *Schlumbergera, etc.*

(i) This section of the garden room is reserved for that splash of brilliant flowers, which you wish to enjoy close up. A selection of flowering plants purchased just as they are coming into bloom e.g.

Begonia Semperflorens–Cultorum Hybrids
Begonia (tuberous rooted)
Billbergia nutans
Campanula isophylla
Campanula fragilis
Convallaria majalis (Lily of the valley
Cyclamen persicum,
Euphorbia pulcherrima (Poinsettia)
Florest's Chrysanthemum
Florest's Cineraria
Hippeastrum,
Hyacinthus
Impatiens walleriana,
Iris reticulata
Justicia brandegeana (Shrimp plant)
Kalanchoe blossfeldiana
Narcissus
Nicotiana alata (Flowering Tobacco)
Pelargonium X*domesticum* (REGAL PELARGONIUMS.)
Pelargonium zonale
Primula malacoides
Primula obconica
Tulipa

(j) This planter contains *Philodendron scandens*, which has been encouraged to climb along the end wall and along the roof beam.

(k) This planter contains two *Scindapsus pictus* 'Argyraeus' which clothe the central roof-support with their attractive, silvery deep green, and silver marked and edged foliage.

(l) This mirror can be attached to the end wall. It greatly adds to the attraction of the garden room, by giving the impression that the plantscape design is on a much bigger scale than it is in reality.

(m) There are two hanging baskets each secured to the underside of the roof support beam. The first hanging basket next to the attic door contains *Chlorophytum comosum* 'Vittatum,' the second hanging basket contains *Nephrolepis exaltata* 'Bostoniensis Compacta' (Dwarf Boston Fern).

(n) This planter contains *Hedera helix* 'Chicago', which has been trained up the wall and along the roof support beam.

(o) This indicates the position of four floodlights on the roof support beam.

(p) This planter containing *Dieffenbachia maculata* 'Tropic Snow'.

(q) A planter containing several members of the MARANTACEAE family, such as *Calathea ornate, Calathea stromata, Ctenanthe amabilis,*

Ctenanthe oppenheimiana, Maranta leuconeura 'Massangeana', *Maranta leuconeura* var. *kerchovean,* all of which are fancy foliage plants whose leaves are patterned in feathery, attractive designs, with generally inconspicuous flowers.

(r) A planter containing *Cordyline stricta,* and *Hedera helix* 'Pittsburgh'.

(s) This planter contains a clump of *Spathiphyllum* 'Mauna Loa'

(t) A planter containing *Monstera deliciosa*, which has been trained to the roof beam.

(u) A carpet of *Aglaonema crispum* 'Silver Queen' with several *Sansevieria trifasciata* 'Laurentii' interspersed as dot plants.

(v) A planter containing *Epipremnum aureum* 'Marble Queen', which have been trained along part of the low wall and over a portion of the low ceiling.

(w) A store cupboard for equipment.

The single wall garden

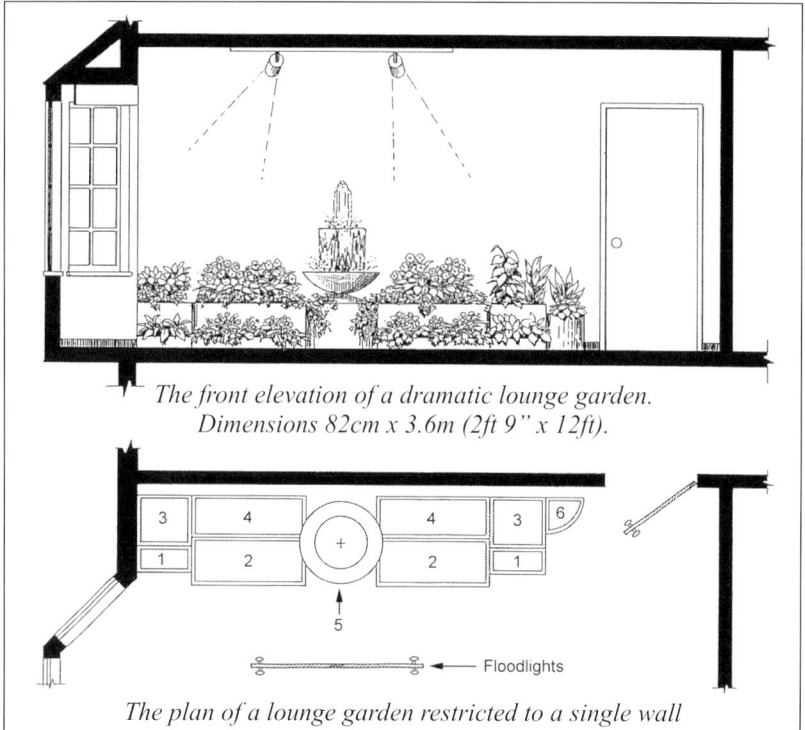

*The front elevation of a dramatic lounge garden.
Dimensions 82cm x 3.6m (2ft 9" x 12ft).*

The plan of a lounge garden restricted to a single wall

Where space is strictly limited, and a whole room cannot be given over to the garden room, you can introduce an indoor-garden into a room, which still has to serve another function. An indoor-garden can be created to dramatic effect against a single wall, in a living room or dining room area, for example. The illustration shows an indoor garden 82cm (33 inches) wide by 3.6M (12 feet) long with the centrepiece of a small indoor fountain. The quietly operating centrifugal pump circulates the water and can incorporate two reflector lights, which add a sparkling attraction, or the centre of the garden can be occupied by an urn or large planter, of similar dimensions, fully planted with fine ornamental plants.

This formal indoor garden can be set out over carpets without any danger of damage as it uses self-watering planters and capillary trays, both of which keep moisture contained.

For Unit layout numbering
See Plan of Lounge Garden Restricted to a Single Wall

UNITS 3-3
Two self-watering planters; 40cm X 40cm X 35cm high (16" X 16" X 14" high).

UNITS 4-4
Two self-watering planters; 87.5cm X 32.5cm X 35cm high (35" X 13" X 14" high).

UNITS 2-2
Two capillary trays approximately; 87.5cm X 40cm X 7.5cm deep (35" X 16" X 3" deep)

UNITS 1-1
Two capillary trays approximately; 40cm X 22.5cm X 7.5cm deep (16" X 9" X 3" deep).

(These capillary trays are equipped with inverted P.V.C. seed trays and capillary matting so they have a water storage reservoir upon which the capillary matting may draw.)

UNIT 5
The plinth for the fountain. 40cm X 40cm X 35cm (16 X 16 X 14 inches high).

UNIT 6
Adjacent to the living room door is a quarter segment of a circular planter with a radius of 30cm (12 inches) and a height of 27.5cm (11 inches).

The Planting Plan

1-1
(1) Two small capillary trays 40cm X 22.5cm X 7.5cm (16" X 9" X 3") deep provide an ideal spot for *Aglaonema* 'Silver Queen' which has foliage, that is almost entirely silvery-grey.

2-2

(2) These two large capillary trays 87.5cm X 40cm X 7.5 cm (35 X 16 X 3" deep) provide the setting for the display of seasonal flowering plants which during late March/early April may well consist of any of the spring flowering bulbs, or such plants *as Kalanchoe* hybrids, *Pericallis* X*hybrida*, (FLORIST'S CINERARIA) *Primula*, e.g *P. Kewensis, P. malacoides, P. obconica*, and P.sinensis, and *Streptocarpus* hybrid 'Weismoor'. All these flowering plants look good when set out against a ground-cover plant like *Hedera h*elix 'Chicago', which can hide the pots from view.

3-3

(3) Two planters 40cm X 40cm X 35cm (16 X 16 X 14 inches high) contains *Peperomia scandens* 'Variegata, *Aphelandra squarrosa* 'Snow Queen', *Schefflera elegantissima*, the slow growing *Hedera helix* 'Little Diamond', and *Philodendron scandens* 'Variegatum', a vigorous climber, which provided with support netting or trellis will develop into useful wall cover.

4-4

(4) The two large planters - 87.5 X 32.5 X 35cm (35 X 13 X 14 inches) high - at either side of the fountain have foliage plants as their main attraction, with just a few flowers to provide a contrast. One or two *Anthurium scherzerianum* will produce exquisite flowers. The other plants consist of *Begonia rex, Calathea makoyana, Dracaena sanderiana, Ficus pumila, Ficus elastic* 'Tricolour' *and Hedera helix* 'Adam'. This *hedera* is to be planted in each planter close to the centrepiece, so that it may be trained around the base of the fountain and down the front of the plinth, linking together the whole of the display on both levels.

(5) The plinth for the fountain. 40cm X 40cm X 35cm (16 X 16 X 14 inches high.

(6) This corner planter - 30cm X 27.5cm (12" X 11" high) contains *Sansevieria trifasciata*.

Some individual planter suggestions for other rooms in the house

(1) 53.75cm (21½") Diameter X 32.5cm (13") high planter

Plants:
1. *Ficus benjamina*
2. *Hedera helix* 'Chicago-variegata'
3. *Hedera helix.* 'Tricolor'
4. *Chlorophytum comosum* 'Variegatum'.
5. *Ficus pumila.*

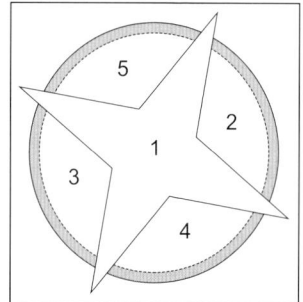

(2) 60cm X 60cm X 35cm high planter (24" X 24" X 14")

Plants.
1. *Schefflera actinophylla*
2. *Aglaonema* 'Silver Queen'.
3. *Cissus rhombifolia* (trailing).
4. *Epipremnum aureum* 'Golden Queen' (trailing).
5. *Aphelandra squarrosa*
6. *Anthurium scherzerianum*

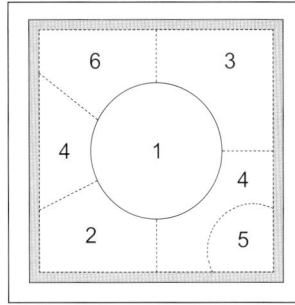

(3) 25.62cm (10¼") diameter X 16.87cm (6¾") high planter.

(This planter is for display on a plant stand or shelf.

Plants.
1. *Sansevieria trifasciata*
2. *Saintpaulia* hybrids
3. *Hedera algeriensis* 'Gloire de Marengo' (trailing).

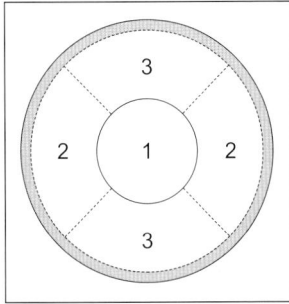

(4) 87.5cm X 32.5cm X 35cm high trough planter (35" X 13" X !4").

Plants.
1. *Ananas comosus*
2. *Hedera. helix* 'Chicago'.
3. *Cordyline terminalis* 'Tricolor.'
4. *Peperomia magnoliae-folia* 'Variegata'.

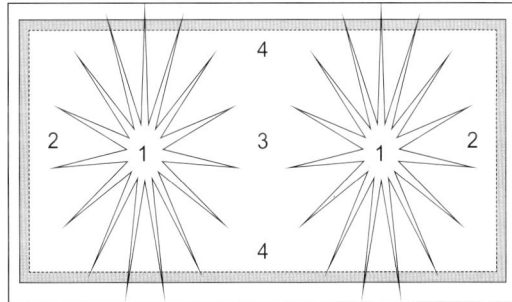

Other possibilities in a garden room, in addition to a **terrarium**, are the introduction of: **A tropical plant case,** (a-practical and indispensable feature), or a heated **orchid case,** under lights, which is adjustable to meet the environmental needs of a larger selection of orchid species than is possible simply in a light garden, or under an adjustable light canopy.

Terrarium see pages 146-148
Tropical plant case see pages 156-157
Orchid case see page 163

THE LIGHT GARDEN

A light garden is designed specially for the cultivation of plants that need a higher level of illumination than is available in a garden room. You can build a light garden as a freestanding structure, or you can convert a shelving unit, bookcase, or room divider. You can also convert a piece of furniture – perhaps a china cabinet or dresser.

See Slide E15. The Royal Borough of Kensington & Chelsea Light Gardens on a windowless corridor.

The light garden principle is the same as for the garden room: you want to provide your plants with the same kind and the same mount of light that is available in their natural outdoor habitats. Fluorescent tubes and compact fluorescent lamps supply the light in a light garden. These lights are attached to the undersides of shelves, or the ceiling of the light garden structure.

The plants in a light garden will be much closer to their light source than the plants in a garden room. If you consider the principle of the point source of light, illustrated below, it will become clear that the illumination levels in a light garden will be very much higher than in a garden room. For this reason, a light garden is the perfect place to display many kinds of flowering plants as well as collections of plants like Bromeliads, dwarf geraniums, Orchids, and Saintpaulias, which need a more powerful light intensity if they are to be really floriferous and thrive.

See Slide E14. A light garden full of tropical plants.

In fact you will need to plan your light garden to accommodate the eventual size of some of the plants you may grow. It is not uncommon for climbing plants to escape from their original growing area, and venture away across the walls or onto the floor. Although sometimes a mixed blessing, this is an encouraging sign, as it means that you are stimulating the most vigorous growth. Some plants will grow too large or spread too much to fit comfortably within a light garden, but there are many species that provide an excellent range of choice. Flowering plants especially, provide an amazing spectacle under the brilliant lighting, producing masses of blooms over long flowering periods, and in some cases all year round.

Point source of light Illustration

Light radiates uniformly in all directions from its point source, and the intensity from the point source of light decreases with the square of the distance of the light from its point source. Thus, a point source of light in a darkened room placed 90cm (3ft) from an object provides that object with 4 times as much light as it would receive if the point source of light were 180cm (6ft) from the object.

LIGHT SOURCE

1m (3ft)

1m² (3ft)

2m² (6ft)

The light garden may be a special area of your garden room, or you can set it up independently in an otherwise dark, unwelcoming corner. It is also the basis of a working garden (see The Working Garden, pages 94-100), and the ideal place for propagation activities. You can develop a special collection, especially of luxurious plants such as orchids, or curious cacti and succulents.

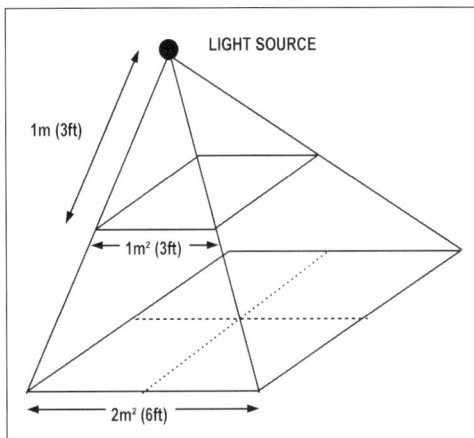

If the light garden is your only indoor garden, and for many readers this may be the case, you can also include more hardy and tolerant foliage plants that would live happily under less intense lighting. These will flourish in your light garden and variegated species will show even more brilliant colours here.

The lighting for a light garden is calculated and placed differently, than in a garden room. Before installing fluorescent tubes, however you will want to read the general information on creating the right environment for a garden room (pages 29-33). Where practical, these suggestions should be followed to make your light garden efficient and easy to manage.

Illuminating the light garden

The electric lighting within the confined space of a light garden can vary from one to five fluorescent tubes, giving a range of light levels from 850 lux to 15,000 lux. This range covers all the species of plants included in The Plant Light Tables (see pages 149-167), with the exception of those plant species which need to spend part of their time, during the warmer months of the year, in the full brilliance of the sun or the dappled shade of a tree or wall etc. The diagrams on these pages show how the fluorescent tubes can be positioned to provide particular lux levels. Calculating the light levels for a light garden is simpler than for a garden room, as shown below.

Comparative light output levels of cool white fluorescent lamps

Although the various manufacturers of fluorescent lamps produce lamps of standard lengths and wattages, the light output varies slightly from manufacturer to manufacturer. The lamps' luminosity also declines with age, and with any accumulation of dust.

In view of these factors, any light meter reading is only an approximation of the lighting potential of a fluorescent lamp. The following light meter readings will, nevertheless, provide you with a fair indication of the light levels that can be achieved using the following light fixtures.

The first thing you may notice is that the light source is very close to the plants, in some cases almost touching their tops. How close to the lights you place the plants will depend on the needs of the plants and the power of the lamps providing the light. The more powerful the light output, the farther from the light source plants may be placed.

You can compensate somewhat for a lower light intensity by leaving the lights on for a longer time. They should not be on for longer than 18 hours, except in one or two special exceptional circumstances, which will be explained later in this book.

Installing the tubes

We have already discussed the advantage of fluorescent lights emitting light evenly along the length of the tube. (See Plants and Light, page 18.) What is not immediately apparent though, is that there is a greater light intensity at the central part of the tube, due to a compounding effect from light emitted on either side. Therefore, to illuminate a long area effectively, you should select the longest tube that will fit the space, rather than using several shorter lengths.

There are fluorescent lights available to fit almost any shelf or box-like space where you may wish to install a light garden. In order to reduce costs and simplify replacement, it is best to use the most common tube lengths- 600mm (24"), 1200mm (48"), and 2400mm (96"). With a shelf only 30cm to 40cm (12" to 16") wide, a single tube may be adequate, providing it is equipped with a reflector to direct all the light downwards.

Ideally, the shelf should be painted white, like the walls and ceiling of the garden room, to reflect light and intensify the illumination. Also useful is a mirror on the back wall, which is almost equivalent to adding a second tube.

If your space is limited, by the depth between one shelf and the next - but more than 30cm (12") - you can cultivate some most beautiful small-scale flowering plants. There is no need to install a reflector for the light, as this would further reduce the depth of your garden area. The ballast unit for regulating the current can be relocated so that the fixture takes up less space, but as the ballast is necessary for the functioning of the light, it must be placed nearby and inside an approved enclosure. (See page 90). Consult an electrician for advice on installing the fittings.

The round light garden for example has its ballast situated in the central tube supporting the lamp hood. (See page 65).

The small 38-watt white light garden has its ballast in the lighting hood.

Where space is really tight the ballast can also be mounted on the back or the side of the light garden unit in an approved unit that complies with the electrical regulations. (See page 90).

The various lamp manufacturers offering fluorescent lamps for sale may well produce lamps of standard lengths and wattages but the lumen rating varies slightly from manufacturer to manufacturer. Lamps also decline in luminosity as they age and unless they are cleaned regularly the light output is reduced still further. In view of these factors any light meter readings are at best only a rough approximation of the lighting potential of the fluorescent lamps being assessed. The following light meter readings will, nevertheless, serve to provide the reader with a fair indication of the light levels which can be achieved under the various lighting fixtures which I am recommedning for use:

1 x 20 watt 600mm (2ft) lamp		
15cm	2600	6"
30cm	1400	12"
45cm	900	18"

2 x 20 watt 600mm (2ft) lamp		
15cm	5600	6"
30cm	2500	12"
45cm	1400	18"

2 x 40 watt 1200mm (4ft) lamp		
15cm	10700	6"
30cm	5800	12"
45cm	3600	18"
60cm	2300	24"
75cm	1700	30"

4 x 40 watt 1200mm (4ft) lamp		
15cm	12900	6"
30cm	9600	12"
45cm	6700	18"
60cm	5900	24"
75cm	3700	30"

Note the quite considerable light meter readings which have been produced as a result of the compounding effect of the white painted wall as indicated in (b) below compared with (a). If a mirror had been used it would have been like adding a further lamp. Both (a) and (b) are equipped with 2 x 20 watt 600mm (2ft) fluorescent lamps.

	(a)		
3000	5600	3000	(15cm)
700	2500	700	(30cm)
450	1400	450	(45cm)

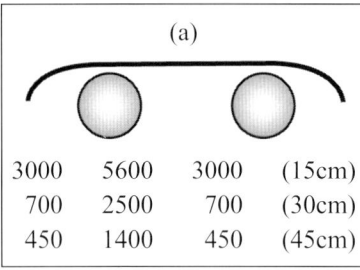

	(b)		
6"	3000	5600	4900
12"	1100	2500	2300
18"	750	1400	1100

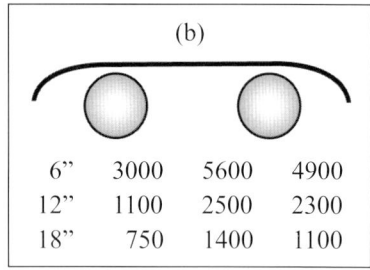

Comparative Light Output Levels

(a) Fitted with 3 x 30 watt Cool White or Warm White 900mm (3ft) flourescent tubes.

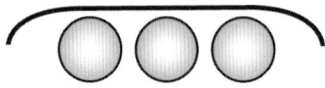

15cm	7500	6"
30cm	3600	12"
45cm	2500	18"

(b) Fitted with 5 x 30 watt Cool White or Warm White 900mm (3ft) flourescent tubes.

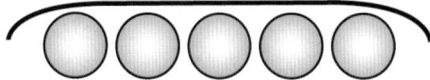

15cm	15000	6"
30cm	7900	12"
45cm	4900	18"

It pays to use the longest fluorescent lamps which will fit your available space. Compare the distribution of light under two 20 watt 600mm (2ft) lamps set end to end under a reflector with one 40 watt 1200mm (4ft) fluorescent lamp.

1 x 40 watt lamp		
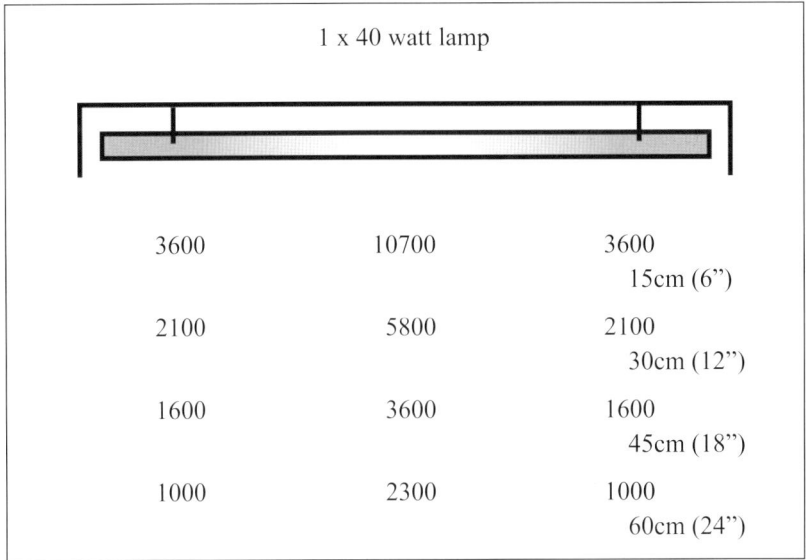		
3600	10700	3600
		15cm (6")
2100	5800	2100
		30cm (12")
1600	3600	1600
		45cm (18")
1000	2300	1000
		60cm (24")

2 x 20 watt lamp				
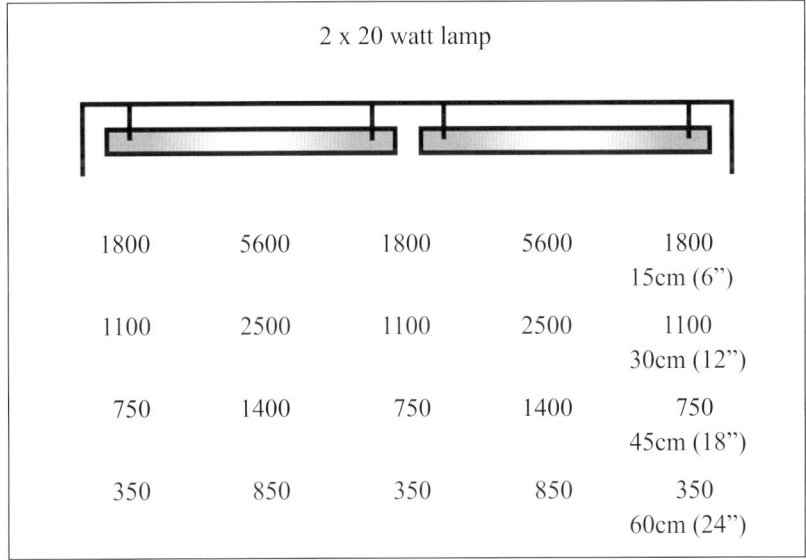				
1800	5600	1800	5600	1800
				15cm (6")
1100	2500	1100	2500	1100
				30cm (12")
750	1400	750	1400	750
				45cm (18")
350	850	350	850	350
				60cm (24")

The assembled light garden ready for use

The light unit is basically a gravel tray with flourescent tubes fitted.

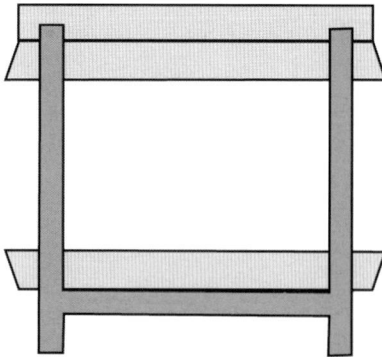

Hood to cover necessary switchgear

Gravel tray for plant display

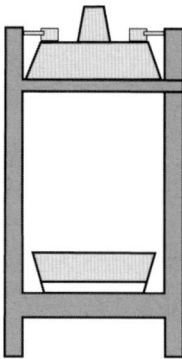

Note the rubber stops for safety

The gravel tray should be white or covered in a reflective material to reflect the light.

An important design factor to take into account when building a light garden is the glare from the fluorescent lights. Whether your lighting consists of a single tube, or two or more fixtures on a wide shelf all of the light should radiate down toward the plants, and must not be allowed to dazzle the eyes of anyone sitting or standing near your light garden. One way to avoid glare from the lights is to install a baffle or valance that shields the light and directs it downwards. This will have the added benefit of concealing the lamps. The depth of the baffle will depend on the height of the light fittings, and the openness of the space they illuminate. Above eye level, a louvred valance will work best to direct all the light downwards. (See page 90)

A Circular Light Garden

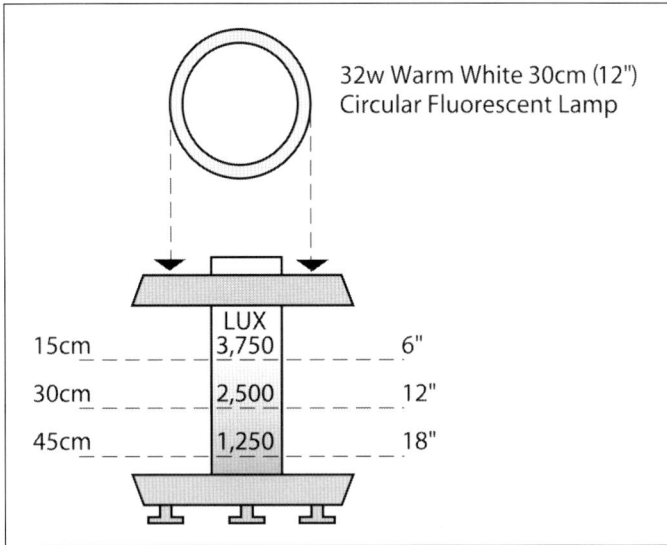

32w Warm White 30cm (12")
Circular Fluorescent Lamp

	LUX	
15cm	3,750	6"
30cm	2,500	12"
45cm	1,250	18"

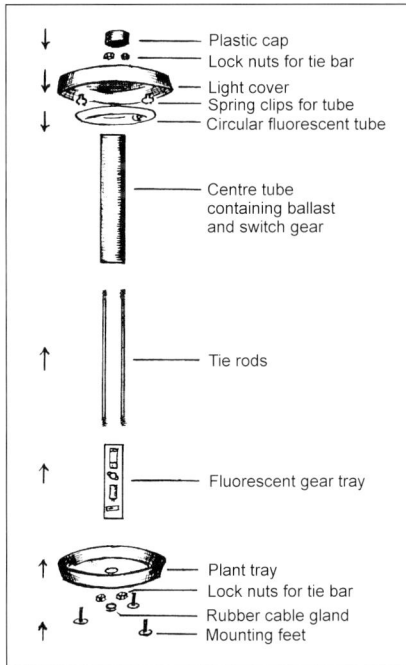

Plastic cap
Lock nuts for tie bar
Light cover
Spring clips for tube
Circular fluorescent tube

Centre tube
containing ballast
and switch gear

Tie rods

Fluorescent gear tray

Plant tray
Lock nuts for tie bar
Rubber cable gland
Mounting feet

The cost of running a light garden

The cost of running your light garden can be calculated as for a garden room (see page 34), taking into account the number and power of the fluorescent tubes and the length of time for which they burn. The recommendations in the **Plant Light Tables** for various light garden species vary from 14 to 18 hours a day, so you can choose to run a small light garden less expensively with the plants that require a lower intensity and a shorter day length, or you can choose to cultivate the more demanding flowering species that need stronger illumination and a full day length of 18 hours. Some readers may choose to start initially by using nothing more than a simple desk lamp, fitted with a fluorescent tube, to provide a few cherished pot plants with some much needed additional light, to see how they respond to this kind of treatment.

See Slide C21. Bottom left *Caladium* 'Candidum', top left *Anthurium andraeanum* 'Brazilian Sunshine', right *Alocasia* X*amazonica*.

See Slide D29. A colourful display of plants in an indoor light garden: *Caladium* 'Candidum' *Crassula ovata*, *Euphorbia milii*, *Impatiens* F1 New Guinea hybrids, carmine, red, and white. *Hyoltelephium sieboldii* 'Mediovariegatum', *Streptocarpus* X*hybridus*, and *Tradescantia*.

Plants for your light garden

A light garden allows you to grow many species of plants that cannot be grown successfully in the lower light levels of a garden room. In the light gardens described in this book plants needing light levels of up to 15,000 lux are included. Any plant that is difficult to grow or bring to flower in the garden room will thrive bathed in the additional light, providing always that both humidity and temperature are appropriate.

It is not only the more fastidious plants needing high light levels that you should consider for your light garden. Many plants will flower more abundantly there, and you will be able to have some species in flower throughout the year. Both flowers and foliage will have a brilliance far beyond what can be achieved under less powerful illumination. Your garden can become a focus of attention, and a source of endless satisfaction.

You will need to position your plants in relation to the fluorescent tubes to obtain the recommended lux level for each particular species. However, you must still watch the reactions of individual plants, and move them up or down according to their responses to their current light level.

If a plant is too far from the light, it will extend its leaves upwards or its foliage will turn pale. Both symptoms indicate that the plants should be moved nearer the tubes. If the plants are spreading their leaves out naturally, leave them where they are.

Since the plants below the ends of the fluorescent tubes receive rather less light than those at the centre, watch for any noticeable differences in the pattern of developing growth. If there is you should change the position of the plants as necessary, so they all share the benefit of higher illumination. You will also need to rearrange your plants when the new growth of one begins to shade other plants.

Flowering species require special attention to light levels. Those that need short-day treatment to bring about flower initiation will be a disappointment if they are left in the light garden full time.

There is a vast array of plant varieties that are suitable for an indoor light garden. Ideally, you should arrange your plants into groups of similar height and with similar light requirements, but if you prefer a mixed grouping of foliage and flowering plants of varying heights, be sure to change their positions every two or three days. They will be competing for the available light and the taller bushier plants will shade the smaller species.

With so many possibilities, it can be difficult to decide which plants to put in your light garden. The following list, while by no means comprehensive, may help you find some ideas to begin your garden plan.

Cacti and Succulent species abound that will thrive in a light garden. And among the flowering plants some outstanding choices for a light garden are, *Anthurium scherzerianum*, and *A. andraeanum*, and several species of *Aphelandra. Begonias* are excellent, as both the fibrous- rooted types, and tuberous-rooted types will produce lovely flowers, *Begonia rex and Begonia. masoniana* look stunning placed among foliage species, and *B. rex* has many available hybrids. *Caladium, Calathea, Coleus*, and *Peperomia* offer much variety among their many hybrids. There are also many attractive *Impatiens* hybrids in a score of different shades of colour, which can be had in flower at any season of the year.

If you wish to cultivate orchids, the hybrids of *Miltonia* and *Phalaenopsis* are two that will reward you with the delicate beauty of their flowers.

Other exciting flowering plants for a light garden include *Sinningia, Saintpaulia, Streptocarpus*, etc., and the cultivation of these plants is covered in detail below.

See Slide H1. *Achimenes* 'Carmencita.' Credit: Ball Colegrave Limited, West Adderbury, Banbury, Oxon OX17 3EY.

Achimenes (Cupid's Bower) Central America.
Gesneriaceae

Achimenes is a small bushy tender perennial herb 15cm (6") in height, which has been the subject of a good deal of hybridisation with the result that there are today dozens of cultivars. It bears small tubular flowers in an array of colours e.g. white, blue, orange, pink, purple, and red during the summer. Although regarded as a greenhouse or conservatory plant, it may also be grow successfully in a light garden.

The scaly rhizomes up to 25mm (1") long should be potted up into shallow pots containing a peat based potting mix. The number of rhizomes required will depend upon the sizes of the pot to be used. An 8.75cm (3½") pot will accommodate five rhizomes, while an 11.25cm (4½") pot will accommodate eight or nine rhizomes. The rhizomes are planted 2cm (¾") deep and spaced out at 1.25cm (½") apart, and watered sparingly.

Cuttings represent the most rapid means of increasing stocks of named hybrids, and these will commence to flower within three months, whereas plants produced from rhizomes will take four months, from potting to flowering. The tips of the shoots removed, when pruning achimenes to induce more compact growth, can be used for propagation purposes. The cuttings will root in 7 to 8 days, in a heated propagation case, and once established, they should be removed from there and their pots spaced out a little in the open light garden, where they are to be grown, so as to ensure a free movement of air about the plants.

Light needs: 10,000 to 15,000 lux 14 to 16 hours per day.

Temperature: 18°C-21°C (65°F-70°F)

Water: Sparingly at first, but as shoots appear more liberally, keeping the compost moist at all times during the growing season, but taking care not to overwater. A dry period will initiate the onset of the dormancy period, so do not let the compost dry out for a short period.

Humidity: Mist the plants daily, morning and night, and create a microclimate by standing the plants on moist peat or pebbles, and water this each day.

Feeding: Provide a dilute liquid feed once every 14 days May/August.

Pruning: Pinch back young shoots to encourage compact bushy growth.

Re-pot: In spring using a peat-based potting mix and start watering again, gradually increasing the moisture as new growth develops. Growth will not start however until the temperature is at a minimum of 16°C (60°F), and should really be in the 18°C to 21°C (65°F-70°F) range.

Propagation: By division of rhizomes, on re-potting, by stem cuttings, or by seed in spring. Use a peat-based potting mix. Place the pots in a heated propagation case with the bottom heat set at 20°C (68°F).

After flowering ceases gradually reduce watering and humidity, until the foliage has died down and the compost dried out, then store in a cool dry place through the winter; minimum temperature 7°C (45°F).

Good Achimenes hybrids include: Cascade Fashionable Pink, soft pink. Cascade Violet Blue, violet blue. Flamingo, scarlet red. Tarantella, carmine red. Snowhite, serenely white.

Begonia

Begonia corallina "Angelwing Begonia";
Begoniaceae

This is one of the best known of the cane-stemmed begonias that is grown indoors as a houseplant. It is of strong upright growth and has large angel wing leaves, which are dark green in colour and spotted white on the upper surface and deep red beneath. It carries large drooping cymes of dark pink long lasting small flowers. When grown in a large pot or shrub tub it can attain 1.8M (6ft) or more in height. When grown in a more constricted pot growth may be 60cm-90cm (2ft-3ft) in height.

This is a very rewarding flowering plant, which can be easily propagated from stem-cuttings, or tip cuttings, when re-potting during the spring, in the open light garden. It can also be propagated from seed in a heated propagation case at 21°C (70°F) at any season of the year. Once established, this begonia may be removed from the light garden completely, and grown near a bright window, or in the pool of light, which spills out from a light garden onto the adjacent floor.

Light needs: 2,300-4,500 lux for 14 to 16 hours per day.

Temperature: Winter minimum temp. 13°C (55°F)

Water: Liberally, but do not flood the potting compost, during the growing season; reduce watering during the wintertime.

Humidity: Create a microclimate about the plant by standing it on a tray of moist peat/pebbles, which is sprayed with water daily, or mist the leaves occasionally.

Feeding: Give a dilute application of liquid feed in accordance with the manufacture's directions every 14 days, during active growth.

Pruning: Tall growing shrubs in tubs and large pots should be pruned back in the spring, to leave a short stump with just two to three buds, to encourage new growth.

Repot: In spring each year, if necessary, using a peat-based potting mix.

Propagation: Stem cuttings root quite easily, and seeds can be sown in a heated propagation case, with the temperature set at 21°C (70°F).

See Slide D13. *Begonia* Semperflorens, F1 'Devon Gems Mixed'.

Begonia Semperflorens–Cultorum Hybrids Bedding Begonia, Wax Begonia.

Begoniaceae

Begonia Semperflorens comes originally from Brazil. This is a small flowered, fibrous rooted plant, which has been subjected to a good deal of hybridization, and it is widely grown as a half hardy summer bedding plant. It is also equally floriferous when grown in an indoors light garden, and may be had in flower at any season of the year.

Seed should be sown thinly on the surface of a moist peat-based mix and not covered, as light is essential for germination. Place the seed pan or seed tray in a heated propagation case at a temperature of 21°C-24°C (70°F-75°F). Maintain a high humidity, but do not saturate the compost with moisture. If necessary, water the containers from the base in a tray of water. Germination will occur in two to three weeks. From seed sowing to the appearance of the first flowers takes some 14 to 16 weeks, under good growing conditions.

If you do not wish to sow your own seed, small trays of Begonia semperflorens seedling may be purchased ready for pricking out, from a garden centre, in the spring. If you have existing plants, which have been bought originally as houseplants, *B.* Semperflorens can be rooted from cuttings in a heated propagation case very easily.

Light needs: 8,000 lux 14 to 16 hours per day.

Temperature: Established plants winter minimum night temp. 13°C (55°F)

Water: Liberally, but do not flood the potting compost.

Humidity: Create a microclimate about the plants by standing them on a tray of moist peat/pebbles, which are sprayed with water daily. Failing either of these, spray the plant tray with water daily.

Feeding: Give a dilute application of liquid feed in accordance with the manufacture's directions every 14 days, starting 4 weeks after potting up the plants.

Propagation: Sow seed, or take stem cuttings, at any time of the year, in a heated propagation case.

Browallia

Browallia speciosa (Bush Violet)
Solanaceae

This plant owes its name to the Lutheran bishop Johan Browallius (1705-55), Bishop of Abo, Sweden, a knowledgeable botanist and a defender of Linnaeus's sexual system. Unfortunately he did not live to learn of this himself.

Browallia speciosa is a shrubby perennial from Colombia, from which small hybrids have been developed.

Browallia speciosa 'Blue Troll' is a small cultivar, which bears a profusion of flowers of purplish blue with a white eye. Height 20-25cm (8-10in.). *B. s.* 'White Troll' is the pure white counterpart to Blue Troll.

They may be either bought as pot-plants, just as they are coming into bloom, or propagated from seed.

Propagation: Sow the seed at any time of the year, at a temperature of 18-21°C (65-70°F) on the surface of a peat/sand seed mix, but do not exclude the light.

When sown at three monthly intervals, *Browallia* will provide a continuous succession of plants.

Pot-up the plants in a freely drained loam based compost mix for preference, using 13cm (5") pots.

Once flowering commences it will continue for many weeks if you provide cool growing conditions.

Light needs: 10,000 lux 14-16 hours per day

Feeding: Provide a weak solution of liquid feed every 14 days, once the plants are established

Temperature 13°C/ 16°C (55°F/ 60°F).

Pruning: Pinch out the growing tips from time to time to promote bushiness, and pick off the dead flowers as they fade.

Water: Keep the compost moist at all times, but do not over wet, as the roots will be damaged by excessive watering. Mist the leaves occasionally.

Discard with the plants once flowering ceases.

See Slide A16. *Caladium* 'Candidum'.
See Slide A18. *Caladium* 'Frieda Hemple'.

Caladium (Angle Wings; Elephant's-ear.)

Araceae

A genus of some few species of tuberous perennial foliage plants from tropical South America.

Caladium X*hortulanum* hybrids make fine indoor plants. They are of a bushy compact habit and some 30cm (12") in height. They bear colourful heart shaped leaves 20cm (8") long and 10cm (4") wide, which hang from long slender stems. Once in active growth the plants can be shunted between the light garden and the garden room, every few days or so, without suffering any setback providing their other cultural needs are met.

Another good idea is to grow the caladium at floor level, once it has fully established its new season's foliage. Place the plant adjacent to the light garden, where it may then gain the benefit of all the stray light, which spills out from the light garden's canopy onto the surrounding floor area. But remember to turn the plant around every day or two, so that the whole of its foliage may be satisfied by this source of illumination. Other garden room foliage plants may be treated likewise with equal success too.

Any light garden enthusiasts who once start taking advantage of this means of satisfying a plant's need for light, will quickly find themselves creating their first interior plantscape feature around the base of the light garden. And once bitten by that bug, they will be keen to extend their activities in that direction!

Light needs: 4,000/7,000 lux 12/14 hours per day.

Temperature: The tubers are stored while dormant during the winter at a minimum temperature of 13°C to16°C (55°F - 60°F).

Re-pot: The tubers are potted up in a moist peat-based potting mix during March and placed in a heated propagation case at 21°C- 23°C (70°F-75°F). When the new shoots appear the temperature is reduced to 18°C (65°F) and they are misted several times a day. The caladium's true foliage colours do not become apparent until some four new leaves have developed.

Water: Water sparingly as new growth begins but increasing as growth gathers pace and the caladiums are placed in the open light garden.

Humidity: Mist plants two or three times daily.

Feeding: Provide a dilute liquid feed every 14 days during active growth.

Propagation: Detach small tubers, when re-potting them up individually in March.

Catharanthus

*Catharanthus roseus** (Madagascar Periwinkle)

Apocynaceae

See Slide D22. *Catharanthus roseus* 'Morning Mist'.

Catharanathus roseus F1 hybrids in the 'Cooler Series' are half-hardy annuals, which not only make excellent compact bushy plants indoors, but also, when hardened off may be planted outside as fine summer bedding plants too.

Sow the seeds on the surface of a peat-based compost mix and cover with 10mm (2/5th of an inch) of medium vermiculite. Place in a heated propagation case at 21°C (70°F) where germination will occur in approximately 14 to 21 days after which they should be grown on in a moderate humidity of 50% in the propagation case until the seedlings are large enough to handle. They are then potted up in 8.75cm (3½ inch) pots containing a peat-based potting mix and placed in the open light garden.

The whole process from seed sowing to having flowering plants takes 12/14 weeks and it is possible to have plants flowering in the indoor light garden at any time of the year.

Catharanthus F1 'Peppermint Cooler' bears crisp snow-white flowers with a dark red eye. These contrast well with the bright green foliage, making the plant a distinctive subject for the light garden or sunny windowsill. Individual flowers are 3.75cm (1½ inch) or more in diameter, and once flowering commences it will continue unceasingly for some 16 weeks or more. Other F1 hybrids in the 'Cooler Series' are 'Blush Cooler' with its deep pink eye against a pastel pink background, and 'Grape Cooler' lavender pink.

Light needs: 10.000 lux for 14 to 16 hours per day.

Temperature: Winter minimum 16°C (60°F)

Watering: Moderately keeping the compost moist at all time but never wet through.

Humidity: Indoors mist the plants daily.

Feeding: Provide a dilute liquid feed once every 14 days while the plants are in active growth and flowering.

Catharanthus roseus is of medical importance too, as it contains alkaloids used to relieve Leukaemia.

See Slide D23. *Euphorbia milii* (Crown of thorns) may be had in flower at all times of the year in the indoor light garden.

Euphorbia

Euphorbia milii, 'Crown of Thorns'

Euphorbiaceae

Euphorbia milii is a delightful flowering succulent plant, with thick angular, sharp spiny stems, elliptic bright green leaves, and scarlet bracts. This is an interesting and undemanding houseplant, which does not need daily misting, and can accept a degree of neglect, when grown in the garden room, where it will flower from spring to autumn, and then take a rest for a while. But when bathed in the more intense illumination of a light garden, it will flower continuously throughout the whole year. It may lose a few of its lower, older leaves, during the winter months, but this is a natural occurrence, and this will in no way detract from its beautiful appearance.

Light needs: When grown as a light garden subject, it will flourish in a light intensity of 8,000 lux to 10,000 lux for 14 to 16 hours each day.

Temperature: Minimum winter temperature, for light garden, year round flowering plants, 18°C (65°F). For spring and summer flowering garden room plants the minimum winter temperature, is 13°C (55F').

Watering: In the garden room, water moderately from spring to autumn, and more sparingly, at other times of the year. In the light garden water moderately throughout the year, but allow the compost surface to dry between waterings. Use tepid water

Feeding: Provide a dilute liquid feed every 21 days, while in active growth.

Re-pot: Re-potting, (in spring and summer time) should only take place every second year, at which time the plant should be given a slightly larger pot. Use a compost consisting of equal parts of peat-based potting mix, and grit or coarse sand.

Propagation: This is by stem-tip cuttings 7.5cm to 10cm (3" to 4") long, in the spring and summer time. Leave the cuttings which will bleed*, for 24 hours to dry, before potting them up in small pots containing a very sandy rooting mix consisting of 25% peat -based potting mix and 75% sand. Watering must be done with tepid water.

*NC. **E. milii,** along with all euphorbias, has a milky white poisonous sap, so wear gloves when taking cuttings, or whenever handling or re-potting these plants

Exacum

Exacum affine (Persian Violet)

Gentianaceae
South Yemen (Socotra)

Exacum F1 Hybrid 'Midget Blue' is a bushy, compact annual plant with glossy green foliage and lightly scented lavender-blue flowers with orange stamens. Height, 12.5cm (5"). There is also a white flowered hybrid 'Midget White' with white flowers and tiny orange stamens.

These *Exacum* hybrids may be either raised from seed, or bought as pot plants, as they come into bloom.

Once in flower this plant needs a lot of nourishment, and should receive a weekly feed of dilute liquid fertiliser. It will remain in bloom for several months and flowering may be prolonged by regularly removing the faded flowers before they set seed.

By sowing seeds at three monthly intervals *Exacum* may be had in flower throughout the year.

Light needs: 10,000 lux for 14-16 hours per day.

Temperature: Winter minimum 13°C (55°F).

Watering: Water moderately. Keep the potting compost moist but never wet.

Humidity: Mist the plants daily.

Feeding: Provide a weekly dilute liquid feed.

Propagation: Propagation is by seed, which may take place at any time of the year. Sow seeds on the surface of a mix consisting of 2-parts peat based potting mix and 1-part sand; and do not cover, temperature 21°C (70°F), and pot into 7.5cm (3") pots of the same mix as soon as the seedlings are large enough to handle.

Treat the plant as an annual and discard it, once the flowering season is at an end.

See Slide D26. *Fuchsia* 'Madam Cornnelissen', rooted from a cutting in the light garden.

Fuchsia (Lady's ear-drops) is native to Central and South America, New Zealand and Tahiti

Onagraceae

Linnaeus named this plant after the German Herbalist and botanical illustrator Leonhart Fuchs (1501-66).

Fuchsias are one of the most popular of pot-plants and hanging basket plants with their gay flowers consisting of four or more swept back sepals and bell-shaped corolla with long showy stamens, on long thin pendulous stalks from the leaf axils. They make an ideal beginners subject for either the garden room or light garden, as nothing could be easier to grow.

If you visit your local garden centre in the spring-time you will find on display a goodly selection of young single and double flowered fuchsia hybrids in 7.5cm to 10 cm (3" to 4") plants pots, and freshly rooted cuttings of the same.

I chose *Fuchsia* 'Display', a bushy type with attractive rose pink/deeper pink flowers as one of my light garden subjects and *Fuchsia* 'Madam Cornnelissen', which is of a pendulous habit and bears delightful double red and white flowers as my other. This latter fuchsia is also suitable for growing in a hanging basket under fluorescent lamps or near a bright window in a garden room.

Once a few stock plants have been initially acquired it is a simple matter to produce further plants by means of cuttings from new growth 5cm (2") long. These will root readily either in a peat-based compost mix or a peat and sand rooting mix, if they are placed in a heated propagation case, in a light garden, with the bottom heat set at 18°C (65°F). Once fresh growth is in evidence remove the rooted cuttings from the propagation case and, having potted them up in 7.5cm (3") pots in a peat-based potting mix, place them in the open light garden where they will flourish bathed in all the light which is available to them, and before you know it they well be starting to produce the first of a great multitude of flowers.

The fuchsia is a day neutral plant, that is to say it is unaffected by photoperiodism or day-length. The flowering season was in the past considered to extend from March to November, but with the introduction of some of the modern hybrids fuchsias may now be had in flower the year round. The secrets for success are these:

Light needs 1, 11, or 111.

Pruning: Judicious pinching back of young shoots to induce bushy growth, or the formation of fresh laterals in pendulous varieties; and the removal of all dead flowers to induce further bud formation.

Temperature: Keep the plants only at cool to average warmth indoors, that is to say within the 13°C/18°C (55°F/65°F) range, and ensure that the temperature does not stray over 21°C (70°F).

Watering: Keep the compost moist at all times during active growth and flowering, while watering sparingly at other times.

Humidity: Keep the air about the plants humid. The latter being achieved by the creation of a microclimate, either by standing the pots on a plant-tray containing a layer of moist peat or pebbles, better still accessed to a capillary watering system, or most basically of all by misting the leaves daily.

Feeding: Provide a liquid feed every 14 days throughout the period of active growth and flowering.

Where fuchsias are used as hanging basket plants choose hanging baskets, which are of the self-watering type.

Impatiens BUSY LIZZIE

Balsaminaceae

Impatiens walleriana is a freely flowering perennial native to Mozambique and Tanzania.

The plants grown today as the ever-popular houseplants, and summer bedding plants, are highly developed hybrids of a continuous flowering habit, and they are treated as tender annuals.

When *Impatiens* is grown in an indoor light garden it will provide a superb display of flowers, at all seasons of the year and is an ideal subject for a beginner to growing under artificial light.

Seed propagated flowering plants can be produced in about three months. Sow the seeds very slightly covered on a peat based compost mix, in a seed tray or pot in a heated propagation case, at a temperature of 21°C-23°C (70°F/75°F).

Germination, will take 10-18 days, and as soon as the seedlings are large enough to handle, they should be pricked out individually into 8.75cm – 10cm (3½"-4") pots and then placed in the open light garden close to the lamps at a temperature of 18°C-21°C (65°F-70°F). The plants will commence to flower freely once their pots are filled with roots.

The *Impatiens* F1 Accent Series has long been popular for its all round performance and won gold medals at the Chelsea Flower Show. Its has deep green foliage, large flowers, and a whole succession of flower buds to ensure continual flowering when this commences, and it is available in a wide array of colours which include: Purple, Violet, Lavender, Carmine Red, Orange, Orange Scarlet, Orange Salmon, Apricot. Salmon, Blush, Deep Rose, Rose, Pink, Pale Pink, Purest White, and mixed colour.

Light needs:7,000 to 10,000 lux 14 to 16 hour per day

Temperature: The winter minimum temperature to keep the plants flowering is 16°C (60°F)

Watering: Keep the compost moist at all times while the plants are in active growth.

Humidity: Mist the plants occasionally, but avoid the open blooms.

Feeding: Do not provide a dilute liquid feed until the first flower buds appear and then apply this once every 14 days, while the plants are in active growth and flowering.

Propagation: This may be by seed, or tip cuttings, which root readily at all times of the year. Plants growing and flowering indoors can be used therefore to supply rooted cuttings to produce plants for the summer bedding display in the garden in due season.

See Slide D32. *Pelargonium* X*hortorum* 'Friesdorf.'(A miniature geranium.)

Pelargonium
Pelargonium X*hortorum*
Geraniaceae

Growing mini geraniums

Miniature geraniums are an excellent choice for the limited space of an indoor light garden, and will provide masses of glorious colour throughout the year.

Miniature geraniums require the same general conditions as large zonal and ivy-leaved geraniums. Miniatures they may be, but in relation to the size of the whole plant, their flowers are large and vivid.

Light Needs: Provide a light intensity of 13,000/15,000 lux 16 to 18 hours per day.

The secret of success lies in the size of the pot you provide for each plant. When starting with rooted cuttings, which should be available from your garden centre, the geranium should be restricted to a 5cm (2") pot containing a peat-based potting mix. When it has established itself and begun to flower continuously, it can be re-potted in a 6.25cm (2½") pot. At the end of the first year, you might consider re-potting the plant into a 7.5cm (3")) pot. Without the root restriction, the plant will grow somewhat large, producing more foliage but it will become less floriferous. Plants treated in this way will be most useful for taking cuttings from to start fresh stock.

Clearly, growing miniature geraniums in such a small amount of potting mix means that the roots of the plants are soon likely to run short of food, therefore start to supply a very, very, dilute application of liquid feed (at the equivalent strength of one teaspoon full of the concentrated liquid feed to a gallon of water) on every fourth occasion when watering the plants after potting them up. Someone with a very few plants of course will not be using the diluted liquid feed by the gallon! But the actual degree of the dilution necessary will be clear from this description.

Six months after potting, the mix will need freshening. Knock the plant out of its pot, and by gently teasing the roots with your fingers, dislodge about 50 percent of the old mix. Follow this with some judicious root pruning to remove a few older roots and encourage fresh root activity. Re-pot the geranium in the same pot and begin feeding as before.

The aim is to produce a compact, short-jointed plant capable of sustained flowering. Always remove the flower stems as blooms fade to encourage new flower development. You will also need to do some careful pruning from time to time, otherwise the stems will become long and spindly, with just a few leaves showing below the flowers. Flowers are produced only on new green growth, not on older, woody stems. You can cut back some of the growing shoots to maintain the plant's bushy habit. This will be only partly effective though, as the geranium must continue to grow upwards if new lateral growths are to provide the plant with a continuous supply of flowers. You will still find some straggly growth when leaves form a rosette behind the growing points of otherwise bare stems.

If a plant is developing this consistently, you can cut most of the stems right back with a pruning knife to encourage fresh growth from the stem base. Leave one or more stems complete with leaves but cut back the rest of the plant to within 5cm (2") of the potting mix. New shoots will quickly develop, and then the remaining old stems can also be pruned so that they too develop new shoots. In this way new growth and flowering potential can be promoted.

Miniature geraniums do not enjoy hot, dry conditions, despite being fond of the sun. Provide a cool environment, with a day maximum of 20°C (68°F) and a night minimum of 13°C (55°F). What the plants like most, to develop their sturdy stems, is fresh but barely moist potting mix around the roots. So be sparing when watering the pots, or you will encourage uncharacteristic soft, sappy growths that are susceptible to fungus attack.

You can create a microclimate, within the immediate area, by placing the pots on a small tray of gravel or peat, better still some capillary matting, and spray this every morning. Alternatively, use a fine spray to mist the foliage daily. Either of these methods will create the humidity necessary for the full development of your plants.

Ideally, miniature geraniums should not be maintained under these conditions for longer than 18 months, as they will begin to lose their flowering momentum. You will be more pleased if you propagate new plants from stem cuttings taken from plants that have been allowed to produce more vegetative growth in 7.5cm (3") pots. Use these to replace your older plants, and treat them as described above for rooted cuttings from a garden centre.

Miniature geranium varieties

'Alcyone.' A bushy plant with dark foliage and double, plum-red flowers.

'Algenon' Slightly zoned mid-green foliage and double, white-based pink flowers.

'Goblin.' Dark foliage and deep red flowers.

'Keepsake.' Very large flowers, purple-rose with white eyes.

'Medley.' A very bushy plant, with dark foliage, and double flowers, white with a distinctive yellow-green tint.

'Orange Imp.' Green foliage and a mass of double orange flowers.

'Red Spider.' Cactus flowered; brilliant scarlet narrow rolled petals; very dark-zoned leaves

'Rosita' Lightly zoned dark green foliage and double scarlet flowers, in "rose-bud" form.

'Snowbaby.' Olive-green foliage and large, pure white flowers.

'Trinket'. A slow-growing plant with small green leaves and double, bright apricot flowers.

See Slide D43. *Saintpaulia* 'Silver Milestone'.

See Slide D45. Bill Carter in his *Saintpaulia* garden room.

Saintpaulia

Saintpaulia ionantha. (African Violet). Tanzania

Gesneriaceae

The African violet was named after the German who discovered it, Baron Walter von Saint Paul-llaire (1860-1910).

Saintpaulia ionantha is a low growing herbaceous perennial, forming a compact rosette of foliage and its flowers are produced on short stems just above these. There are now-a-days numerous named cultivars, including miniature and trailing kinds, with a bewildering assortment of flower forms ranging in colour through white, pink, red, blue and dark purple.

Propagation may be by seed or by the vegetative means of leaf-stem cuttings, but as the numerous named cultivars do not come true from seed, the latter is the principal method of propagation.

Mature leaves, which are firm and of good colour, are used. The stems (petioles) are cut at a slant to 2.5cm to 3.75cm (1 to 1½ inch) long and the leaves are stuck in a peat/sand propagating compost 5cm (2") apart, with stalks erect, in such a way that the leaves do not touch each other. Place the pots of cuttings in a light garden propagator, with the bottom heat set at 21°C (70°F). Plantlets will then form on the stems, after four or five weeks, and in 10 to 12 weeks they will be ready for potting up.

Each leaf-stalk cutting may have some three to five or more young plantlets attached to it and the whole lot is then potted up as one plant, in 5cm/6.25cm (2"-2½") pots containing a peat based compost and grown on in the open light garden Then, as the roots of the plants fill the pots, move them on into pots one size larger, but bear in mind that Saintpaulia plants like to be kept slightly pot-bound.

This method of planting the whole of the plantlets on a leaf stem into one pot will result in the development of large plants with many more flowers than would be the case, if each plantlet was, potted up individually. The plants are then grown on at a temperature of 18-23°C (65-75°F) and the pot sizes are gradually increased as is appropriate to the needs of the particular Saintpaulia cultivar concerned. Many plants grow and bloom quite happily in 10cm (4") pots while in the case of large growing types 20cm (8") pots may be necessary. However, miniature Saintpaulias should remain in their 5cm/6.25cm (2"-2½") pots and when it becomes necessary to re-pot them, the way to proceed here is to cut the lower third of the root-ball away at the time of re-potting and then, having filled the lower part of the pot with fresh compost, re-pot the plants in this.

The whole process from leaf stem cuttings to flowering plants takes 7-8 months.

The propagation of flowering Saintpaulia plants from seed takes some 9-10 months. The seed is sown in light on the surface of a peat-based compost, at a temperature of 21°C (70°F), with high humidity, in a heated propagator. Germination will take 4 to 6 weeks. Once the seedlings are large enough to handle, they are potted up into 5cm/6.25cm (2"-2½") pots, containing a peat based compost, and grown on in a light garden in the same way as the vegetatively propagated plants.

Light Needs: 6,500 lux, 14 to 18 hours per day. At this light intensity plants will continue to grow and flower throughout the year.

Water: The compost should be kept moist but never soaked at all times. If the compost dries out too much then the roots of the plants will be damaged. Use tepid water. To prevent foliage damage; always water the pots from the bottom.

Humidity: Surround the pots with moist peat, or place them on a tray of pebbles and keep these wet at all times, to create a microclimate about the plants.

Feed: Except during the resting period give a _weak_ application of liquid feed ever 7/10 days.

Propagation: This may be by seed or by leaf-stem cuttings.

See Slide E1. *Sinningia* 'Jester Mixed' F2 Hybrid, flowering, in the light garden.

Sinningia

Sinningia speciosa **(Florist's Gloxinia)**

Gesneriaceae

The botanical name of one of our most loved plants is based on that of Wilhelm Sinning (1792-1847), a Prussian horticulturalist and botanist, who was the curator of the Botanical Garden in Bonn; whilst its common name is based on that of Benjamin Gloxin a Strasbourg Physician.

Sinningia speciosa is a tuberous rooted perennial plant with rosette forming velvet textured foliage, and bell-shaped, lavender, purple, red, or white flowers in the wild, but few *S. speciosa* are in cultivation today. The plants generally in cultivation are in fact hybrids of this, and bear flowers of mixed colours.

Gloxinia hybrids may be grown from seed into flowering plants in 11.25cm (4½") pots in 5/6 months in an indoor light garden. The seeds are extremely small (26,470 seeds per gram.), and some care is called for when they are sown onto the surface of a finely graded peat-based potting mix, which has been previously moistened. Place the seed container into a heated propagation case at a temperature of 22°C (73°F) until germination is complete. At this temperature the seedlings should be ready for pricking off in four to five weeks. This is firstly into 8.75cm (3½") pots, and later into 11.25cm (4½") pots using the same peat-based potting mix. At the time of potting up the seedlings into individual pots they are moved from the propagation case into the open light garden, to continue their development.

When the flower buds have formed in the crown of the plants and enlarged to the point where they are clearly visible, it will be necessary to remove any leaves, which have also developed in the crown. This has to be done otherwise they will displace some of the flower buds and result in plants of unbalanced appearance.

When the resulting plants are well budded, a more uniform plant may be obtained, by removing the first two flower buds, just as they begin to show colour, thus encouraging more of the other buds to develop and flower at one and the same time.

Light needs 9, 000 lux for 15/16 hours per day.

Temperature: Night temperature 20°C (68°F) and a little higher by day.

Water: Water from the base of the pots to keep the compost moist at all times, but never allow it to become saturated. Take care to keep the foliage and the crown of the plants dry.

Feed: Provide an occasional weak dose of liquid feed, at only 25% of the recommended strength, during their growing period, to avoid a build up of salt levels in the compost to a point where root damage may result.

Although the vast majority of gloxinias are grown from seed nowadays they may also be grown from tubers.

The tubers may be started into growth from December onwards. They are placed in boxes containing moist compost at a temperature of 20°C (68°F) and once they have produced a good root system they are potted up into 12.5cm (5") pots and then grown on in the same manner as the ones grown from seed.

Tuber-grown gloxinias make somewhat larger and more vigorous plants with the result that the removal of crown leaves from between the developing buds will call for more attention. When grown under artificial light the plants are discarded with once flowering ceases, and fresh tubers purchased for the following year.

Gloxinias grown under artificial light do not form tubers.

See Slide E6. *Streptocarpus* F1 'Royal Mixed' in a large light garden.

Streptocarpus

Streptocarpus (Cape Primrose)

Gesneriaceae

Streptocarpus **Xhybridus**, although greenhouse perennials, may be grown in the home provided they are given a bright light away from direct sunlight, and are ideal candidates for cultivation in an indoor light garden.

Plants are usually propagated from seed or leaf cuttings.

Seed propagated flowering plants can be produced in 5/6months.

Sow the seeds on the surface of a peat based compost, in a seed tray, pot etc., in a heated plant propagator, and do not exclude the light, temperature 21°C-23°C (70°F/75F) After germination, when the seedlings are large enough to handle, prick them out into other seed trays, or smallish plant pots and grow them on at 18°C-21°C (65°F/70°F).

See Slide E4. *Streptocarpus* F1 'Royal Mixed'; seedling growth stimulation may be necessary.

Streptocarpus can sometimes be a bit stubborn about making growth in the early stages of their development, but a process of jumping the plantlets forwards can overcome this. That is to say patching the plants out complete with a clump of their original compost, onto the surface of another pot or seed tray containing fresh moist compost. This may need doing more than once in order to get them over their initial lack of growth, but each time they are treated thus, some discernible growth will occur.

Lower the temperature to 16°C-18°C (60°F/65°F) from the time the plants are large enough to be potted up individually into 7.5cm (3") pots in the open light garden. *Streptocarpus* X*hybridus* are only shallow rooted plants so when they are ready for moving on again into firstly 12.5cm (5") pots, and finally 15cm (6") pots use half pots for this purpose.

Vegetative propagation is by leaf sections. A mature leaf is taken from a plant and the mid-vein removed. The two pieces of leaf are then placed length-wise in a peat/sand rooting mixture, which is kept moist, in a heated propagator set at 21°C (70°F). The leaf sections will root in three or four weeks, and in another four weeks plantlets will appear along the cut edges, but these should not be transplanted until they are large enough to handle easily, in a further four weeks, making a total of three months. By this means of propagation a fresh batch of flowering plants in a 10cm (4") pot can be obtained in six months.

Light needs: 9,000/10,000 lux for 15/16 hrs per day.

Temperature: Minimum winter night temperature 16°C (60°F).

Water: The compost should be allowed to dry out slightly between waterings' during active growth and flowering, but kept on the dry side when the plants are resting periodically. (Plants are easily injured when over watered.)

Feed: To ensure vigorous flowering give an application of liquid feed at half the recommended rate once every 14 days

Streptocarpus F1 'Royal Mixed ' colour range of flowers, includes red, and rose shades, in addition to the normal blue and lavender tones.

The *Streptocarpus* 'Wiesmoor' hybrids are also good for cultivation in the indoor light garden. They bear beautiful waved and fringed flowers in colours of lavender, mauve, pink, and white.

Summer bedding plant propagation for the outdoor garden

While the garden room may not be able to fulfil all the functions of the greenhouse, with the introduction of light gardens, and heated propagation cases, it does go some way towards rendering the latter as being something of an expensive anachronism. This is particularly so where the propagation of plants from seed and the rooting of cuttings is concerned, for bedding plants, propagated under the influence of fluorescent lamps, in the warmth of the garden room, give better results than from those obtained in the greenhouse. There is a faster rate of growth, so seed sowing dates may be delayed by a couple of weeks or so, yet the resulting plants still be every bit as sturdy as those with the longer growing period, by the time bedding out takes place. Furthermore, the plants need not occupy a light garden for more than a few weeks as, once pricked out and growing well in their pots or trays, they can be moved, in early April, to a cold frame in the garden. Here they are protected by the glass and on cold nights a piece of tarpaulin sheeting, or something similar, may be placed over the top of this, to give extra protection. In early May the top of the light should be removed altogether, during the daytime, and only replaced at night, if clear skies should suggest that frost is likely. The plants will then be hardened off and ready for planting out in early June.

BEDDING PLANT PROPAGATION - IN THE INDOOR LIGHT GARDEN
Seedlings and young plants 8,000 lux 16 hours per day.

Crop Plant	Time sown	Temp	Germination days	Observations
Ageratum houstonianum	Mid March	18/21°C (65/70°F)	10/14	Sow-thinly on surface.
Antirrhinum majus	Late Feb	21°C (70°F)	,,	,,
Begonia **S**emperflorens	Jan/Feb	21/23°C (70/75°F)	,,	,,
Begonia Tuberhybrida Hybrids	,,	,,	,,	,,
Calendula officinalis cultivars	March	18/21°C (65/70°F)	7/14	Sow lightly covered.
Dahlia hortensis	March	16°C (60°F)	14/21	Sow seeds individually in pots covered with 10mm of compost.
Dorotheanthus bellidiformis syn. *Mesembryanthemum criniflorum*	March	18/21°C (65/70°F)	14/21	Sow seeds pressed into the surface of compost.
Impatiens hybrids	March	21/23°C (70/75°F)	10/18	Sow lightly covered.
Lobelia erinus	Early Feb	18/21°C (65/70°F)	14/18	Sow seeds pressed into the surface of compost.

Lobularia maritima syn. *Alyssum maritimum*	,,	,,	14/16	Sow-thinly on surface
Pelargonium zonale	Jan/Feb	21°C (70°F)	14/21	Sow lightly covered.
Petunia hybrids	March	16/18°C (60/65°F)	10/15	Sow on surface.
Phlox dummondii	,,	,,	14/21	Sow lightly covered.
Salpiglossis sinuate	Mid March	18/21°C (60/65°F)	10/14	Sow lightly covered.
Salvia splendens	Mid/Feb	21/23°C (70/75°F)	18/21	,,
Senecio cineraria 'Silver Dust'.	March	18/20°C (65/68°F)	7/10	Sow lightly covered.
Tagetes patula.	April	18/21°C (65/70°F)	8/15	,,
Tagetes tenuifolia.	,,	,,	,,	,,
Verbena x*hybrida*	March	,,	18/21	Sow lightly Covered.

When starting the seeds into growth in a heated propagator, placed within a light garden, this has several benefits.

1. It avoids the costs of heating a greenhouse, and the vagaries of the weather to which the plants would be exposed i.e., periods of dull, cloudy, or foggy conditions.

2. The seeds can be started into growth several weeks later than might otherwise be the case, with a steady light intensity of 8,000 lux for 16 hours per day, once germination occurs.

3. The resulting seedling can then be pricked out, into small plant-pots or seed trays, as appropriate, and grown on in a light garden for a few weeks, in the warmth of the garden room until such time as the weather becomes milder, when the bedding plants may be placed outside in an un-heated cold-frame, for growing on, and hardening off, prior to being planted out in the garden in early June.

Once germination has taken place keep the seedlings within 15cm (6") of the fluorescent lamps, so as to ensure stocky compact growth.

If your indoor garden is not equipped with a heated propagation case you could consider buying one, as the simplest models are inexpensive to purchase, and very cheap to operate, consuming no more than 20 watts to 30 watts of electricity per hour, when in use. Alternatively, providing you already have a light garden at your disposal, you could consider buying in a few bedding plant seedlings, ready for pricking out, and start the procedure from that stage. You will find many garden centres, and some super-market stores, stock small trays of bedding plant seedling, and do a brisk trade in these, during the early months of the year.

Some seedlings may also be purchased in the form of 'Miniplugs', that is to say individually grown seedlings in tiny tapered plugs. These are easily pulled out and transplanted into plant-pots or trays. There are also 'Speedlings'. These are similar to the former only the plantlets are a little older, and ready for potting up. In either case the seedlings and the plantlets are bought in easy to handle strips, and can be transplanted without root damage to check subsequent growth.

The trays of seedlings most readily available in the U.K. are the following:

Ageratum

Antirrhinum

Begonia

Dorotheanthus bellidiformis, syn. *Mesembryanthemum criniflorum*

Dahlia hortensis

Impatiens

Lobelia

Lobularia maritima, syn,. *Alyssum maritimum*

Petunia

Pelargonium

Stocks

Salvia

Senecio cineraria 'Silver Dust,' syn., *Cineraria maritime*, 'Silver Dust'

Tagetes

Verbena

All you have to do is to prick them out into seed-trays, or plant-pots, containing a peat-based compost, and give them the benefit of the light and warmth of a light garden until they get established, and put on some growth, then you can put them out into a cold frame in the garden, during early April. But do remember to place a piece of tarpaulin, straw matting, or other insulation material, over the glass each evening until all fear of night frost has ended.

Vegetative propagation

The availability of a heated propagation case and a light garden, in the garden room/working garden, will also prove a valuable asset, when it comes to the rooting of a few chrysanthemum cuttings, or dahlia cuttings during the earlier months of the year.

Chrysanthemums propagation

Chrysanthemum cuttings need to be rooted in February/early March, and should be secured from the old chrysanthemum stools, of the previous year, which have been given the protection of a cold frame, during the winter. If you have no stock plants of your own, you will be able to buy rooted cuttings, either from a local garden centre or from a specialist chrysanthemum grower. In either case, clear labelling of the propagation material is essential, right from the outset, to prevent any possibility of a mix up at some stage, during the course of their cultivation.

The chrysanthemum is almost hardy in the U.K., and even in a cold frame, where the old stools were cut back before Christmas, they will be found to have started producing new shoots from the base of the old stems, both above and below the soil, and it is from these that the cuttings will be selected. The ones most suited to quick rooting, are the succulent, short-jointed, leafy cuttings. These are removed with a sharp knife, and should be some 5cm (2") long. There is no need to trim back the leaves, to create a length of clear stem, or cut the stem back to a joint (node), before inserting the cuttings 2.5cm (1") deep, and 5cm (2") apart, in a 50/50 peat and sand rooting mixture, (without the use of any growth-promoting substances). The cuttings are then placed in a heated propagator, with the bottom heat set at 16°C (60°F), in a light garden, with a light intensity of 8,000 lux for 12 hours per day. Rooting will occur in 14 to 18 days. Once this has been achieved, it is important to move the rooted cuttings from this mixture, which is devoid of any plant nutrient, and pot them up individually in 8.75cm (3½") pots containing a peat-based potting mix. They are then placed in the open light garden for a few days, to settle down in their pots, prior to being moved into a cold frame-here they are hardened off, and in late April/early-May, planted out in the open garden.

Dahlia propagation

Dahlias may be propagated from seed, by division of the crowns, or by cuttings.

The cheapest and simplest way to propagate dwarf varieties of dahlias, these are the ones used as summer bedding plant subjects, is from seed (see page 125). However, this method cannot be recommended for other types, as seed rarely produces plants which come true to type, so recourse to vegetative means of propagation is necessary, either by division of tubers, or raising plants from cuttings.

Tubers, which have been stored in a frost-free place, from the previous autumn, are started into growth in late March, in the warmth of the working garden, at a temperature of 16°C to 18°C (60°F to 65°F). The tubers are bedded into a box, or boxes, of moist peat, with the old crowns just protruding above the peat's surface. When moistening the peat, care must be exercised not to moisten the crowns themselves.

Good labelling is important at this stage to prevent the possibility of the various dahlias cultivars from becoming mixed up at some point.

The eyes from which new shoots develop, usually only occur at the base of the previous years stems and not on the tubes, so when these are seen to be beginning to develop, the tubers should be divided up into two or three pieces, each of which should have at least one eye attached to it. Each piece of tuber is then potted up in a peat-based potting mix, and placed in a light garden with a light intensity of 8,000 lux for 12 hours per day until the end-April, when they are transferred to a cold frame in the garden, and planted out in early June. During the summer each of these sections of tuber will produce a full sized root for lifting in the autumn.

Where rather more dahlia plants are required from the old tubers, the eyes are allowed to develop until the shoots are 8.75cm (3½") long. These are then removed, making a cut, with a sharp knife, about 1.25cm (½") above the tuber, so that further fleshy shoots may arise from the part remaining. The cuttings should be approximately 7.5cm (3") long, with a cut made just beneath a node (joint), and inserted in a 50/50 peat and sand rooting mixture, in a heated propagation case with the bottom heat set at 16°C-18°C' (60°F-65°F'), in a light garden, with a light intensity of 8,000 lux for 12 hours per day.

Rooting takes place in about three weeks, after which time the cuttings should be potted up individually in 10cm (4") pots, in a peat-based potting mix, and placed in the open light garden with a light intensity of 8,000 lux for 12 hours per day. The dahlias will grow quickly in their pots, and will starve, unless the compost has been fortified with a slow-release fertiliser, or is given a dilute solution of a liquid fertiliser every 14 days.

In late-April/early May the dahlias should be transferred to a cold frame in the garden. But remember to place a piece of tarpaulin, straw matting, or other insulation material, over the glass each evening, until all fear of night frost has ended. The dahlias are planted out into the flower borders in early June.

LIGHT GARDEN DESIGNS

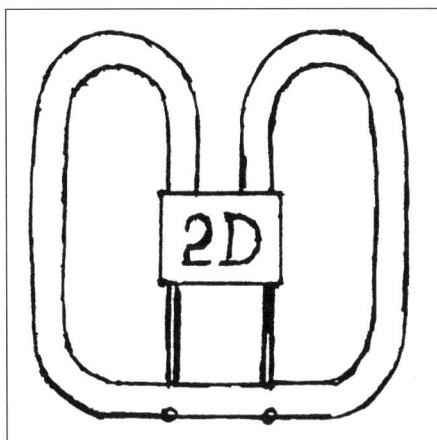

The 2D type fluorescent lamps.
A very suitable light source for the smaller light garden.

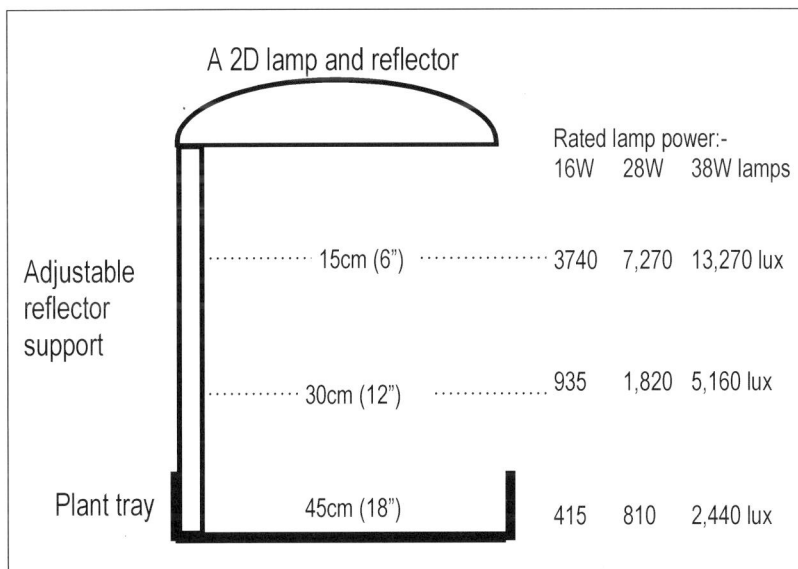

A 2D lamp and reflector

	Rated lamp power:-		
	16W	28W	38W lamps
15cm (6")	3740	7,270	13,270 lux
30cm (12")	935	1,820	5,160 lux
45cm (18")	415	810	2,440 lux

Adjustable reflector support

Plant tray

A louvred fluorescent ceiling fitting	Lamps with reflector to direct light downward.
3 ballasts (see page 61)	Parawedge louvre
A lounge garden restricted to one wall	11cm (4.5in) valance
	7.5cm (3in) valance

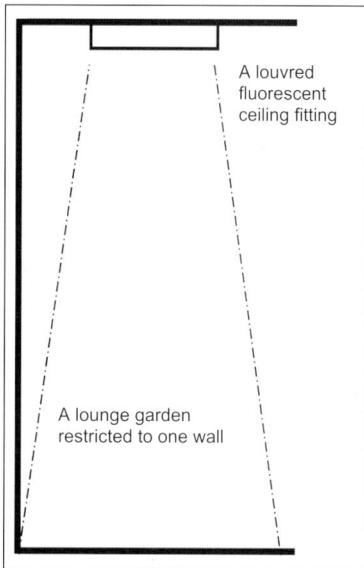

A louvred fluorescent ceiling fitting, for a lounge garden restricted to one wall.

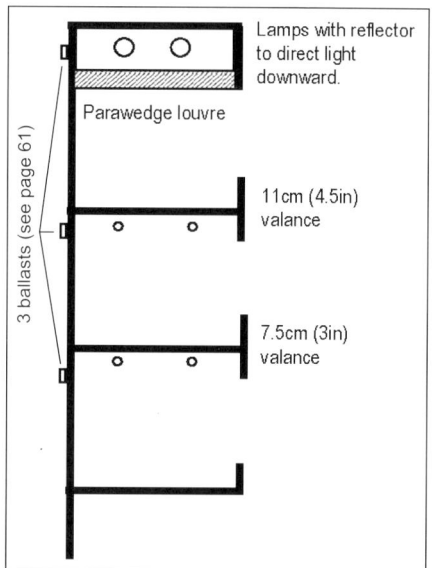

The valance varies in width depending upon the height of the light above floor level.

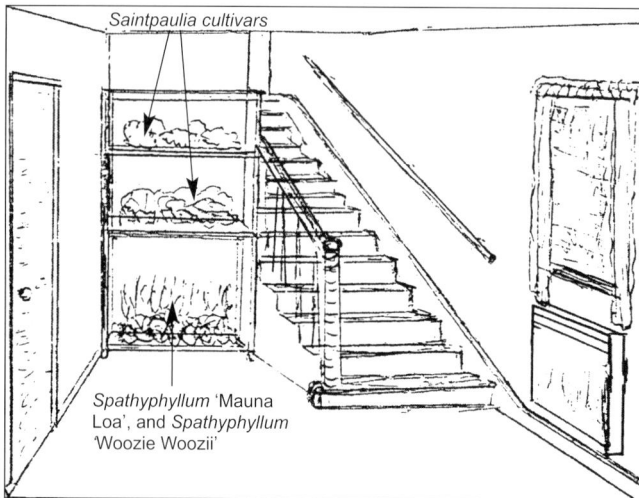

Saintpaulia cultivars

Spathyphyllum 'Mauna Loa', and Spathyphyllum 'Woozie Woozii'

This indoor light garden was installed in a small entrance hall of a townhouse. It is seen from the front door. The entrance hall is 2.1m (7feet) wide and 2.1m (7feet) deep.

A dresser converted into an indoor light garden. This too could likewise fulfil the same function in an entrance hall, or alternatively it could form an interesting feature for a dining room, even serve as a room divider in a large room, if so desired.

An open room divider offers considerable potential for an indoor light garden. All that is needed is the introduction of some fluorescent lamps with reflectors to the lower surface of the top three shelves, and some plant trays, and it will be immediately ready to receive the plants it will hold.

The choice of available plant material is considerable, providing that you only purchase small specimens initially. Some of these plants can then be moved on into the garden room, as they grow too large for their light garden to accommodate. The following selection only serves as an example of what may be included:

Begonia rex 'Silver Queen'.
Begonia bowerae
Begonia masoniana
Calathea makoyana.
Cissus discolor
Codiaeum variegatum var. *pictum*
Ficus sagittata 'Variegata'.

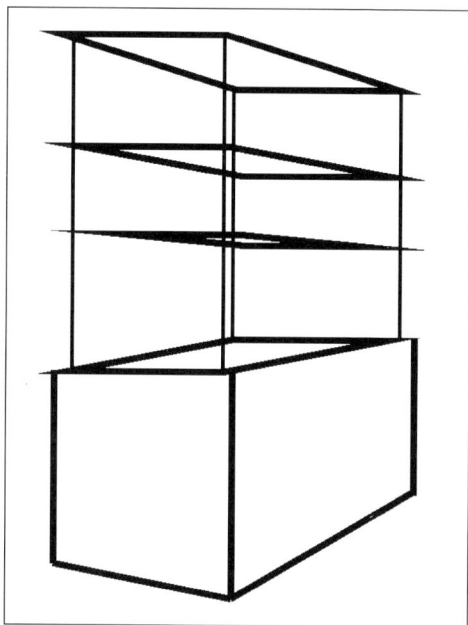

A room divider light garden.

Nephrolepis exaltata 'Fluffy Ruffles.'
Plectranthus forsteri 'Marginatus.'
Solenostemon scutellarioides syn. *Coleus blumei*
Coleus: C. 'Buttermilk', *C.* 'Firebrand', *C.* 'Picturatum,' with a low creeping habit, *C.* 'Royal Scot' and *C.* 'Scarlet Rainbow' (Slide C9).

A bromeliad garden

Bromeliads are some of the easiest plants to grow, and they are at the same time some of the most spectacular. But with limited headroom between the shelves it is as well to stick to some of the smaller growing species and cultivars of cryptanthus, and tillandsia such as:

Cryptanthus are the dwarves amongst the bromeliads:
C. acaulis
C. bivittatus 'Minor'
C. bivittatus 'Pink Starlite
C bivittatus 'Tricolor'
C. zonatus' Zebrinus', Plus many more cultivars

Tillandsia is a large genus of bromeliads of divers size and shape and there are hundreds of the small ones among them which all do well in confined spaces under artificial light:

T. albertiana
T. andreana
T. bergeri
T. caput-medusae
T. crispa
T. cyanea
T. ionantha
T. magnusiana
T. plumosa

A pelagornium garden

A garden full of miniature geraniums, which may be kept in flower throughout the whole year. There are some wonderful cultivars from which to make your selection. 'Alcyone,' 'Orange Imp,' 'Snowball', etc.

A small light garden for a studio apartment

See the colour slide (D26) of the small white light garden with a 38-watt lamp.

Even if you live in a studio apartment you can still find space for an indoor light garden, if you want one.

There are lots of other flowering and foliage plants, which would be suited to these settings. Among them are *Impatiens, Kalanchoe, Pelargonium, Primula, Schlumbergera, Caladium, Cissus, Coleus* etc., plus any of the crops suggested in the section, Growing Your Own Food.

THE WORKING GARDEN

A working garden is based on a combination of the garden room and light garden principles, and serves a similar function to an outdoor greenhouse. It is not a display area, but a small room or other small space reserved for plants to be propagated or maintained. It is intended to be a purely practical environment, rather than an elegantly designed one.

You can set up a working garden with benches and shelving anywhere you have the space. A part of a basement, or a laundry area, is ideal. Directions for installing fluorescent tubes are exactly the same as for the light garden in a shelved unit (see page 58). You can provide up to 15,000 lux within each compartment or shelf. But any necessary electrical work, should be undertaken by a qualified electrician; in the interest of safety.

If you are willing to go to a little more expense, you can set up an adjustable lighting rig that can be moved up and down to accommodate the heights of growing plants.

As with the garden room you should paint the walls, ceiling and shelf space white to reflect all the available light towards the plants and make sure the floor covering is non-slip and easy to clean. Ideally, storage space for containers, potting mix, and equipment should be inside the working garden itself, perhaps underneath the workbench or on the lowest level of shelving.

If your working garden is fully enclosed, and especially if the door will be kept shut, except when you are working with plants, you will need to install an exhaust fan into one wall to ensure a free air circulation around the plants. If space is restricted, and you need to place the garden within a plantscape that is on show, it may be possible to screen it with a group of tall plants, or to locate it within a shelving unit or a room divider.

Growing edible crops is a particularly rewarding aspect of indoor-gardening. While small tomato plants or herbs can be a delightful visual feature of your light garden, you may prefer to keep food crops in their own area, away from foliage and flowering species grown only for their appearance. Here the working garden comes into its own, as an indoor kitchen garden that will provide you with produce throughout the year.

Propagators, seed trays, and plant cuttings waiting to root are not particularly attractive, so it is useful to be able to carry out propagation work separately from your display areas. A trickle irrigation system (see page 96), which you may also want out of sight, can provide a steady supply of moisture to each pot or tray of seedlings. Further information on equipment and techniques for a working garden is contained in the following chapters on Watering Systems, Propagation, and Growing Your Own Food.

WATERING SYSTEMS

A day-to-day check of water requirements in your garden may be one of the particular pleasures of indoor gardening, if you have leisure to treat your plants individually and, more important, if your water supply is close by. Or you may regard watering plants as a tiresome but necessary chore, especially in a large and well-stocked garden room. In this case, you may want to develop a more efficient watering system.

Self-watering planters or capillary watering devices are the solution. They also benefit the plants by allowing them to take up just the amount of water they need, avoiding the dangers of over or under watering. In the working garden, where new plants are being propagated and a range of other plants are developing, you can install a simple trickle irrigation system that is directed to every pot and regulates the water supply.

All these systems are easily set up and maintained, and require no electricity. They can store enough water to meet your plants requirements, for several days, or even a week or two, providing a worry-free answer to the question on maintaining your garden when you are away from home.

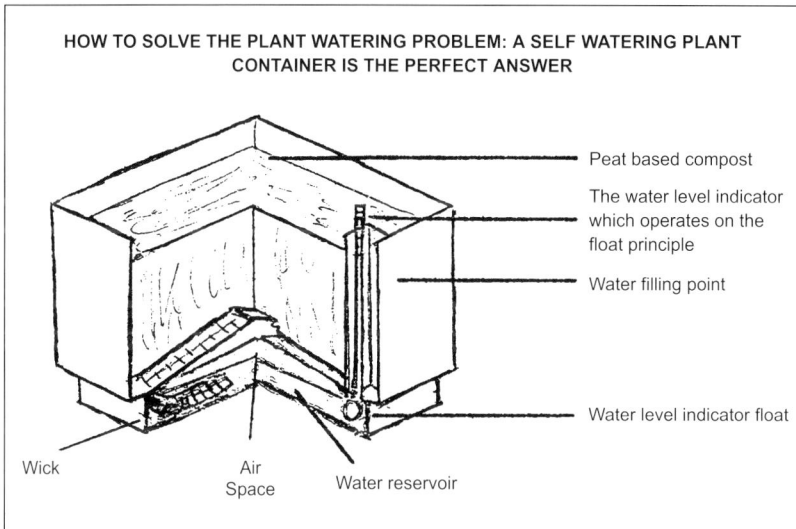

HOW TO SOLVE THE PLANT WATERING PROBLEM: A SELF WATERING PLANT CONTAINER IS THE PERFECT ANSWER

Peat based compost

The water level indicator which operates on the float principle

Water filling point

Water level indicator float

Wick

Air Space

Water reservoir

These planters are available in a range of sizes and shapes, and, while relatively expensive, they will give years of useful service. If you do plan to leave plants in these containers unchecked for a long period, you can extend the safe time without having to provide additional water simply by spreading plastic sheeting over the surface of the planter, and tying it around the sides with string.

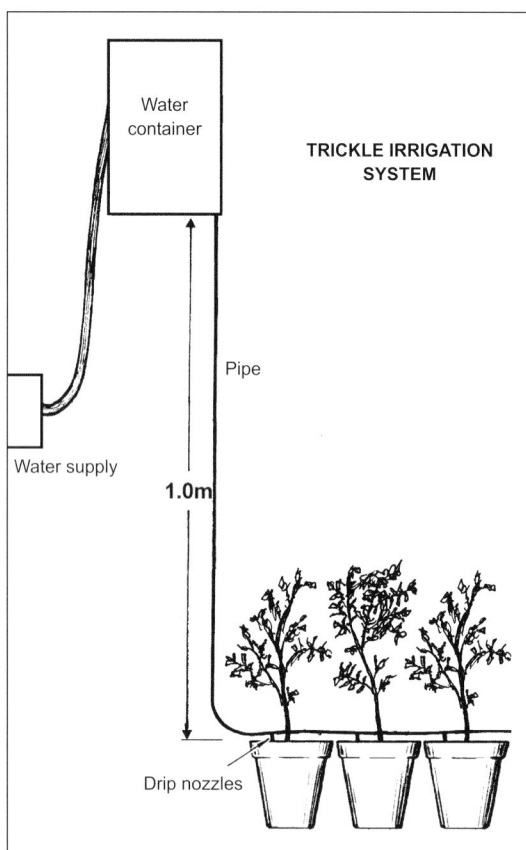

Water container

TRICKLE IRRIGATION
SYSTEM

Pipe

Water supply

1.0m

Drip nozzles

Self-watering planters work on the principle of capillary watering. Each planter consists of a container for potting mix fitted with a reservoir for water underneath. Water is supplied to the potting mix by a wick, at the same rate as it is used by the plants or lost through evaporation from the mixture's surface. An air space just beneath the mix ensures that the roots of the plants can breathe freely, as they would if growing in the open ground. A water-level indicator shows whether the reservoir is full or becoming drained.

Self-watering planters are very reliable once they are made fully operational. However, you must use extra care when first filling the container with the potting mix and planting either a single plant or a group of plants. Do not fill the reservoir beforehand. When you have put in the potting mix, firm it lightly and introduce the plants in the usual way. Water it generously from the top; making sure that it is wetted right through.

Leave the planter without any further water for about five days; then pour water into the reservoir until the water-level indicator shows that it is full. Do not over fill the reservoir. This blocks the air space at the base of the mixture, and fresh air is essential to the well being of the plant's roots.

Once the wick has absorbed some moisture from the damp mix, and water is available in the reservoir below, a further supply will be drawn up automatically by capillary action. You need not add more water until the water-level indicator registers a considerable drop in the existing supply. The most common reason for improper functioning of a self-watering planter is disturbance of the wick at the planting stage, so follow the procedure with care from the initial stages.

Such containers are particularly useful for the large permanent foliage plants in the garden room-palms, shrubs, and tall-growing indoor trees. Self-watering hanging baskets are also available for both indoor and outdoor usage. These are very useful devices, as plants suspended in the air tend to dry more quickly than potted plants, or may be forgotten in the normal routine of watering.

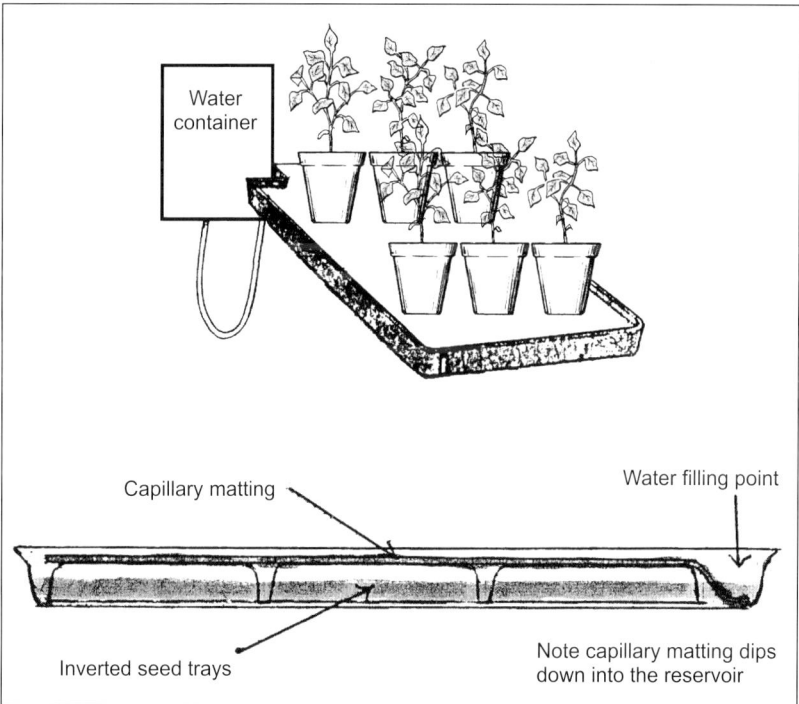

Diagram of a capillary watering system

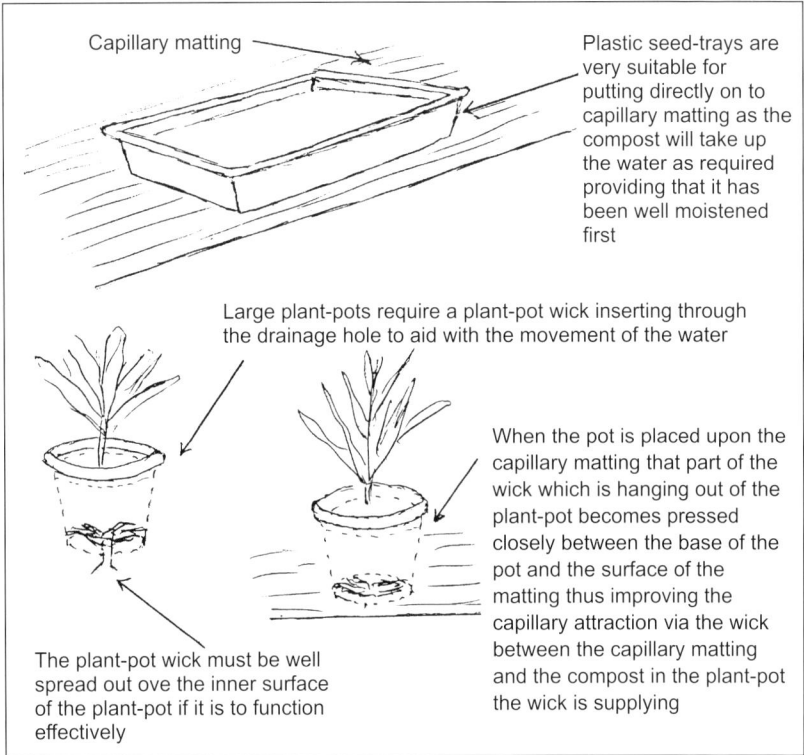

Capillary matting

Plastic seed-trays are very suitable for putting directly on to capillary matting as the compost will take up the water as required providing that it has been well moistened first

Large plant-pots require a plant-pot wick inserting through the drainage hole to aid with the movement of the water

When the pot is placed upon the capillary matting that part of the wick which is hanging out of the plant-pot becomes pressed closely between the base of the pot and the surface of the matting thus improving the capillary attraction via the wick between the capillary matting and the compost in the plant-pot the wick is supplying

The plant-pot wick must be well spread out ove the inner surface of the plant-pot if it is to function effectively

Board with holes for plant-pot wicks

Kitchen sink or washing bowl

Treasured pot-plants can be kept supplied with water whilst one is away on holiday simply by equipping them with wicks and placing them on a board over a sink or washing bowl.

The capillary system of watering plants has done a great deal to increase the potential of indoor gardening. It is based on the use of a thick felted fabric, or capillary matting, which draws up water from a reservoir, and supplies the moisture to the base of the plant pots standing on the matting. With this system, you can design a sophisticated plantscape and maintain it with the minimum of effort. A capillary watering system answers another important plant need; water evaporated from the moist matting, creating humidity around the plant's foliage.

If you intend to use capillary watering extensively, plot out the design of the whole room on graph paper, with full details of the plants' placement. If you apply this system to small, individual groupings of plants, the watering arrangement is easily accomplished.

The matting must be placed with one end in a tray of water. If the plants stand in a tray on a shelf or bench, the matting can be laid out along its entire length and then be lapped over the edge of a reservoir set at one end. Be sure to lay the capillary matting on a smooth, horizontal surface. For a more complex plantscape, you will need to arrange trays of suitable shape and size, and cut the matting to fit, leaving enough matting to overlap into the reservoir. You can place the trays directly on the floor or raised up, on plant stands. Remember that in all cases the success of capillary watering depends on the trays being absolutely level.

Capillary watering kits or self-contained systems are available, some of them quite small. They are suitable for a small-scale light garden, or plants displayed on a narrow shelf or windowsill.

Over time, the matting becomes affected by algae and takes on a rather unpleasant appearance. While the matting will only be visible during the early stages of your plants' growth, and algae is quite harmless, you can prevent it if you prefer. You simply need to exclude all light from the matting. Some capillary watering systems include a sheet of plastic for covering the matting, which is black on one side and white on the other. You place it black side down and cut V-shaped strips, curling them back to accommodate the bases of the pots. This method also prevents water evaporating from the matting, so the water supply lasts longer than it otherwise would.

One limitation of capillary watering systems is that the take up of moisture becomes progressively less effective with larger pots-those 15cm (6") or more in diameter, but pots up to 15cm (6") in height are usually satisfactory You can anticipate this difficulty and put a wick into the base of each pot before adding the potting mix. You can buy wicks for this purpose, but woven bootlaces are perfectly adequate. Wet the wick before use and coil it around the inner base of the pot, threading one end through the drainage hole then add the potting mix. The protruding end of the wick will take up water from the capillary matting when the pot is set into place. You must always make sure, though, that the potting mix is well watered before the pot is positioned on the matting.

Some species that require a dormant period may be best removed from the matting during dormancy, so that they do not absorb too much moisture. You will have to remember to water them occasionally and to provide sufficient humidity so that the dormant plants do not suffer from leaf burn.

In the working garden, if for some reason it is inconvenient to use matting, or you need an instant solution, simply provide each plant pot with a long bootlace wick, and group them on a slatted shelf just above the surface of a water filled bowl, or bucket with the wicks dangling into this.

With a water supply like this, you can leave the plants unattended for quite long periods, and they will receive all the water they require. This arrangement is not particularly elegant, but its appearance will not matter in the privacy of your working garden.

Preventing moulds

Peat-based potting mixes are not generally subject to the growth of moulds on their surface. With self-watering planters or capillary matting, the surface is generally on the dry side once they are fully functioning properly. To help prevent the possibility of mould, you can create free air movement within the potting mix by working its surface with a hand fork or old dinner fork. If there is still a problem, perhaps because of local climatic conditions, simply place a thin layer of perlite or hydroleca (a form of inert aggregate) over the surface of the mix. This will prove very effective to prevent mould growth.

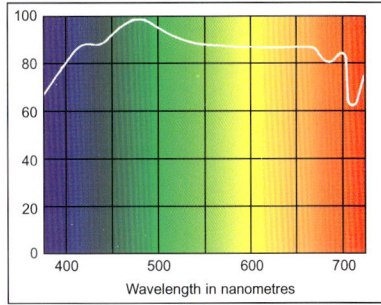

D25. This slide illustrates the point that all the light energy that illuminates our indoor plants today comes from the same source, the Sun. The only difference is that the electric power produced by the power station in the background, the chimneys of which can be seen to the left of the picture, is creating its electricity from the coal, gas or oil, formed from the remains of the fauna and flora that once basked in the Earth's sunlight millions of years ago. It is using the stored energy of the sunlight - while the tree in the foreground is receiving all its energy directly.

The spectral energy distribution of sunlight. The sunlight reaching the earth whilst appearing white to our eyes is composed of all the colours of the rainbow, from dark violet to dark red, and just like any artificial light source it has its own spectral energy distribution curve. (See lamp graphs, pages 17-18). However, in the case of sunlight its energy distribution curve is not constant, on the contrary this varies with the time of day. In the morning and evening the prevailing colours are red and yellow whereas in the middle of the day it is mainly blue.

H42. *Spathyphyllum floribundum* 'Woozie Woozii'.

A19. *Begonia masoniana.*

B11. *Epipremnum aureum* 'Marble Queen'.

H8. *Anthurium andraeanum* 'Brazilian Sunrise'.

H25. *Euphorbia pulcherrima* 'Marble Queen' (Poinsettia). A short term indoor plant.

A42. *Cordyline terminalis* 'Kiwi'.

A8. *Fatsia japonica* 'Variegata'.

B6. *Dracaena deremensis* 'Lemon and Lime'.

B50. *Schefflera arboricola* 'Jacqueline'.

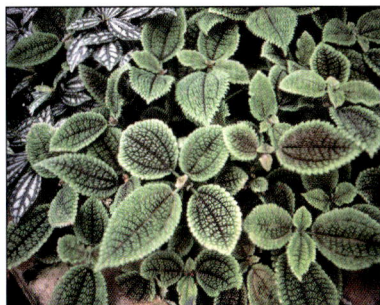

B41. *Pilea involucrata* 'Moon Valley'.

F46. *Asplenium nidus.*

A48. *Cyperus alternifolius.*

A9. *Araucaria heterophylla.*

E15. The Royal Borough of Kensington & Chelsea light gardens on a windowless corridor.

E14. A light garden full of tropical plants.

H1. *Achemenes* 'Carmencita'. Credit: Ball Colegrave Limited, West Addersbury, Banbury, Oxon OX17 3EY.

F15. *Neoregelia* 'Madam Van Durme'.

F41. *Aporocactus flagelliformis*.

A16. *Caladium* 'Candidum'.

A18. *Caladium* 'Frieda Hemple'.

D23. *Euphorbia milii* (Crown of thorns) may be had in flower at all times of the year in the indoor light garden.

D22. *Catharanthus roseus* 'Morning Mist'.

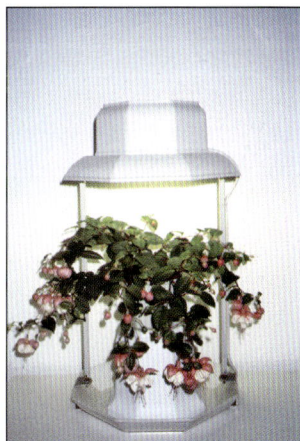

D26. *Fuchsia* 'Madam Cornnelissen', rooted from a cutting in the light garden.

D32. *Pelargonium* X*hortorum* 'Friesdorf'. (A miniature geranium).

D43. *Saintpaulia* 'Silver Milestone'.

E4. *Streptocarpus* F1 'Royal Mixed'; seedling growth stimulation may be necessary. (See text page 82).

E1. *Sinningia* 'Jester Mixed' F2 hybrid, flowering, in the light garden.

E6. *Streptocarpus* F1 'Royal Mixed' in a large light garden.

D45. Bill Carter in his *Saintpaulia* garden room.

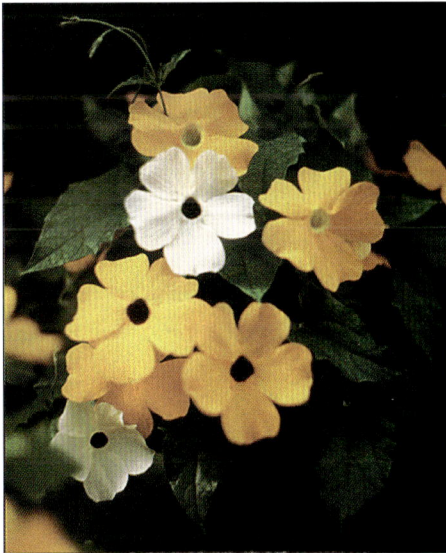

E12. *Thunbergia alata* 'Susie Mixed'.

C26. A Gold Medal winning display of exotic foliage plants on the grand scale at the Chelsea Flower Show 1988.
The exhibitor - Anmore Exotics.

Rear left *Anthurium crystallinum,* rear right *Dieffenbachia maculata* 'Tropic Snow', rear left *Dieffenbachia Xbausei*, and *Dieffenbachia maculata* 'Neptune', next to these a small touch of *Calathea veitchiana*, near to these is *Peperomia* 'Columbiana' and this is followed by a patch of *Ctenanthe amabilis*, which meets up with a patch of *Calathea veitchiana*, whilst in the centre front is *Dracaena deremensis*, and at the middle right front is *Fittonia verschaffeltii* var. *argyroneura.*

D9. A light garden with two propagation units and some recently rooted plants.

C21. Bottom left *Caladium* 'Candidum', top left *Anthurium andraeanum* 'Brazilian Sunshine', right *Alocasia* X*amazonica*.

D29. A colourful display of plants in an indoor light garden: *Caladium* 'Candidum', *Crassula ovata*, *Euphorbia milii*, *Impatiens* F1 New Guinea hybrids, carmine, red, and white. *Hyoltelephium sieboldii* 'Mediovariegatum', *Streptocarpus* X*hybridus*, and *Tradescantia*.

C16. Exotica general view.

C19. Top left *Dracaen marginata*, top right *Calathea zebrina*, 'White Butterfly', left centre *Tradescantia zebrine*, top centre *Codiaeum variegatum*, bottom left *Adiantum raddianum*, bottom *Primula acaulis* with blue, orange and yellow flowers, right *Fittonia verschaffeltii* var. *argyroneura*, centre *Syngonium podophyllum.*

H43. *Spathyphyllum* 'Mauna Loa'.

D1. A small low cost heated propagation unit.

D2. A larger more expensive heated propagation unit with variable temperature control.

D3. *Begonia rex* leaf propagation in a heated plant propagator.

D5. *Begonia rex* plantlets ready for potting up individually.

D6. *Begonia rex* plants growing in a light garden.

E10. This slide shows a number of *Streptocarpus* F1 'Royal Mixed' in flower. These plants have all been propagated vegetatively from a single *Streptocarpus* leaf.

E46. The Cucumber F1 hybrid 'Patio Pik' - 4 pots of seedlings immediately after germination has taken place.

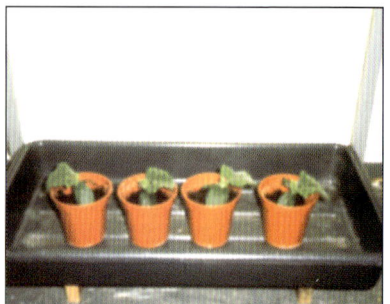

E47. The Cucumber F1 hybrid 'Patio Pik' after 7 days light garden treatment.

E48. The Cucumber F1 hybrid 'Patio Pik' after 14 days light garden treatment.

E50. The Cucumber F1 hybrid 'Patio Pik' after 28 days light garden treatment.

E27. The Tomato F1 hybrid 'Minibel' plants displaying a crop of ripe fruits in early June.

A40. *Codiaeum variegatum* 'Volcano'.

B3. *Dieffenbachia maculata* 'Pluto'.

B27. *Monstera deliciosa* 'Variegata'.

B21. *Fittonia verschaffeltii* var. *gigantea.*

G9. *Miltonia* 'Sherpa'.

T50. *Caladium lindenii.* This *Caladium* is an ornamental evergreen species with thin leathery leaves that is native to tropical South America.

F8. *Fascicularia bicolor.*

B36. *Philodendron* 'Champagne'.

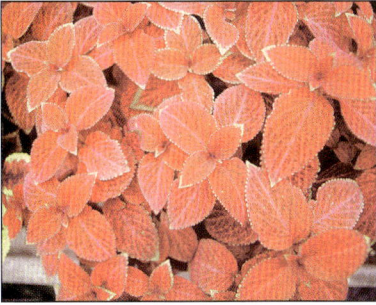

C9. *Solenostemon scutellariodes* 'Scarlet Rainbow'.

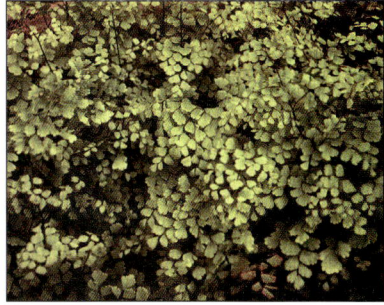

F15. *Adiantum raddianum* 'Maidenhair fern'.

C1. *Schefflera arboricola* 'Variegata'.

G15. *Phalaenopsis* hybrids flowering in the light garden.

A10. *Asparagus setaceus*.

A47. *Cycas revoluta*.

A6. *Alocasia cuprea* and beneath this a
carpet of *Strobilanthes dyerianus*
'Persian Shield'.

D13. *Begonia* Semperflorens, F1
'Devon Gems Mixed'.

F48. *Nephrolepis exaltata*
'Bostoniensis compacta'.

CARE FOR PLANTS

Successful plant cultivation of any kind calls for a through understanding of the needs and preferences of the plants concerned. In an indoor garden, you must create conditions that meet the basic requirements of the plants and encourage healthy growth, for while they are adaptable to some extent, they cannot over-come a lack of essential elements within their environment. Understanding the various functions by which plants live, and grow, is the key to their care and conditions that you must provide.

Indoor-plants are most likely to die because environmental factors and the individual care that they receive are not well suited to their requirements. Often the damage caused to a plant is the result of good intentions: over-watering, is a good example, and is the most common error in plant care. It is not always wise or possible to develop a strict routine of tasks in the indoor garden. You should follow the few basic guidelines below, but the key to success lies in being sensitive to your plants' responses to the treatment they are receiving.

Photosynthesis and respiration

The importance of light for photosynthesis was discussed in a previous chapter. Photosynthesis is the process by which plants convert light into essential nourishment. Without sufficient light, the process stops, and the plants die.

Respiration reverses what occurs in photosynthesis. In this process the plant breaks down glucose in the presence of oxygen, and releases carbon dioxide and water. This activity continues in light and darkness, although photosynthesis predominates while the plant is receiving light. The energy created in respiration changes some of the glucose into protoplasm, a jelly-like substance which lines the walls of plant cells and which is the living material of plants.

Normally air contains only about 0.033% (330 ppm) carbon dioxide, and if a large number of plants in a room need it for photosynthesis, they may reach a stage when they are literally suffering from carbon dioxide starvation. This problem is caused by lack of air circulation around the plants, and can easily be resolved by using a small fan to produce a gentle, draft-free air movement around the plants. If there is no carbon dioxide for the plants to assimilate, the process of photosynthesis will cease. Where only a few plants are in a room, they are not likely to suffer from this problem.

The amount of carbon dioxide given off by plants is infinitesimal and does not affect the purity of the air we breathe.

Root system

The root system of a plant serves two main functions: it anchors the plant securely, and it absorbs water and nutrients from the soil, which are channelled upwards for use within the plant. Soil particles are infiltrated by the root hairs-tiny, elongated single cells situated at the tips of the roots, which are constantly being replaced as the roots grow. The hairs take up a film of moisture, containing dissolved nutrients, which cover the soil particles. The roots must also be able to breathe, and the moist particles of soil should be separated by tiny air spaces. This is why overwatering is dangerous to plants, for if soil is waterlogged the roots can no longer breathe and they cease to function. If, on the other hand, the soil becomes dry, and the film of moisture around each particle is thin,

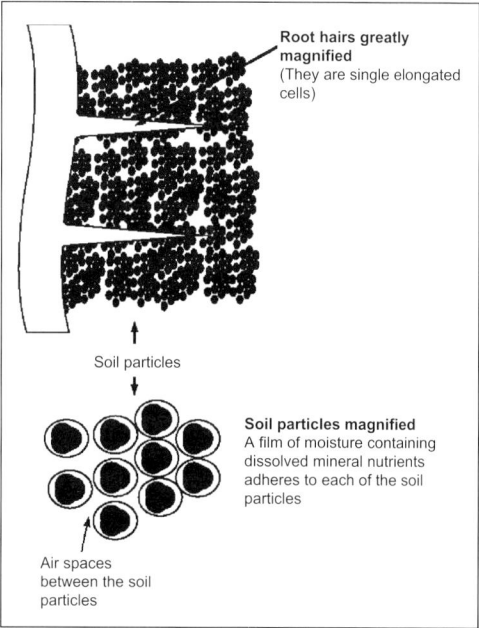

Root hairs greatly magnified
(They are single elongated cells)

Soil particles

Soil particles magnified
A film of moisture containing dissolved mineral nutrients adheres to each of the soil particles

Air spaces between the soil particles

the roots hairs cannot absorb enough to supply the plant's needs. Either condition leads to wilting because stems and leaves are deprived of both moisture and nutrients.

The roots of plants may also serve as storage organs for example; the begonia, dahlia and potato plants; the tuber allows the plant to survive through its dormant period and promote healthy new growth once activity resumes.

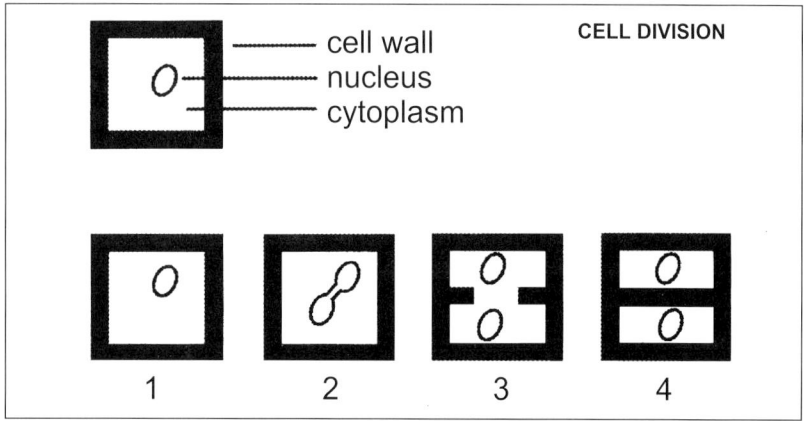

cell wall
nucleus
cytoplasm

CELL DIVISION

1   2   3   4

As growth takes place there is continuous activity below and above ground, in the very young cells at the tips of the roots and in new leafy shoots, as the formation of new cells is from the division of plant cells, which already exist. A plant cell, in the shoots and roots of plants, is of cube-shape and one thousandth of an inch or less in size. Each one of these cells contains protoplasm and embedded within the protoplasm is the cell nucleus.

Essentially what takes place is that first the nucleus divides into two forming two nuclei and then the cytoplasm divides itself into two separate portions, one half of which surrounds each of the two new nuclei and, while this is taking place, the original cell itself develops a new cell wall in the centre of the existing cell effectively dividing it into two separate parts, and these two new cells, thus created, then grow to the size of the original cell.

This process is stimulated by a plant hormone, a substance produced by the plant, which is present in a minute quantity within the cytoplasm surrounding the nucleus of the cell. This is just one of a number of such hormones within the plant which control all aspects of growth and development. At the appropriate times, they stimulate the production of tuberous roots, or bring about flower bud initiation, or cause the plant to bend towards the light if it is in a shady place.

How the structure of a plant develops

While the young cells in the growing points of the plant may all be similar in size and shape, the older cells in older parts of the plant may be as much as 10 or more times larger than this, and may have developed in all directions, creating cells more or less spherical in shape, but they still consist of the same elements, cell walls, cytoplasm and nucleus, which is always embedded within the cytoplasm, but here the cytoplasm has vacuoles (cavities) in it which develop as the cell grows larger. These vacuoles contain cell sap. Such modified groups of cells as these, when gathered together form a tissue called **parenchyma** and food storage tissue is usually composed of these parenchymatous cells such as those in the begonia tuber, the dahlia tuber, the potato tuber, and the fleshy parts of the fruit of the apple for example.

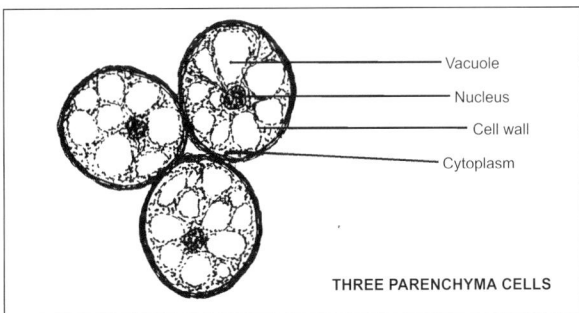

THREE PARENCHYMA CELLS

103

Other older cells may also enlarge in one direction only, becoming longer but not necessarily any wider than when initially formed. They may also have thicker cellulose walls. Such cells are called fibrous cells, and serve to give a plant greater strength in those parts of it in which they occur.

If the stem of a geranium is dissected horizontally and a cross section of this is then examined with the aid of a hand lens, or a microscope, groups of fibrous cells can be seen arranged in circles. These are the stem's veins (vascular bundles) which are formed for the conveyance of water and dissolved nutrients from the root of the plant to the leaves (the factory of the plant) and they are then used to transfer the products of photosynthesis to other parts of the plant where they are employed in respiration, or some other process, or are to be stored for future use.

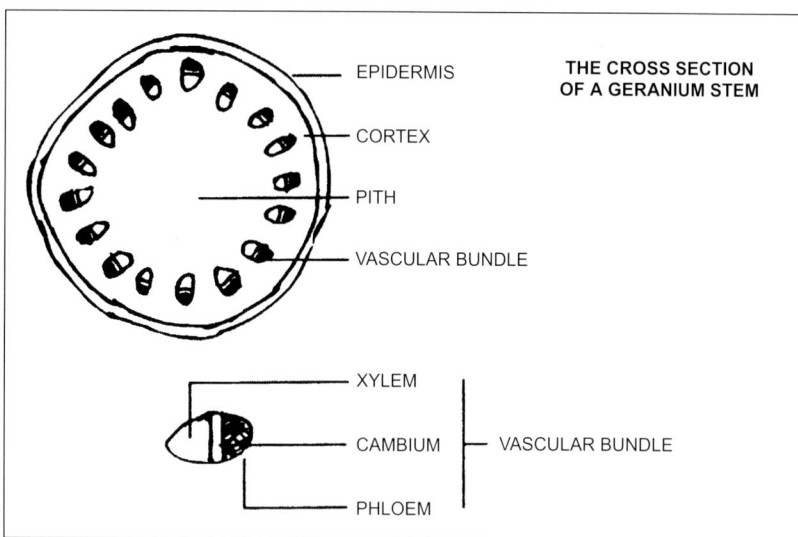

EPIDERMIS

THE CROSS SECTION OF A GERANIUM STEM

CORTEX

PITH

VASCULAR BUNDLE

XYLEM

CAMBIUM — VASCULAR BUNDLE

PHLOEM

In the stem of a plant the fibrous cells composing the vascular bundles are arranged in groups to the outside of the stem as illustrated, and they fulfil both the requirement for transportation of water and food materials from one part of a plant to another and at the same time provide the stem with increased strength.

Each vascular bundle is comprised of two sets of tubes. The tubes nearest the outside are composed of long thin-walled cells, which form the **phloem**, which transfers food materials from the leaves to other parts of the plant where they are needed. While those on the inside are long thicker walled cells which form the **xylem**, which transfer water absorbed by the root hairs to other parts of the plant where it is required.

In between these two layers of cells is a third layer of cells, and this is called the **cambium** layer. These cells are capable of division and multiplication, just-like the ones in the tips of the roots and shoots of the plant, and when a cell on the out side divides one of the two cells formed as a result of this becomes part of the phloem, while the other cell remains part of the cambium. When a cambium cell divides on the inside, likewise one of the cells forms part of the xylem while the other remains part of the cambium. This process of cell division continues all the time the plant is growing.

None persistent stems

While the same regions are to be found in the stems of all young plants, the vascular bundles are not necessarily arranged in a ring within the stem, neither do they always have a cambium layer associated with them. In the

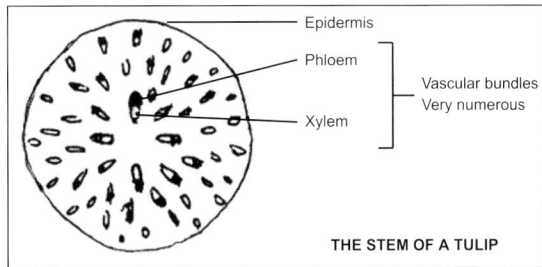

THE STEM OF A TULIP

stems of some plants the vascular bundles may be scattered throughout the stem and it is not possible to divide the parenchyma into cortex and pith. Amaryllis, narcissus, and tulips are examples of such plants.

Secondary thickening of the stem

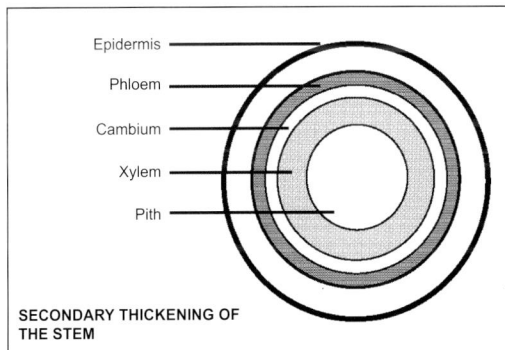

SECONDARY THICKENING OF THE STEM

In the stems of plants that live for years (perennial plants), a process of secondary thickening of the stem takes place. The structure of the stem becomes modified, as the cambium layer in each of the vascular bundles spreads out laterally to meet up with the cambium of the other vascular bundles, which are also doing likewise. Once the cambium meets up and forms a complete ring within the stem, it begins to produce more xylem and phloem, so that each of these also forms a complete ring within the stem, instead of being confined to the original vascular bundles. Azalea, ficus and schefflera are examples of such ornamental indoor plants.

Potting mixes

Most of the plants growing outdoors will be quite happy with the soil into which their roots have thrust, but this same soil will not be satisfactory when used in indoor pots and planters that are not subjected to the elements. There are many different types of natural soil, they can be described as stony, gravely, sandy, loamy, silty, or clay soils. Their fertility is equally variable. If you were to insist on growing indoor plants in such soils the results would be very disappointing.

Over the years great efforts have been made to produce quality potting mixes for seed sowing and potting, with the end result that today's gardener can choose from a number of readily available mixes that will ensure excellent results. In addition, these commercial mixes have been sterilized, which eliminates the chance of introducing pests or diseases into your indoor garden.

Some consist of loam, peat, and sand, while others are based on mixtures of various grades of peat. They are all fortified with the necessary plant nutrients, which are gradually released, as the plants require them. Moisture retention in potting mixes is adequate for the plants' needs, and also provides satisfactory drainage so that the roots can breathe. I recommend the use of a peat-based potting mix because I have experienced consistently good results with it over a number of years. Generally, you can use it in small and medium sized pots straight from the bag. In larger planters, I usually incorporate perlite as this increases air-holding capacity while ensuring a more even distribution of the root system throughout the planter.

Some environmental considerations

Temperature

A plant's ability to grow and flourish also depends on a suitable temperature. Some plants require cool conditions with a minimum temperature of 7°C (45°F), while others flinch at a minimum temperature of 13°C (55°F). You should aim to keep your garden room, or garden area within a room, between 16°C to 21°C (60°F to 70°F) during the day, with a nighttime minimum temperature, of 10°C(50°F), except where otherwise indicated. Tropical and sub-tropical plants will grow quite well within this temperature range. Indoor plants exposed to wide temperature ranges rarely flourish for long.

It is far better to keep your room temperature at 18°C (65°F) or thereabouts, than to allow it to stray above 21°C (70°F). Overheating is more likely to be a problem, during the winter when people are more concerned about keeping their homes warm, than it is in the summer.

Humidity

Humidity is an important factor in the successful cultivation of indoor plants. For some species, the correct degree of humidity can be the key to success or failure, and they will have to live permanently in a humid micro-climate. Moisture in the air helps leaves to remain cool and fresh. A combination of high temperature and low humidity can cause browning of leaf tips or margins, so watch for these symptoms.

The air entering an apartment or house from outside may have a relative humidity of around 50% to 55%, and this is fine for the majority of plants. In a cold climate, or a hot dry one, the humidity will be much lower. If a central heating system is in operation, there will be a rise in temperature, with a decline in relative humidity, and this may have a harmful effect on the plants. The problem is likely to be most acute when the temperature outside is below freezing, with a consequently high rise in the temperature of the air gaining entry.

If your indoor garden is a very modest affair, perhaps occupying just a tiny space on a bookshelf, it will take only a few moments each day to spray the plants' leaves with water from a small mist sprayer. If your garden is large, you can create a more humid microclimate by standing the plant containers on trays covered with fine gravel or peat, and spraying them with water each morning. During the course of the day the water will evaporate, creating a humid atmosphere around the plants.

In a garden room, you will need more extensive means of maintaining a humid atmosphere. Most large planters have their own water reservoirs that provide moisture to the potting mix as the plants' roots draw upon it. You may have other plant containers standing in trays on capillary matting (see page 97), which provides water to the roots of the plants. Some of this water will evaporate and provide extra humidity.

You must also be careful not to make your garden room too humid, however-not so much for the sake of the plants as for your house. This is especially important when your garden is in a living room, as furniture, and fabrics may suffer deterioration if very humid conditions prevail over a long period. When cultivating exotic plants that need a high humidity level, it is best to grow them in a glass or plastic sided, self-contained terrarium, with the lamps above them. (See page 146)

An electric humidifier will certainly solve the problem of dry air in your garden room. If the room is heated, by a central heating unit a humidifier may be the only way to provide plants with a suitable humidity, especially during colder months.

Watering and feeding

The amount of water a plant needs at any particular time will depend upon its innate requirement, the temperature and ventilation within the room, the season of the year, and the stage of the plant's growth cycle. Watering is not a simple routine that can be carried out daily or weekly at the same hour, and applied routinely to all plants in your collection.

As over watering is the greatest danger to indoor plants, it is better to err on the side of caution. If the potting mix is dry, it is easy enough to add a little water, but it is difficult to correct conditions for a waterlogged plant. If root damage has already occurred, the plant cannot be revived. Over watered plants literally drown in their potting mix, as the roots cannot breathe.

Check the potting mix with your fingers, and, if you are still not sure if the plant needs water, study its overall appearance. If it looks healthy and there is no sign of yellowing or wilting, delay watering for a day or two.

Persistent under watering is also a cause of failure in indoor cultivation, so it is important to check the mixer frequently. To correct under watering, stand the pot in water until the potting mix gradually draws up enough moisture, but do not leave it so long that the roots become saturated. For a large collection of plants, the best solution may be to provide self-watering systems (see page 95), which allow the plants to take as much water as they need.

When watering, never use cold water, which will shock the plant. You should always allow the water to warm to room temperature before giving it to your plants.

Over feeding is another common mistake. A well balanced potting mix supplies most of the mineral nutrients the plant is likely to need for some time. Additional plant food does not necessarily make the plants grow bigger or better. A build up of feed in the potting mix over and above what can be used immediately will have a detrimental effect on the plants.

The early sign of overfeeding is what looks like scorched leaf margins. If the accumulation of unwanted food continues, the concentration of chemicals (whether from chemical or organic fertilizer) in the potting mix will be so high that the plant will die of poisoning. In general, a plant should not need additional nutrients for several weeks following re-potting. Do not give a plant food during a dormant period. The highest requirement occurs during active growth, when the plant is producing new leaf shoots or developing flower buds, or fruit.

When feeding your plants, keep strictly to the manufacturer's instructions regarding recommended dosage. There are numerous plant foods available, and they come in all forms, from tablets and plant sticks that are placed in the pots, to foliage feeds sprayed over the leaves. There are the traditional soluble powders that are mixed with water before application, and the liquid preparations that usually require dilution and then are watered into the potting mix. Liquid feeds are generally recommended because they are watered into the potting mix, unlike tablets or plant sticks, and their application can be regulated quite easily.

Plant health and hygiene

One of the great advantages of indoor gardening is that the plants are not exposed to the diseases and pests that may attack outdoor plants; nor do they have to rely on the vagaries of weather for the right degree of warmth, light, or moisture to suit their needs. Under the controlled environment of your indoor garden, there is no reason why plants should not live out their lives in permanently healthy attractive conditions.

Regular examination and cleaning of your plants is a necessary task. It consists mainly of checking for damaged leaves and stems, and removing dead foliage or flowers. This material, would otherwise lodge in the living plant or accumulate on the surface of the potting mix to present a potential source for subsequent pests and disease infection.

Leaf cleaning should be carried out gently and only as strictly necessary. Wiping away dust gathered on the leaves with a small sponge, a fine cloth, or soft-haired paintbrush, depending on the size and texture of the plant leaves. A few plants are averse to having their leaves touched or wetted, so always check individual care instructions before handling foliage.

Many of the evergreen plants on sale as indoor plants have been given an application of leaf-shine to clean the leaves and add a deeper lustre to the foliage. However, in your indoor garden, a healthy plant will have a healthy appearance and will not need constant polishing, as this can cause harm to the foliage.

Chemical products for plants should be avoided as far as possible to protect human health. Many of the pests that affect plants growing outdoors do not affect indoor plants so the usual wide spectrum insecticides and fungicides are not recommended in this book. If in any doubt about the health risks of using such substances indoors, it is best not to apply such substances indoors, Apply them out doors instead and then keep the affected plant or plants in quarantine elsewhere until they recover. If you keep; a watchful eye over your plants and immediately remove any plant that looks sick or infested with insects, you will find it a much safer and generally more effective way of dealing with the problem. Good hygiene is the basic philosophy behind preventing sickness in plants.

Safe health remedies

Troublesome insects do occasionally find their way indoors through an open window or an air conditioning system, but this should be a rare occurrence under garden room conditions.

The most likely way in which pests or diseases can gain a foothold among your plants is when they arrive on new plants that are placed too quickly among your established ones. Reputable plant growers and suppliers take care to produce healthy stock, but the plant may have travelled some distance by the time you buy it, and may have come in contact with insect pests or diseases.

Always inspect plants carefully for signs of disease before you buy them, and check the undersides of leaves for insect eggs. Keep new plants in isolation from your others for two weeks after bringing them home. This allows time for hidden problems to develop. If they do, you can treat the plants before giving them a permanent place in your indoor garden.

At the first sign of insect infestation in your garden room, remove the infected plant from the room. Aphids and whiteflies can be removed from many plants with just a bowl of water. For other insects, you can use a small paintbrush to dab a touch of methylated spirit on the invaders. This will solve the problem quickly. A very effective insecticide is a simple pyrethrum powder or spray, and it is virtually non-toxic to humans and other warm-blooded animals.

Red Spider Mite can be more of a problem to control as the adult female is a barely visible, eight legged, reddish-green colour, and only about 1/60th of an inch long, and the male is slightly smaller. Mite infested leaves turn silvery grey or yellowish in colour, due to the destruction of the chlorophyll, and the margins of the leaf may die. In general, hot dry conditions favour mite infestation. Common hosts include *Anthurium, Codiaeum, Cordyline, Dieffenbachia, Dracaena, Maranta*, and palms.

This is a serious infection because trying to rinse the mites off the leaves and in the leaf joints is not really all that successful, so another technique has to be adopted.

Take the affected plant outdoors to a well-ventilated area and spray it with malathion. When the spray dries, rinse the leaves with clean water. If after treatment and keeping the affected plants in isolation the infestation persist, destroy the plant.

Scale insects can occasionally infect foliage plants in the garden room and become a bit of a problem, particularly on such species as *Codiaeum, Ficus*, and palms. They can be easily recognised by the shell that covers the body, which is between 1.5mm and 3mm (1/16" and 1/8") in diameter. These attack leaves and stems, sucking plant juices, causing stunting, leaf discolouration and death of tissue. Honeydew is also excreted. The best way to eradicate this insect pest is by the application of methylated spirit to the infested areas with the aid of either a cotton-wool pad or a small paintbrush.

Few diseases attack, the leaves and stems of plants growing in the indoor garden, due to the lower humidity indoors. Any infection, which may occur, is likely to come from newly acquired plants, which were diseased before arrival. To avoid this possible risk, isolate the new plants initially, to ensure that they are in good health, before introducing them into the garden room. Where it is found that a disease is present, spray the plants with a suitable fungicide, to eradicate any existing problem and prevent its spread. Be careful not to over water plants, avoid wetting the leaves, and don't crowd them together.

The general care of plants, however, does include one other factor, which is more difficult to define. Some people are credited with having green fingers because every plant they cultivate seems to flourish. These gardeners can effect the most startling transformations even in diseased or exhausted plants.

Much has been said in recent years about the benefits of talking to and cherishing indoor plants to encourage them to grow. Many years of plant cultivation have proved to me that the difference between the gardener with green fingers and the one without is nothing more than a genuine interest in the plants and the desire that they will thrive. Talking aloud to plants is not really necessary. The infusion of life is due to a more subtler, sympathetic connection between gardener and plant.

THE IMPORTANCE OF INDOOR PLANTS
AS AIR-FILTERS

Indoor plants are not simply pleasing to the eyes and soul; scientific studies have revealed that they are also beneficial to our health, and well being. They improve the quality of the air we breathe by their action in consuming the chemical pollutants that lurk in our homes.

The air in our homes and offices has been declining in quality over the last 50 years, according to some reports. And it is estimated to be some five to ten times more polluted now than the air outdoors! This is due in part to some of the modern building materials now widely employed, and the hard and soft furnishings introduced into buildings. In addition the electrical equipment, such as radios, televisions, electric blankets, computers, printers, fax machines, photostat machines, household cleaning agents, etc., all these contribute to the problem. Hazardous gases are given off from carpets, furniture, glues and resins, paints, wallpaper, particleboard, (used to make furniture), chipboard, plywood, foam insulation, upholstery, curtains, and electrical equipment. All these things have been found to spread airborne contaminants which are not easily dispersed, and can damage human health when present at levels above 0.1 part per million in the air. This can cause a whole range of symptoms to develop, from irritation of the eyes, nose, and throat, to coughing, headaches, dizziness, nausea, skin rashes, and respiratory problems.

In his book, **'Eco-Friendly House Plants'**, (Phoenix Illustrated, George Weidenfeld & Nicolson Ltd., 1996. ISBN 0-75380-046-2), Dr. B. C. Wolverton, a former NASA scientist, who spent many years studying plants abilities at improving indoor air quality, explains how houseplants support colonies of microbes on, and about their root systems, which can degrade volatile organic chemicals, how some of the pollutants in the air are absorbed by the leaves, and are either digested or translocated to their roots, where they serve as food for the microbes, how air pollutants are also drawn down into the soil as moisture about the roots is drawn up by the plants, and water evaporates from the soils surface. He also recommends the growing of indoor plants in hydroculture, as this makes them more effective air purifiers*. (See Hydroponics for Ornamental Plants pages 141-145.)

Dr. Wolverton lists a number of houseplants, which have been tested for their ecological benefits. And undoubtedly their numbers will continue to increase, as more research work is undertaken in this area.

Some plants are, of course, better at removing one pollutant rather than another from the indoor air:

Nephrolepis exaltata is top of the list, at the moment, for its removal rating for Formaldehyde, while *Chrysanthemum morifolium, Dracaena deremensis* 'Janet

Craig', *Chamaedorea seifritzii, Nephrolepis obliterata* (Aptly named I think!), and *Phoenix roebelenii*, are also good at the removal of this toxin.

Phalaenopsis sp. is effective in the removal of both Toluene, and Xylene from the indoor air.

Rhapis excelsa is a good plant for the removal of Ammonia, and a reasonable one for the removal of Formaldehyde from the indoor air.

See Slide H43. *Spathyphyllum* 'Mauna Loa'.

Spathiphyllum sp. has an ability to remove Acetone, Methyl alcohol, Ethyl acetate, Benzene, Ammonia, and other chemicals from the air. What a splendid plant species this is to have in the indoor garden, and to think it also produces such beautiful flowers into the bargain, under low light conditions!

In the light of this evidence, I believe that the time has come when we must cease to regard indoor plants as being purely ornamental, for they are not. They are living air filters with an essential role to play in human health and well being, in both the home and the office environment.

Amongst the plants listed in The Plant Light Tables of this book (pages 149-167), are to be found plants species, which Dr. Wolverton recommends make good air filter plants. Each one of these plants has had an asterisk placed next to its name, for easy identification, when selecting species, and cultivars of plants, for indoor cultivation, e.g., **Nephrolepis obliterata.* Some readers may choose to start initially, by selecting from amongst those plants, which are known to consume the chemical pollutants that lurk in their homes.

PROPAGATION

Gardening provides a way to participate in the continuous natural cycle of life and growth, and this is what makes it such an absorbing pastime. The ability to propagate plants from seed, or to encourage new growth from established plants, greatly increases the potential of an indoor garden. With fluorescent lighting, and a heated propagation case, you will be able to produce replacement plants at all seasons of the year, making your garden nearly self-sufficient.

If your garden room happens to have a good expanse of glass, and is on the south side of your property, then summer will provide conditions similar to those of a greenhouse, with plenty of light, warmth, and humidity. You should be able to reduce your costs for lighting and heating during warmer months, and the only extra equipment you will need is the simplest type of domed plastic propagation case. Set in a bright spot, these cases will enable you to propagate many kinds of plants with success.

If your garden room does not have such ideal conditions, during colder months, you should place a heated propagation case immediately beneath the fluorescent lamps. It can be a permanent feature in your light garden, or you can design a propagation unit as a separate working garden area e.g., in a small room basement or attic.

Propagation cases

The simplest type of propagator is nothing more than a plastic seed tray equipped with a clear plastic dome that fits neatly over the top; and generally this dome incorporates one or more hand-operated ventilators. You can convert it to a heated propagation case by installing a moulded plastic panel containing a heating cable, which is available as a kit. The panel is the same size as the seed tray and has plastic feet. To install it, simply place the panel on your shelf feet down, and mount the propagator on top. When the panel cable is plugged into the nearest wall socket, it will supply the seed tray with gentle warmth, using only 16-watts of electricity each hour. This type of propagator is simple to operate, and fits in a small indoor garden unit.

See Slide D1. A small low cost heated propagation unit.

There are two disadvantages to this simple propagation unit, however. The case itself holds very little material, and it does not have a thermostat by which you can regulate the degree of heat beneath the seed tray. To meet the needs of a number of different plant species, you will eventually need a larger and more versatile piece of equipment.

See Slide D2. A larger more expensive heated propagation units with variable temperature control.

The larger and more sophisticated propagation units are considerably more expensive.

An alternative to buying one ready for use is to assemble a unit from the necessary parts, which your local garden centre should be able to supply. A home-made propagator can be just as efficient and versatile as a ready made one, although commercially manufactured units are generally designed to be

A HOME-MADE PROPAGATION CASE

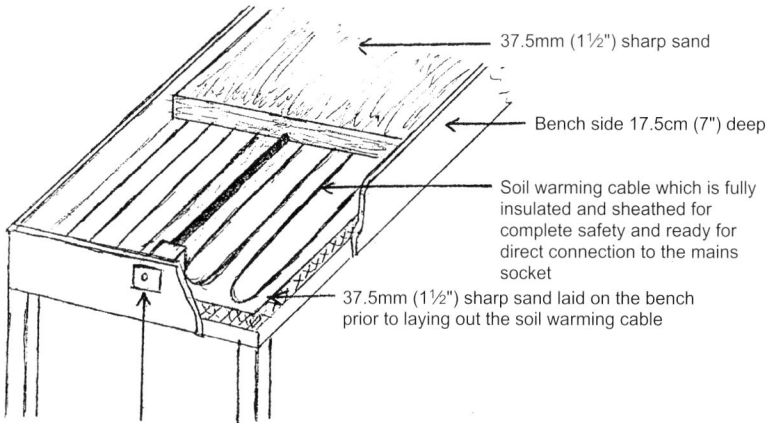

37.5mm (1½") sharp sand

Bench side 17.5cm (7") deep

Soil warming cable which is fully insulated and sheathed for complete safety and ready for direct connection to the mains socket

37.5mm (1½") sharp sand laid on the bench prior to laying out the soil warming cable

Thermostat and rod some 2.5cm (1") below the surface of the sharp sand. The thermostat should have a wide temperature control range, i.e. 10°C-27°C (50°F-80°F) to meet all propagation needs

A MIST PROPAGATION UNIT

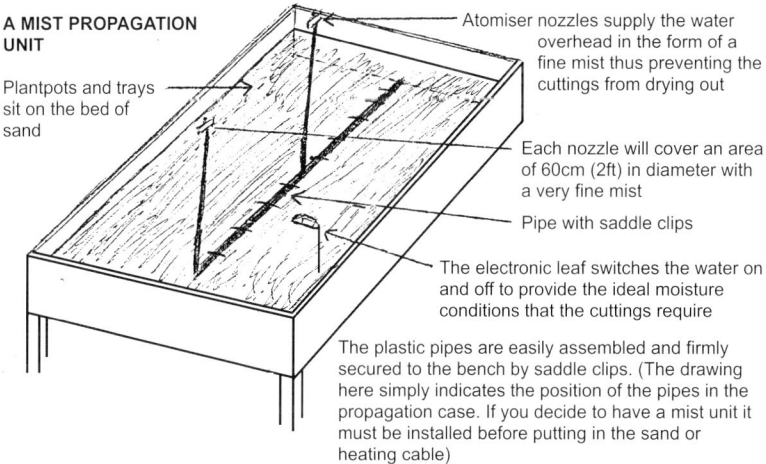

Plantpots and trays sit on the bed of sand

Atomiser nozzles supply the water overhead in the form of a fine mist thus preventing the cuttings from drying out

Each nozzle will cover an area of 60cm (2ft) in diameter with a very fine mist

Pipe with saddle clips

The electronic leaf switches the water on and off to provide the ideal moisture conditions that the cuttings require

The plastic pipes are easily assembled and firmly secured to the bench by saddle clips. (The drawing here simply indicates the position of the pipes in the propagation case. If you decide to have a mist unit it must be installed before putting in the sand or heating cable)

compact with a neat appearance to suit garden rooms and light gardens. In your working garden, a homemade propagator is perfectly adequate, and will be even more effective if you add a mist watering system, as illustrated.

A mist propagation unit

The plastic pipes are easily assembled and firmly secured to the bench by U-shaped clips. (The drawing here simply indicates the position of the pipe in the propagation case. If you add a mist unit, it must be installed before the sand or heating cable.)

Propagating from established plants

The basic methods for producing new plants from existing plants are taking cuttings from leaves or stems; the division of plants; the removal of offsets or plantlets; and by air-layering. The drawings on the following pages serve to illustrate these techniques.

See Slide E10. *Streptocarpus* propagated vegetatively from a single leaf.

Leaf cuttings

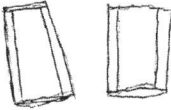

Sansevieria

Use leaf cuttings for the rapid multiplication of this plant if it is not large enough to provide offsets. Cut the leaf into sections 5cm (2") long, and insert right way up in small pots containing peat/sand potting mix and put them into a heated propagation case.

A bottom heat of 21˚C (70˚F) is necessary to promote the development of new roots and new shoots. Under these conditions, rooting will take about one month.

Variegated Sanseiveria cannot be propagated successfully from cuttings because they revert to the common green form of this plant.

Pot your rooted Sansevieria when they have produced three leaves, and carefully cut away the remains of the old leaf.

Foliage Begonias such as *B. masoniana* and *B. rex* are also propagated from leaf cuttings

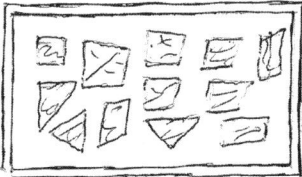

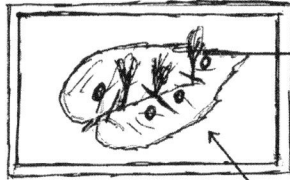

New plants

Here we see an example of vegetative propagation in progress. A *Begonia rex* leaf has been detached from the parent plant and laid flat in a tray of moist peat/sand mix, and a number of transverse incisions have been made, at well spaced intervals, through the leaf's major leaf veins, with a sharp knife. The tray has then been placed in a propagation case where it has been maintained at 21˚C (70˚F). The result of this is that the leaf has begun to root and produce new shoots.

It is also possible to cut a *Begonia rex* leaf up into sections of 1.25cm to 2.5cm (½" to 1") square, with each encompassing a portion of a major leaf vein. These sections are then laid flat with the upper surface of the leaf uppermost, on the moist peat/sand propagation mix, and plantlets will develop from these in a few weeks if given the same rooting conditions. This is one of the most productive propagation methods.

A new plant growing from a small section of leaf.

New roots forming from cut edge of the begonia leaf.

Set the propagators bottom heat at 21˚C (70˚F) to promote rooting.

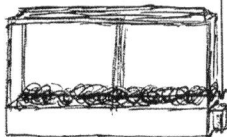

The light intensity needed to promote satisfactory rooting is 5,000/6,000 lux for 16 to 18 hours per day.
Pot up the resulting plants complete with any bits of old leaf, which may be present, as soon as they are large enough to handle. Then put them back in the propagator to encourage growth.

Streptocarpus. This plant may be propagated from leaf cuttings and by division of the plant.

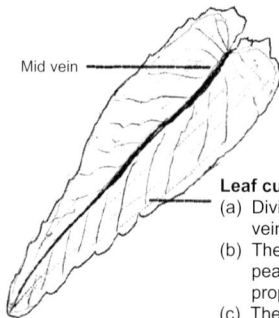

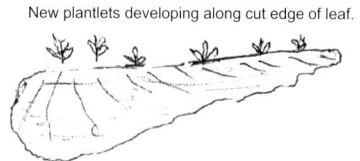

Mid vein

New plantlets developing along cut edge of leaf.

Leaf cuttings

(a) Divide the leaf in two down the middle, and remove the mid-vein entirely.

(b) The two pieces of leaf are then placed lengthwise in a peat/sand rooting mixture, which is kept moist, in a heated propagator set at 21˚C (70˚F).

(c) The leaf sections will root in three or four weeks, and in another four weeks plantlets appear along the cut edges, but these should not be transplanted until they are large enough to handle easily, in a further four weeks, at which time you can pot them up individually into 10cm (4") pots.

(d) The remains of the leaf will be fit to use again for a second batch of plantlets, so put it straight back in the propagation unit again.

Division of the plant

Well cared for plants will last for several years but they become rather tired by the end of the second year.

The easiest way to revitalise them is by division of the roots in the spring time and the provision of some fresh compost.

Leaf bud cuttings

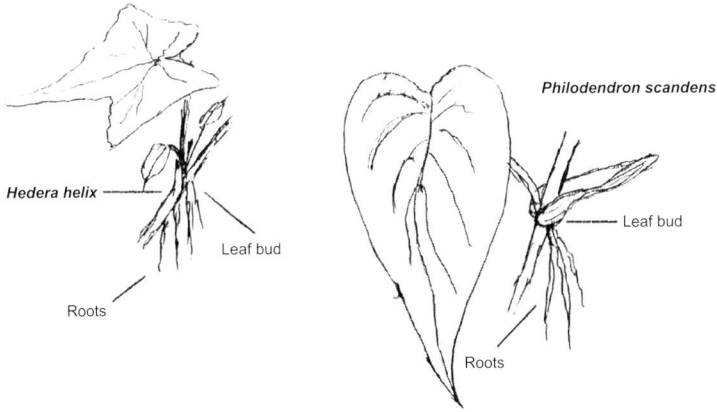

Hedera helix —————— Leaf bud

Roots

Philodendron scandens

Leaf bud

Roots

Both **Hedera helix** and **Philodendron scandens** can be propagated from leaf bud cuttings, as shown. Roots will be produced readily. Established pot plants with plenty of top growth will provide suitable propagation material. Insert each leaf-bud cutting in an individual small pot containing equal parts peat and sand, and place in a propagation unit, with the temperature set at 21˚C (70˚F). Once the plants have nicely filled these small pots with their new roots and shoots, re-pot them in 7.5cm (3") pots containing peat-based mix, and remove them from the propagator and treat them in the normal way.

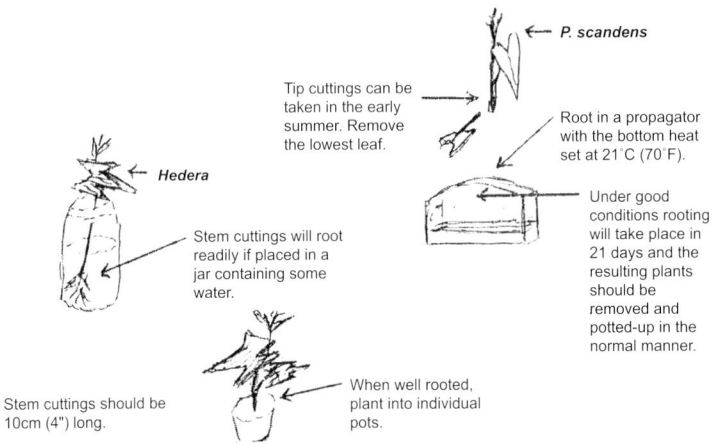

← **P. scandens**

Tip cuttings can be taken in the early summer. Remove the lowest leaf.

Root in a propagator with the bottom heat set at 21˚C (70˚F).

← **Hedera**

Stem cuttings will root readily if placed in a jar containing some water.

Under good conditions rooting will take place in 21 days and the resulting plants should be removed and potted-up in the normal manner.

Stem cuttings should be 10cm (4") long.

When well rooted, plant into individual pots.

Stem cuttings

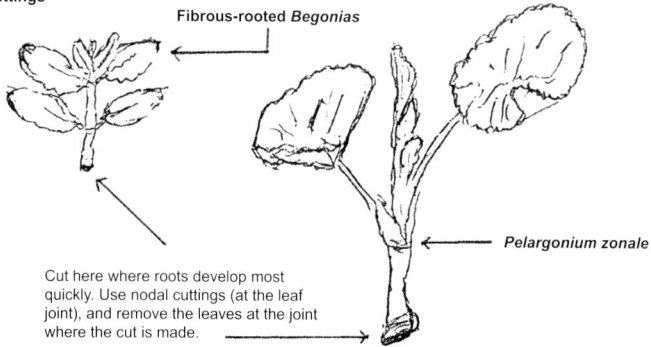

Fibrous-rooted *Begonias*

Pelargonium zonale

Cut here where roots develop most quickly. Use nodal cuttings (at the leaf joint), and remove the leaves at the joint where the cut is made.

Fuchsia. Take inter-nodal (between leaf joint) stem cuttings of this plant, as they will root more successfully.

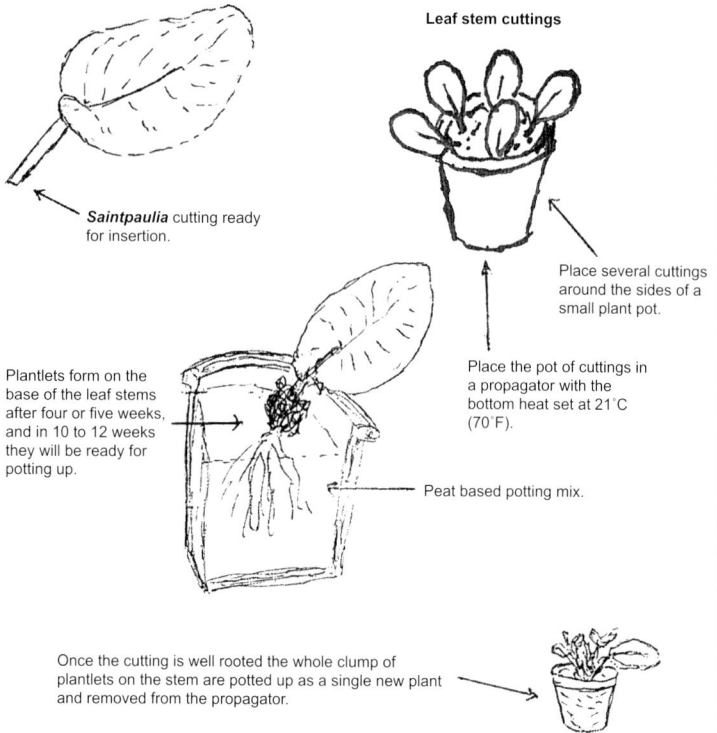

Leaf stem cuttings

Saintpaulia cutting ready for insertion.

Place several cuttings around the sides of a small plant pot.

Place the pot of cuttings in a propagator with the bottom heat set at 21˚C (70˚F).

Plantlets form on the base of the leaf stems after four or five weeks, and in 10 to 12 weeks they will be ready for potting up.

Peat based potting mix.

Once the cutting is well rooted the whole clump of plantlets on the stem are potted up as a single new plant and removed from the propagator.

120

Stem Cuttings

Schlumbergera truncata, syn. *Zygocatus truncata.*

Propagate during the summer by cutting a stem section consisting of 2 segments at the joint.

Lay the cutting on one side for 48 hours to allow the cut surface to dry.

Schlumbergera truncata

Place the cuttings in a seed tray in a propagation case. Set the bottom heat at a temperature of 21˚C (70˚F) but do not cover them with a plastic or glass dome. Keep in a good light, but not direct sunlight.

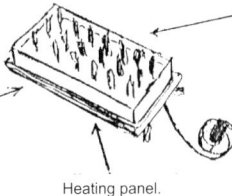

Heating panel.

Insert the cuttings to half the depth of the lower segment in a half-sand and half-peat based potting mix. If they tend to fall over, insert a small bit of cane to keep them upright. (If you push them too deeply into the mix, they may rot.)

When new roots have formed, pot the plants up in 10cm (4") pots containing a peat-based potting mix, and place in a light garden.

Root formation takes several weeks to occur so it is pointless watering rootless cacti cuttings. However, misting the stem segments will maintain the humidity and delay the shrivelling process, thus giving the cuttings some additional time to root successfully.

Also *Enchinopsis spachiana* and *Opuntia basilaris*

If this one is getting too big cut off the top and use this as a cutting.

For propagation purposes select one section of stem and cut it off at a natural junction.

General Advice:
Proceed as for Zygocactus with regards to propagation requirements including depth of insertion into compost.

Echinopsis spachiana

Opuntia basilaris

121

Aspidistra elatior and *Cyperus altenifolius*

Aspidistra elatior

Cyperus alternifolius

Propagate by division of the clumps.

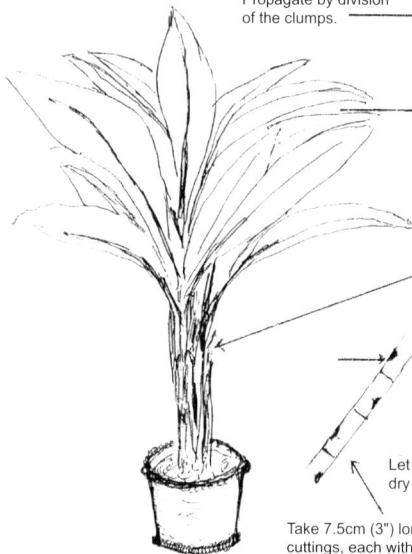

Dieffenbachia maculata

The sap of *Dieffenbachia* plants is poisonous. Wear gloves when taking cuttings, so that no sap gets on the skin.

All *Dieffenbachia* tend to lose their lower leaves, as they grow larger. If you want smallish plants filled with leaves right down to the pot, you will have to propagate fresh ones from the older plants or buy new plants.

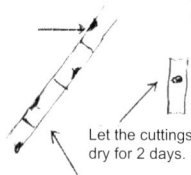

Let the cuttings dry for 2 days.

Insert stem cuttings in a propagation unit in peat-based potting mix, and set the bottom heat at 21˚C (70˚F) to 27˚C (80˚F). Keep moist.

Take 7.5cm (3") long stem cuttings, each with a leaf joint.

You can also prune back the over-large plant to encourage new growth.

An example of the new plant when rooted.

122

Propagation by division of the roots.

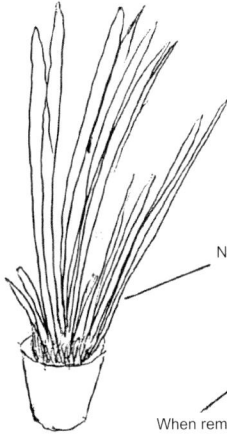

A good pot of **Sansevieria** ready for division of the plant.

Note how the pot is packed with leaves.

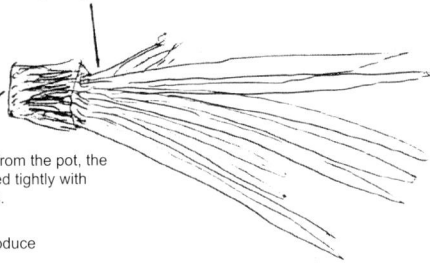

When removed from the pot, the root ball is packed tightly with roots and shoots.

Careful dissection with a sharp knife will produce several rooted young shoots (offsets).

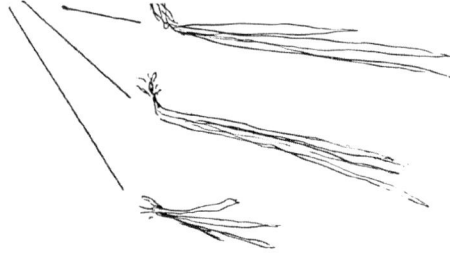

Plant these in individual pots to form new plants. ————

Plantlets and offsets are two methods of plant propagation that do not need a propagator.

Saxifraga stolonifera

A plantlet detached from its ———— runner and potted up to form a new plant

——— Runners.

——— Plantlets complete with roots.

Examples of instant new plants without the aid of a propagation case.

Air Layering with Plastic

Some plants such as **Cordyline, Dieffenbachia, Dracaena,** and **Ficus** may grow very tall, with just a few leaves at the top of the stem.

The solution is to encourage the growth of fresh roots from the stem in close proximity to the existing foliage leaves.

In early summer, make an upward cut in the stem with a sharp knife 7.5cm to 10cm (3"/4") beneath the lowest leaf. This will encourage the growth of fresh roots from the stem, close to the existing leaves.

Save the stem after the top has been cut off. It will produce new shoots from dormant buds, and these can be the source of more new plants.

Keep the cut from closing and healing back together again, by placing a wedge of peat or a small stone between the cut surfaces.

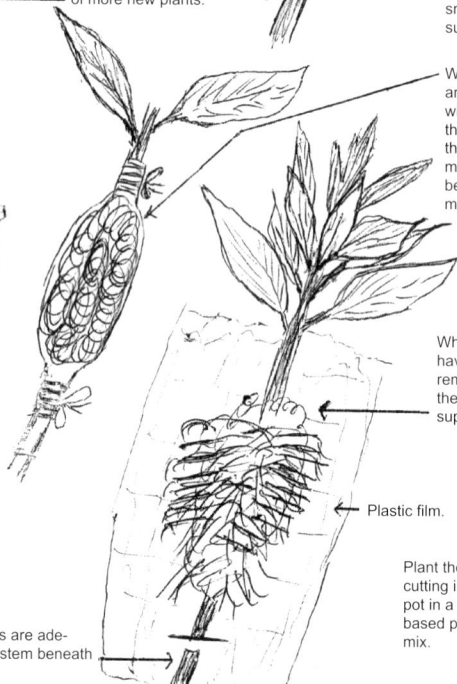

Wrap a thick layer of moist peat around the stem. Hold it in place with a sleeve of plastic film. Tie the plastic in place a little beneath the cut in the stem. Then pack more moist peat into the sleeve, before tying the top to prevent moisture from escaping.

When you can see that roots have filled most of the sleeve, remove the plastic. Then examine the roots to ensure that they can support the top growth.

Plastic film.

Plant the rooted cutting in its own pot in a peat based potting mix.

When the roots are adequate, cut the stem beneath the root ball.

124

Sowing seed

Basically, a seed is a tiny plant in a small container. It is very much alive, but resting until the time and conditions are right for it to awaken. To keep this embryo plant alive during this stage of its existence, there is a supply of stored food within the seed case. When the seed is sown and provided with moisture and warmth, the seed case bursts open and the roots begin to probe their way down among the compost. At about the same time, a tiny shoot emerges from within the seed case, pushing its way upwards in search of the light.

During the course of this activity, the only supply of food available is within the seed case. If the light is not found fairly quickly, enabling the shoot to open its seed leaves and produce fresh supplies of food, it will die.

Sowing seed therefore calls for some care, and it is in this initial stage that the success or failure of the seeds to germinate will be decided. Generally failure results from sowing seeds too deeply in the compost, so always read the sowing instructions on the seed packet very carefully before you begin.

It is especially difficult to germinate fine seed evenly over the surface of a seed tray. Often, a great deal of the seed falls between the particles of the seed compost and is buried too deeply to survive the effort of reaching the surface.

Begonia seeds are extremely tiny, with a seed count of over 60,000 seeds per gram (⅛th of an ounce). The amount of seed in the average packet is far above your immediate requirements, even though the visible quantity may seem infinitesimal.

Fine seed should be dusted over the surface of a seed compost that has already been firmed into position and watered with a fine rose on a small watering can. Bring the seed packet close to the compost's surface, as the slightest draught catching the falling seed will spread it unevenly or blow it right away from the tray. Do not try to cover fine seed with sand, as is sometimes suggested.

Less fine seeds present fewer problems, providing there is enough light to enable the seedlings to produce stocky growth, enough moisture to meet their needs, and the correct temperature for germination. A slight covering of sifted seed compost or sand will not prevent the necessary penetration of the light between the particles, but will hold the seeds down while germination takes place, encouraging the roots to make their way down into the compost. Otherwise, there is a tendency for the root growth to push the seed upwards, leading to poor seedlings, When judging the amount of covering to provide, the rule of thumb is a covering equal to twice the diameter of the seed.

Another common mistake is the assumption that seeds will only germinate if they are placed in the dark. While it is true that some seeds require a warm, dark environment until they germinate e.g. *Calendula* and *Salpiglossis*. This is not the case with all plants that are grown from seed. *Browallia, Exacum,*

Kalanchoe, *Primula*, and *Streptocarpus* are some popular flowering plants that must receive a certain amount of light after sowing to ensure a good level of germination.

Most summer bedding plants will germinate in the light, and many others do equally well in the light or darkness, in their early stages. In a greenhouse, these plants would need protection from the sun, but this is not necessary in a garden room with its much lower intensity of fluorescent lighting e.g., 400 lux to 2000 lux.

For those plants that do require light to germinate, there is no one level of light intensity that is correct for all kinds of seeds. Day length and light intensity must be linked with temperature and humidity to achieve the best conditions for any particular seed variety. However, you can germinate seeds successfully with a light intensity in the region of 700 lux to 1,500 lux.

Do not cover the seeds of the following plants:

Achimenes cultivars
Begonia Semperflorens
Begonia (tuberous rooted)
Browallia speciosa
Calceolaria (outdoor varieties)
Campanula isophylla
Campanula fragilis
Exacum affine
Hypoestes phyllostachya
Kalanchoe blossfeldiana
Lobelia erinus
Mimulus x*hybridus*
Nicotiana alata (Flowering Tobacco)
Petunia X*hybrida*
Saintpaulia ionantha
Sinningia speciosa
Solenostemon scutellarioides syn. *Coleus blumei*
Streptocarpus xhybridus

If you would like to make an early start with bedding plants that will be going out into the garden later, provide the seedlings and young plants with a light intensity of 8,000 lux for 16 hours per day.

If you are an absolute beginner, it may be better to start with a seed kit. This is a seed tray ready-sown with seeds, which just needs watering and the warmth of a propagator to start the seeds into activity. Once you have confidence in starting new plants from seed by this method, you can become more adventurous in choosing from among the packeted seeds.

Preventing fungal infection in seedlings

Damping off describes the effects of a number of very destructive fungi-*Pythium ultimum*, and *Rhizoctonia solani*, primarily, and to a lesser extent, *Botrytis cinerea* and *Phytophthora sp.* which attack and kill young seedling in the early stages of germination. Pre-emergence damping off rots the seeds before any growth can get started. Post-emergence damping off attacks the stems of the seedlings at or near the surface of the compost, causing them to topple over and collapse.

A good quality seed compost, and potting compost (and multi-purpose mix for both seed sowing and potting) will be free from all pests and diseases, giving the plants an excellent start. Seeds should always be sown very, very thinly, over the surface of the compost. Thick sowings, lend themselves more readily to invasion by fungal diseases, and once they have gained a foothold all the seedlings in the seed tray very quickly become infected and die. Where the sowing is thinner, and the resulting seedlings further apart, a fungal infection will spread more slowly. If you keep a close eye on your seed trays, day by day, you will be able to eradicate infected seedlings by scooping them out of the seed tray and destroying them, or you can transfer the unaffected seedlings into other seed trays to prevent them becoming infected as well.

Take care when watering seed trays. Water the compost initially, leaving it to drain for a few hours before sowing the seed. After sowing, all watering of the seed container has to be done from the bottom. Avoid wetting the surface of the mix, or watering germinating seedlings from above, as this will encourage an invasion of the universally present airborne fungus spores and the onset of damping off disease.

You will need to keep the seeds in a warm place where they can germinate rapidly, and begin to thin them out as soon as they are large enough to handle.

Plants You Can Propagate From Seed

Indoor plants you can propagate from seeds, with the aid of an illuminated and heated propagation case, include:

Plant Name	Germination Light/Dark requirement	Germination Temperature °C - °F
Abutilon pictum 'Thompsonii'	D	20°C - 68°F
Achimenes cultivars	L	21°C - 70°F
Begonia Semperflorens	L	21°C - 70°F
Browallia speciosa	L	20°C - 68°F
Catharanthus roseus	L	21°C - 70°F
Coffea arabica	D	22°C - 73°F

Plant Name	Germination Light/Dark requirement	Germination Temperature °C - °F
Coleus blumei	L	20°C - 68°F
Cuphea ignea	D	21°C - 70°F
Exacum affine	L	16°C - 60°F
Grevillea robusta	D	20°C - 68°F
Hypoestes 'Pink Splash'	L	20°C - 68°F
Impatiens walleriana	D	21°C - 70°F
Kalanchoe blossfeldiana	L	21°C - 70°F
Pelargonium zonale	L	21°C - 70°F
Saintpaulia ionantha	L	21°C - 70°F
Schefflera arboricola	D	23°C - 75°F
Sinningia speciosa	L	20°C - 68°F
Streptocarpus X*hybridus*	L	21°C - 70°F
Thunbergia alata	D	20°C - 68°F

Propagation by seed – General observations

Fluorescent lamp.

Immediately germination takes place bring the seed-pan into close proximity to the fluorescent lamps 10 to 15cm (4" to 6") distant). This will ensure short compact growth.

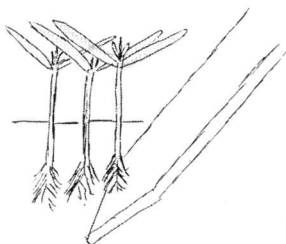

Raise the seed-pan on a box or upturned plant pot.

Once the seedlings are big enough to handle they should be pricked out without delay, thus minimising any check to their growth.

Use great care when removing the seedlings from the seed-pan. The ideal tool for this purpose is a seed label. Loosen and lever the seedlings from the pan without causing injury to their tiny fragile roots.

A pencil makes a good dibber for pricking out seedlings.

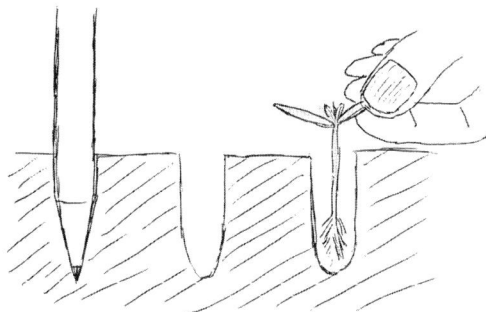

Always hold seedlings between one's finger and thumb.
Never hold a seedling by its stem as this causes injury and may result in its death.

Prick seedlings out 5cm (2") apart in each direction and flick a little of the compost into the hole around the fragile roots with the tip of the pencil. Never try to firm the compost about the roots either with one's finger or a pencil.

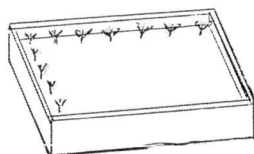

A light watering in with a can with a fine hose will provide all the firming of the compost necessary.

When the seedlings have been pricked out they are returned to the close proximity of the fluorescent lamps again.

129

GROWING YOUR OWN FOOD

Indoor gardening readily extends to the cultivation of useful as well as decorative plants. Germinating seeds indoors under artificial lighting offers the opportunity for an early start on vegetables and salad crops for your outdoor garden. But you also have the realistic prospect of growing edible crops to healthy maturity entirely within your indoor garden. Fresh salad crops-lettuce, tomatoes, radishes, mustard and cress-will flourish under fluorescent lamps, and you can grow a fine range of culinary herbs, many on a year round basis, to add distinctive flavours to your meals. Even if your light garden is small, you can accommodate edible plants, and enjoy the practical rewards, as well as the interest, of cultivating them.

There is a special pleasure from homegrown foods; that is enhanced when you harvest fresh produce that is out of season, or highly priced in the stores. You can produce salad crops year-round by providing intense illumination over relatively long periods. In some cases you will have to keep the lights on 24 hours a day, for several days or even weeks. Since fluorescent lighting is an economic source of light energy, the cost of raising food crops from seed will be little more than that of growing foliage and flowering plants.

Culinary herbs

Today herbs are enjoying a new popularity for the fresh and delicate flavours they add to both hot and cold dishes. These plants like the sun, and traditionally have been grown in pots on sunny windowsills. If you grow herbs in your light garden, many will produce a year-round supply of fresh leaves. Those that remain seasonal will need a rest period during the year, with an especially abundant and healthy crop during their growing season.

Herbs grown outdoors under natural conditions generally develop into tall or spreading plants, but this need not be a problem in an indoor garden. If you carefully remove growing tips by pinching them out between finger and thumb, you will encourage compact, sturdy plants. These will fit into your light garden, close to the fluorescent lamps, and will flourish as long as they can enjoy a light intensity of 8,000 lux to 10,000 lux for 12 to 14 hour per day. Apart from their culinary value, many herbs are very attractive in their own right, and will also give a delicate scent to your garden area.

Basil (*Ocimum basilicum*) is a half-hardy annual, originating from tropical Asia and Africa, used widely to flavour salads, soups, and cheese or vegetable dishes. Herbalists regard it as an aid to relief of nervous tension, and this can be easily raised from seed in the light garden. Sow the seeds very thinly in two or three 11.25cm (4½") pots, and when they have germinated, thin out the seedlings so there are only three in each pot. Basil does not respond successfully to transplanting, so this should be avoided. Keep the seedlings within 15cm

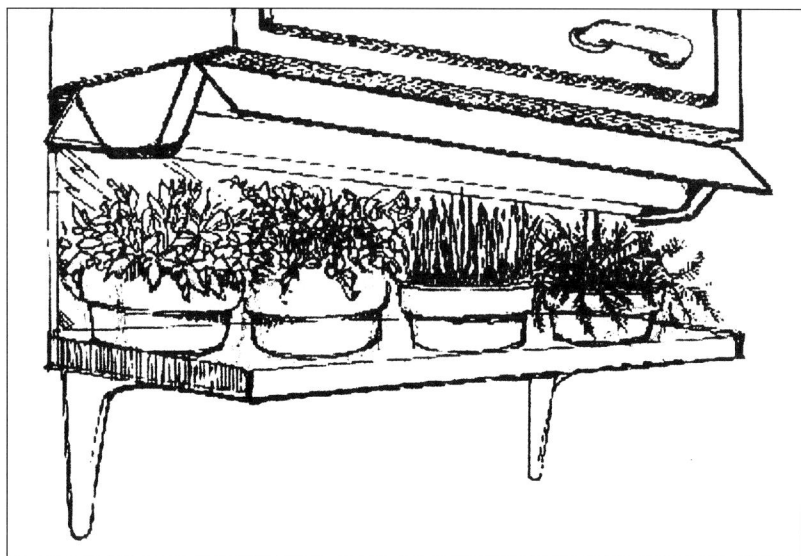

Drawing of a herb garden that is ideally suited for a spot within a fitted kitchen where fluorescent lamps can be attached under one of the wall units as illustrated, or in a laundry area.

(6") of the fluorescent lamps, to ensure compact, sturdy growth. Gradually lower the pots as the foliage develops, always keeping the tips of the shoots at the same distance from the lamps.

In order to maintain a regular supply of basil throughout the year, you will need to make several sowings. Time the second and subsequent sowings to coincide with the first signs of decline in the existing crop. Apart from its culinary value basil is worthy of a spot in your light garden because its leaves give off a delightful aroma, with the added bonus that the plant repels flies.

Chervil (*Anthriscus cereifolium*) is a hardy annual native to Europe, which you can enjoy throughout the year simply by sowing seed at three-month intervals. Its feathery foliage has a delicate aniseed flavour, and can be used in salads, or as a garnish for meat and fish dishes.

Sow the seeds thinly and transplant the seedlings, when they are large enough to handle, into 10cm (4") pots, and keep the growing tips of the developing plants approximately 15cm (6") from the lamps.

Chives (*Allium schoenoprasum*) is widely distributed throughout the northern hemisphere. It is a hardy perennial and a diminutive member of the onion family. It has long, narrow, tubular leaves with a mild onion flavour delicious in egg and cheese dishes, salads, and soups.

Although chives can be grown from seed, it takes two years before the plants are a useful size. It is best to buy a few plants from a garden centre in 11.25cm (4½") pots in the late winter just before new growth is about to start. Put these straight into your light garden to encourage renewed activity, and you will soon have a supply of fresh new leaves. They will grow up to 25cm (10") tall. Lower the plants as necessary to keep the leaf tips 15cm (6") from the lamps. In the middle of the growing season, pinkish flowers will appear. You must remove them straight away to encourage further leaf production.

Chives will not produce fresh leaves throughout the year. The plants must have a resting period, and will die down naturally in the autumn each year. However, they will have a longer season under indoor cultivation than if they were grown outdoors.

Stop watering during their resting period, but just damp the compost from time to time to prevent it from drying out completely. Clumps of Chives require re-potting every year, during the resting period. Every second year at this time, you can propagate additional plants by dividing the clumps.

Marjoram (*Origanum majorana*), originally from North Africa, is a half-hardy annual that forms a bushy little plant only 20cm (8") high. It is sweet yet, spicy, often used in meat dishes to bring out their full flavour. Fish dishes, salads, and soups will also benefit from a small addition of this herb. You can use its leaves and flowers either fresh or dried, but the herb has a much stronger flavour when dried. Herbalists recommend marjoram for the relief of high blood pressure, headache, and neuralgia, and also as a mild laxative.

You can raise plants from seed in a light garden at any time of year. Make further sowing as soon as the existing plants show signs of fading. Sow only a few seeds at one time, and these will germinate rapidly. Once they are large enough to handle, they should be transplanted individually in 7.5cm (3") pots. Keep the tips of the leaves close to the lamps at all times, as they need all the light you can provide.

Mint (*Mentha spicata*) is a hardy perennial, native to Europe, the leaves of which are used to make sources and jellies. It is also used as a garnish, sprinkled on new potatoes, peas, beans, carrots, meat, and fish dishes, and in salads. As a herbal remedy, it is recommended for the relief of indigestion.

While you can grow mint from seed, the best way to introduce it to your light garden is to buy several roots in 11.25cm (4½") pots from your local garden centre, in late winter. In the warmth of your light garden, new shoots will soon develop, and you will have mint available for use after about one month. Keep the tips of the shoots within 15cm (6") of the lamps.

Mint bears small spikes of purple flowers at the height of its growth period. Remove them as soon as they appear, to direct the plant's energies into producing more tender, leafy shoots, and to induce additional root development that will sustain the next year's growth.

Unfortunately, mint cannot be produced throughout the year, as the plant must be allowed to die down naturally in the autumn to rest, but its season of availability is much longer indoors. Re-pot the plants annually just as renewed growth begins. Propagate by dividing the roots at this time, or by cuttings obtained during the early part of the growing season.

Parsley (*Petroselinum crispum*) is a hardy biennial from central and southern Europe that is treated as an annual. Used as flavouring or garnish in a great many dishes, it is also a highly nutritious vegetable, rich in iron and vitamins A and C. By making successive sowings, starting new seeds as soon as existing plants show signs of fading, you can have parsley throughout the year from your light garden.

The germination of parsley seeds is very slow. In order to speed up the process as much as possible, soak the seeds in luke-warm water for 24 hours before sowing. Parsley does not respond well to transplanting, so it is best to sow a few seeds in the top of several 7.5cm (3") pots. Thin out the plants as they develop, leaving one in each pot.

As each plant grows too big for its original container, re-pot in a 12.5cm (5 in pot) pot. Handle it carefully, to avoid disturbing the roots. Keep the tips of the leaves close to the lamps at all times. To stimulate new growth, pick a few leaves frequently from each plant.

Rosemary (*Rosmarinus officinalis*) is an evergreen shrub, which comes from southern Europe and Asia Minor. It has narrow, grey-green leaves from 2.5cm to 5cm (1" to 2") long. It is used to complement beef stews, lamb, veal, pork, and poultry dishes. When grown outdoors, it reaches a height of 1.8M (6ft) but in a light garden it will remain quite diminutive if you trim it regularly. You can keep a rosemary plant in good health producing its fine aromatic leaves over many years.

Begin by purchasing one or two small plants from a garden centre. If you like, you can increase your stock by growing additional plants from stem cuttings. Grow the plants in 11.25cm (4½") pots, and keep the tips of the shoots within 15cm (6") of the lamps.

Sage (*Salvia officinalis*) is a hardy perennial, sub-evergreen, aromatic shrub, native to southern Europe. You can buy plants from a garden centre in 8.75cm (3½") pots, to add to your light garden at any time of the year. The leaves can be used, either fresh or dried, with pork, goose, duck, and other meat dishes. They also add flavour to fish, and cheese dishes, and to vegetables like cabbage, carrots, and onions.

Herbalists recommend sage to relieve sore throats, laryngitis, and hay fever. Its purple flowers are an added attraction, and you need not remove them when they appear.

When the shrubs begin to become too big for their pot, re-pot them in 12.5cm (5") pots. Remove the tips of the shoots, when growth begins, to encourage short, sturdy, bushes. Cut the stems back lightly when flowering has finished to induce the production of fresh leafy shoots. Replace the existing bushes with younger more vigorous stock at the end of every second year.

Thyme (*Thymus vulgaris*) is another low-growing, bushy perennial with aromatic leaves, which you can also buy as small plants in 8.75cm (3½") pots. It is extensively used fresh, or dried, in poultry stuffing, with pork, lamb, and fish dishes, and in soups.

You can start to cut the stems when they are about 7.5cm (3") long, taking care to remove just a few from each bush at any one time. This will stimulate the production of new shoots for future use without weakening the bushes. Be sure to keep the tips of the leaves within 10cm (4") of the lamps in your light garden.

As the thyme continues to grow, it will need more space for its roots, and must be re-potted in a 12.5cm (5inch) pot. To propagate, divide the plants at the time of re-potting. If you eventually find that the stock is becoming less vigorous the best thing to do is to purchase fresh plant stock.

Culinary herbs

Light Needs: 8,000 lux/10,000 lux 12/14 hours per day

Basil (*Ocimum basilicum*)
Chervil (*Anthriscus cereifolium*
Chives (*Allium schoenoprasum*)
Marjoram (*Origanum majorana*)
Mint (*Mentha spicata*)
Parsley (*Petroselinum crispum*)
Rosemary (Rosmarinus officinalis)
Sage (*Salvia officinalis*)
Thyme (*Thymus vulgaris*)

Cucumbers (*Cucumis sativus*)

Cucumbers can be raised from seed in an indoor light garden ready for subsequent planting in a greenhouse, a garden frame, or the open garden, when weather conditions will permit.

The seed should be sown three weeks before it is anticipated that it is a safe time for setting out the plants in their intended cropping position.

The seed is sown singly, on its' side, 1.25cm (½") deep, in 8.75cm (3½") pots containing moist peat/based potting mix. The pots are then covered with black polythene to induce humidity, at a temperature of 18°C/24°C (65°F/75°F).

Germination occurs in 3/5 days, and the pots are then brought into the light and placed in a light garden with a light intensity of 13,000/15,000 lux for 12/24 hours per day, for 15 plus days.

It is interesting to note that cucumber plants appear to be insensitive to day length for flowering, providing that their other cultural requirements are satisfactory. Indeed I have continued this treatment for up to 28 days without any adverse effect to the plants.

See Slide E46. A close view of four pots of cucumber seedlings.

See Slide E47. The same cucumber plants after some 7 days of growth under the fluorescent lamps.

See Slide E48. The same plants after 14 days of growth under the fluorescent lamps.

See Slide E50. The Cucumber F1 Hybrid 'Patio PiK' in its final pot ready for removal from the indoor light garden and putting out on the patio to start fruiting. Due to the poor weather conditions prevailing in the year 2000, the cucumber plants remained in the light garden for 28 days.

Take care not to disturb the roots of the cucumber plants when they are being set out in their final cropping positions.

Mustard and Cress

Black Mustard (*Brassica nigra*), and Common Garden Cress (*Lepidium sativum*).

Mustard and Cress have long been grown indoors on the kitchen windowsill as a delicious addition to salads.

Years ago, the technique was to germinate the seeds on a piece of damp cloth spread over the surface of a saucer. This was a source of fascination to generations of children, who would observe the tiny seedlings growing, and harvest the leaves simply by cutting them with a pair of scissors. Today Mustard and Cress can be produced with much greater precision in a light garden, if they receive 8,000 lux on a continuous basis for 24 hours per day from when germination occurs.

The seed is sown in plastic seed trays containing 3.75cm (1½") of peat-based potting mix. This is firmed into the trays and moistened with water before sowing takes place. The Cress is then sown in one tray and the Mustard in another*. Sow the seed evenly and thickly over the surface of the trays and cover the seed trays with black plastic to exclude the light and help retain moisture. Leave them in the warmth of your garden room like this for two days (48 hours). Then remove the plastic covering from the trays to expose the germinating seedlings to the light, and place them in a light garden 10cm to 15cm (4" to 6") from the lamps, at a temperature of 21°C (70°F). After 3 days of constant illumination at this temperature the crop will be 5cm (2") high and ready for cutting. Where, however, these precise illumination and temperature requirements cannot be satisfied, the crop may take a day or so longer to mature.

If the Mustard and Cress are grown under ordinary room conditions, on a window ledge the crop may take some 10 to 14 days to mature.

* The benefit to be gained by sowing the mustard and cress separately is that when ready for cutting one can mix in whatever proportion of each one prefers.

Radishes (*Raphanus sativus*)

Radishes are another catch crop that you can grow successfully in a light garden throughout the year. They will need a light intensity of 13,000/15,000 lux 24 hours per day over a period of 21 days or more, and a steady temperature of 18°C (65°F). The best types for indoor cultivation are the early forcing varieties, such as 'Saxerre' or 'Saxa', both of which produce round, bright red roots that look good and taste delicious.

The seed is sown 1.25cm (½") deep and 3.75cm to 5cm (1½" to 2") apart, in half pots, or similar, with a minimum of 7.5cm (3") depth of peat based potting mix, at a temperature of 18°C (65°F). Use pelleted seed if you can obtain it. It is easier to handle and enables you to sow more efficiently. After sowing moisten the potting mix, and cover the seed trays with thick black plastic. Leave in the warmth of the garden room for 2 days in the dark, for germination to occur, and then place the pots in the light garden under the fluorescent lamps which are to remain lit for 24 hours per day.

Under normal room temperatures, the radishes should be ready for pulling some 21 days from the date they were placed in the light garden. Once you have harvested the crop, discard the mix and do not use it for another crop. With regular weekly sowings in fresh potting mix, you can produce a continuous supply of crisp, tasty radishes.

Salad Bowl Lettuce (*Lactuca santiva*)

Lettuce can only justify its presence as a light garden crop in the winter months, when a supply of fresh green leaves (not hearted lettuce) can be harvested from the plants.

While it is not practicable to raise good quality headed lettuce in a light garden, it is perfectly possible to cultivate lettuce using the "cut-and-come-again" technique of harvesting leaves. This method of cultivation is not limited only to the production of the non-hearting 'Salad Bowl' variety, which provides an abundance of fresh green foliage for use in salads. Any of the common lettuce varieties such as 'All The Year Round' can be grown in a light garden in the same way. You will obtain several crops of leaves from each plant, and they will be every bit as tender and tasty as outdoor lettuce.

If available, purchase pelleted seed to make it easier to sow. Grow the lettuce in 8.75cm/10cm (3½", 4") pots. Sow the seeds 1.25cm (½") deep and two or three to a pot, in a peat-based potting mix which has been firmed and then moistened prior to sowing. The end of a pencil will do to bury the seeds in the pots and cover them from the light. Temperature: 16°C/18°C (60°F/65°F). The seeds will germinate in 6 to 12 days.

Once germination is seen to be occurring, move the pots into the light garden and place them 15cm (6") from the lamps to ensure sturdy, compact growth, at a light intensity of 8,000 lux to 10,000 lux for 24 hours per day for the first 11 days. Then reduce the day length to 14 hours per day. From this time onwards do not increase the day length or the plants may bolt to seed.

Thin the seedlings out as soon as they are large enough to handle, leaving just one to each pot, and as the plants grow space out the pots to give them plenty of room,

Water the compost moderately at all times to keep it moist, but never saturated with water. Create a microclimate, around the plants, by standing them on a bed of peat or pebbles and spray this with water daily. If the plant pots are to stand directly on the plant tray, spray this with water several times a day.

Give a dilute dose of liquid feed every 14 days starting from the time when the lit period for the lettuce is reduced to 14 hours per day.

Start cutting leaves for use as soon as there are enough of a suitable size. Remove only the largest leaves from each plant, to stimulate the rapid development of new leaves.

If you have space for successive sowings, you can produce a continuous, small-scale supply of fresh lettuce.

Tomatoes (*Lycoperscion lycopersicum*).

You can propagate tomato plants from seed in an indoor garden at any time of the year. If your garden room has the benefit of some natural light from a south-facing window, you can sow tomato seeds in the spring that will flower and fruit quite happily on the window-ledge. In the autumn, you can make a further sowing to fruit in a light garden during the winter.

The choice of tomato variety is all-important for obtaining the best results, and it is the dwarf compact F1 hybrids, which are most suited to indoor cultivation, where space is a limiting factor. The F1 hybrid 'Minibel' is one such cultivar, and it produces a good crop of 1.8cm to 2.5cm (¾ to 1 inch) diameter fruits-the delicious and popular cherry tomatoes.

If you would like a crop of December fruiting tomato plants in a light garden, sow the seeds at the end of July. Soak the seeds firstly in water for 24 hours, and then allow them time to dry for a couple of hours before sowing them in a half-pot of peat-based potting mix and slightly covering with fine sand, or vermiculite. Leave them to germinate in the garden room for 4 or 5 days, at a temperature of 18°C/21°C (65°F/70°F), and when this occurs move them into a light garden with a light intensity of 13,000/15,000 lux for 14 to 16 hours per day*.

Growth will take place fairly quickly, and as soon as the seedling are large enough to handle, (after a further 3 days) they should be pricked out individually into 8.75cm (3½") pots. It is essential that this is done at the earliest moment when the seedlings can be handled, as at this stage, the tomatoes will suffer the least possible check to their future growth. The tips of the young plants should be kept some 10cm to 15cm (4" to 6") from the fluorescent lamps, so as to ensure sturdy, compact, short jointed growth.

As the tomato plants continue to develop they will need moving on into 15cm (6") pots, using the peat-based potting mix, and given more space between them.

Do not be misled, by the tomato plants' rapid development, into thinking that you could induce even more rapid growth by increasing the day length. Too much light can have as serious an effect at this stage, as too little, and a dark period each day, is important to the tomato plants. They require some 8 hours of darkness in each 24-hour period, and at the same time as much light as your light garden can afford them, so do remember to dust the lamps and their reflectors at frequent intervals, to remove the dust, but always do this when they are switched off and cool.

Maintain a temperature within the range of 16°C to 21°C (60°F to 70°F) and see that the compost is always kept moist but never over wet.

See Slide E27.   The Tomato F1 hybrid 'Minibel' plants displaying a crop of ripe fruits in early June.

The plant tray in the light garden should be sprayed with water several times a day to provide the necessary humidity so essential to the success of this crop. Better still stand the pots on a piece of capillary matting and moisten this daily to provide an appropriate microclimate for the plants.

When the first truss of flowers begins to show colour, start misting the plants two or three times daily to encourage the setting of the fruits. It is also beneficial if one gently taps or shakes the plant stems for a few moments each morning to further encourage pollination to occur.

138

When the first newly sett fruits are in evidence start giving the plants a dilute liquid feed once each week.

Pay special attention to the water requirements of any plants, which may be growing in hanging baskets and check them every day. Those which are growing on capillary matting and have had an artificial wick inserted into the base of their plant-pots can obtain water as they require it, and you need only apply the weekly liquid feed to the surface of the moist potting compost in which they are growing.

As the trusses of fruit ripen and the plants near the end of their useful life some yellowing of the leaves may commence, but at this stage it is simply a matter of allowing any fruits remaining to finish ripening and then discarding with the plants.

Two other dwarf bushy F1 Hybrids worth growing in the light garden, are 'Florida Petit', and 'Tiny Tim'.

* If pelleted tomato seed is sown it will take some 6 to 8 days before germination occurs.

SOME FOOD CROPS FOR THE INDOOR LIGHT GARDEN:

Plant species	Period of days treatment after seed germination	Light intensity lux level	Illumination (in hours) per 24-hours period	Temperature °C (°F)
Mustard and Cress	4/5 days, this is a catch crop	8,000	24	21°C (70°F)
Radishes	Until harvested (another catch crop)	13,000/ 15,000	24	18/21°C (65/70°F)
Lettuce (Salad Bowl)	11 days then reduce lighting to	8,000/ 10,000 "	24 14	16/18°C (60/65°F) "
Tomatoes	Throughout growth	13,000/ 15,000	14 to 16	18/21°C (65/70°F)

Indoor propagation of outdoor vegetable crops in late winter/spring:

Early Cauliflowers Use pelleted seed and sow directly into 8.75cm (3½") pots.	14	13,000/ 15,000	12	18°C (65°F)

The resulting plants can then be set out in a garden frame to grow on and be hardened off for subsequent setting out in the open garden, or they can be grown to maturity in a garden frame. Possibly intercropped with spring maturing lettuce.

Plant species	Period of days treatment after seed germination	Light intensity lux level	Illumination (in hours) per 24-hours period	Temperature °C (°F)
Cucumber Sow seeds individually, in 8.75cm (3½") pots	10/28	13,000/15,000	24	21°C (70°F)
Tomatoes	10/28	13,000/15,000	14 to 16	18/21°C (65/70°F)

The resulting pot grown plants then go out into the greenhouse, the garden frame, or open garden when the weather conditions are suitable.

HYDROPONICS FOR ORNAMENTAL PLANTS

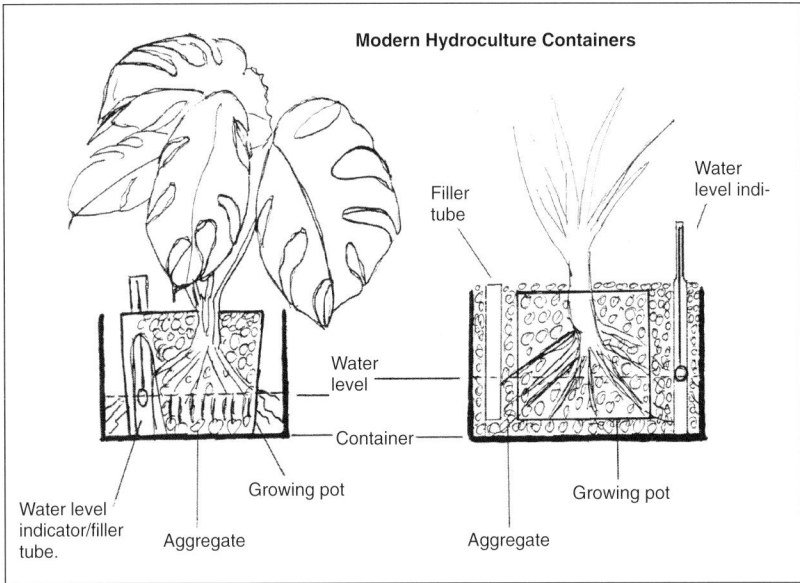

Modern Hydroculture Containers

Filler tube

Water level indi-

Water level

Container

Growing pot

Growing pot

Water level indicator/filler tube.

Aggregate

Aggregate

Modern indoor gardening techniques are enabling us to use some very different methods from the more traditional ways of growing plants. The term "hydroponics" is used to describe the method of cultivating plants in nutrient-enriched water. The concept is not a new one, as it has been practised for over sixty years. It is a simple way of growing indoor plants successfully in the garden room.

While the cultivation of indoor plants in peat-based potting mixes is less expensive, hydroponics does have other benefits, and is gaining in popularity.

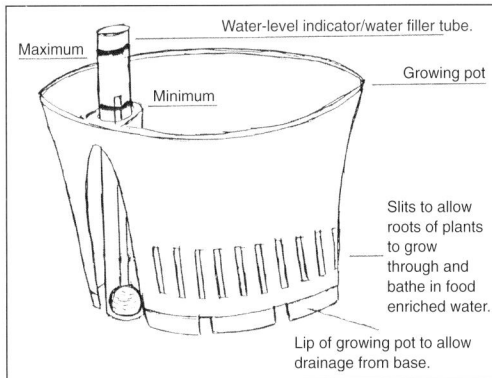

Water-level indicator/water filler tube.

Maximum

Growing pot

Minimum

Slits to allow roots of plants to grow through and bathe in food enriched water.

Lip of growing pot to allow drainage from base.

Admittedly hydroponic containers are initially costly, but they will remain serviceable for many years.

Plants grown in this way can never be over-watered or under-watered. The nutrient-enriched water ensures that all the plants' nutritional requirements are fully satisfied. A single dose of specially prepared, slow release hydrofeed, which is a long-term nutrient feed based on synthetic ion exchange resins, will keep plants healthy and in active growth for several months at a time, providing the light level and temperature are appropriate, topping up the hydroponic container's reservoir with tepid water is only necessary about every 21 days, and the presence of this water has the added benefit of reducing the dropping of leaves.

The plants have their roots supported in an inert sterile aggregate of baked clay pebbles, perlite, or vermiculite, with selected grades chosen to meet the needs of the particular plants. These aggregates provide excellent root anchorage, and also serve as a reservoir for the food-enriched water. Furthermore, they will not change their shape or be chemically affected by the plant nutrient solution that washes over them. Occasionally white crystals (from lime in hard water areas) may form on the surface of the aggregate, but these are easily rinsed off with tap water, or can be hidden by turning over the surface layer of aggregate.

Hydroponic containers are available in various sizes. Some accommodate just a single plant, while others will hold several. A group of these containers can be arranged together, and by combining different sizes you can create a fine plant display.

A hydroponic container consists of an inner pot (the growing pot), and an outer pot or container, which contains food-enriched water. There is also a water level indicator and a water filler tube. In a small hydroponic container, this may be attached to the inner pot. In a larger one, it may either be attached to the outer container, or be freestanding, supported by the aggregate between the inner and outer container. Some water-level indicators only show the water level within the reservoir, while others also prevent water getting in by the water filler tube once the water-level indicator is registering, maximum. This feature is a useful refinement to look for when you are purchasing hydroponic containers. In the very small units, there are no tubes at all, and you must use your own judgement about when to add water.

Do not rush to top up the reservoir as soon as it indicates that the water is at the minimum. It should register the minimum level for three or four days before you add more water. The roots of the plants need to breathe as well as to absorb moisture, and the delay in watering allows this to take place. Without being allowed this breathing time, the roots would simply die*. (See page 112, The Importance of Indoor Plants as Air-filters)

The inner pot holds the aggregate in which the plants are first placed. The pot itself has many slits low down on its sides, which allow the roots of the plant to grow through and bathe in the reservoir of enriched-water.

The plant species and cultivars you choose to grow hydroponically need to be of a reasonable sized, with a good root system. The best time of year to transfer them from soil-or peat based potting mix, is after their resting season, when you can see renewed growth. Maintain the room temperature at about 18°C to

21°C (65°F to 70°F) for five or six weeks, until the plants become established in their new growing medium.

After choosing your plants, knock them from their pots and gently wash their roots in tepid water to remove all traces of potting mix. You must be very meticulous in this task, as even just a few small particles of mix can result in the rotting of these roots, followed by the plant's death. For the same reason, remove any damaged plant roots at this time, using a sharp knife.

Next, place a layer of aggregate in the bottom of the inner pot. Spread some of the roots of the plant out over it, with some of the longer roots threaded through the slits in the sides of the pot. Then, gently introduce more of the aggregate and work it down between the roots as you fill the pot. If the water-level indicator is attached to the inner pot, slot it through the hole near the upper rim of the pot before lowering the inner pot into the outer container. Finally, fill the container's reservoir through its filler tube/water level indicator with tepid water. Leave it for about three weeks, until it indicates the need for more water, before you add a dose of a specially formulated commercial hydrofeed.

During the first few weeks, there may be some settlement of the aggregate, so you may need to do some topping up to bring it level with the rim of the pot once more. It is very beneficial to mist the leaves of the plants once or twice daily, until they show signs of fresh new shoot growth and additional roots.

Once established in the aggregate, you can leave the plants undisturbed for a long time. This system permits a good deal of top growth with a smaller root system than would be necessary if the same species were grown in potting mix. However, a stage may be reached when some plants become too top-heavy and unstable for their containers and have to be moved to larger ones.

Some pots have a mark on the outer container to indicate maximum water level with this pot; you are expected to use your own judgement on when to add water. These containers can be highly satisfactory once you have some experience in hydroponics.

Suitable plants for hydroponics

While all plants that can be grown in soil-based and peat-based mixes can be grown in hydroponic units, you will find this system of cultivation particularly useful for the following long-lived foliage plants:

Aglaonema (all cultivars)
Araucaria heterophylla
Calathea makoyana
Chamaedorea elegans
Cissus rhombifolia

See Slide A40. *Codiaeum variegatum* 'Volcano'.

Ficus elastica 'Schrjvereana'.

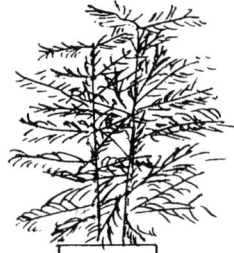

Araucaria heterophylla.

Ficus benjamina.

Philodendron bipinnatifdum.

Yucca elephantipes.

Dracaena marginata.

Codiaeum variegatum var. *pictum*
Dieffenbachia maculata 'Tropic Snow'

See Slide B3. *Dieffenbachia maculata* 'Pluto

Dieffenbachia maculata 'Pluto'
Dracaena deremensis 'Warneckii'
Dracaena fragrans 'Massangeana'
Dracaena marginata
Epipremnum aureum
Fatsia japonic
Ficus benjamina
Ficus elastica 'Schrijveriana'
Howea forsteriana

See Slide B27. *Monstera deliciosa* 'Variegata'.

Monstera deliciosa
Pandanus veitchii
Philodendron bipinnatifidum
Philodendron erubescens 'Green Emerald'.

See Slide B36. *Philodendron* 'Champagne'.
See Slide C1. *Schefflera arboricola* 'Variegata'.

Schefflera arboricola
Yucca elephantipes

THE TERRARIUM

A terrarium is a garden enclosed within a glass bottle or glass case, and it serves to accommodate a collection of plants which relish high humidity-a microclimate wherein the air around their leaves contains a lot of moisture at all times.

A terrarium makes an ideal low maintenance garden, one that can be left, without either water or maintenance, for long periods, once it has been established. But the plants will eventually call for some maintenance, as some become too large for their place within the terrarium, and have to be removed and replaced by smaller species. Others may be trimmed back to a more suitable size once more.

Whatever type of container is used as a terrarium, it must be made meticulously clear before use for this purpose, as bacteria will thrive in the high temperature and humidity of such an enclosed environment. For this reason too it is important to use a peat based potting mix, not a soil based one.

The growing medium in the base of the terrarium consists of three distinct layers. The first of these is the 12.5mm (½") drainage layer, which is placed there to enable excess moisture to drain from the peat based potting mix, away from the roots of the plants This can be composed of tiny pebbles, or crushed rock.

The second layer is a thin layer of charcoal, a highly absorbent material. Its purpose is to keep the compost sweet.

The third layer is the peat based potting mix - the growing medium, which is to be the home for the roots of the plants. Enough of this is introduced to fill about one third of the bottle or case.

Each layer is levelled and firmed lightly, before the next one is added.

When confronted with a narrow mouthed bottle, which is being used as a terrarium, it is advisable to use a funnel as the means of introducing the materials to the bottle.

Other tools necessary to carry out this work, are a tea spoon tied to a piece of bamboo cane, a dinner folk tied to a bamboo cane, and a bottle cork, attached to a bamboo cane. This latter is for firming the compost and other materials. A bent loop of wire with a bit of sponge attached to it will serve well enough to clean up the inside of the bottle, once the planting work is completed

The actual planting, should always start at the outside and finish up in the centre. Make a small hole with the aid of a bit of bamboo cane, where a plant is to be placed and leave room for its future growth. And then drop the plant down through the neck of the bottle, and fluff it around with the end of the cane until it is located in the hole where it is to be planted. Once there, firm it lightly into place with the bottle cork.

When the planting work is finished, and the bottle suitably cleaned up on its inner surface, add water, sufficient to wet the compost without also flooding the drainage material in the base. This can be a bit of a tricky task in the first instance, and it is better to water in small quantities, until the correct balance is reached, rather than over do it. For over doing this will most certainly cause the roots of plants to rot.

The objective is to add sufficient water to the compost for plant growth, and at the same time initiate the rain cycle, which will maintain the terrarium's high humidity.

At this stage the top of the terrarium should remain slightly open for a few days, to enable any excess moisture to escape and the atmosphere within reach a proper balance. The top is then closed up, and subsequently only opened slightly, if moisture continues to form on the glass and does not dissipate each morning.

Rectangular terrariums are much easier to deal with, as one can access them easily, and no special tools are required. The ground can be landscaped into hills and valleys, and small bits of rock added to provide a more natural appearance.

Light needs: 7,000 lux, for 14 hours a day, under fluorescent lamps. Do not use incandescent lamps, as these will give off too much heat and cause a rise in the temperature of the air in the terrarium, to the detriment of the plants.

Temperature: A temperature within the range of 18˚C to 24˚C (65˚F and 75˚F) is ideal for the tropical plants in the terrarium, and this will not be difficult to maintain within the garden room.

Water: This should only be provided subsequently, if the plants within the terrarium are observed to wilt slightly, and moisture formation on the glass is no longer to be seen. Water is usually only needed at several month intervals.

Feed: Give a dilute liquid feed, at only one tenth of the recommended strength, every four months. The aim here is not to stimulate the plants to start growing quickly, but merely to maintain their original stature. For this reason, the first application of liquid feed should not be given until four months after the terrarium has been first established.

Terrarium Plant Species

Select from the following list and buy small specimens:

Adiantum hispidulum
Adiantum raddianum
Adiantum reniforme
Aechmea miniata discolor
Asplenium bulbiferum
Asplenium nidus
Begonia bowerae 'Nigromarga'

147

Begonia prismatocarpa
Begonia pustulata
Begonia rex
Calathea micans
Chamaedorea elegans
Chlorophytum comosum 'Variegatum'
Cissus antartica 'Minima'
Columnea microphylla 'Diminutifolia'
Cryptanthus bivittatus
Cryptanthus zonatus
Dracaena sanderiana
Ficus pumila 'Minima'

See Slide B21. *Fittonia verschaffeltii* var. *gigantea*.

Fittonia verschaffeltii
Gesneria cuneifolia
Hedera helix (small leaved species) e.g; *H. h.* 'Glacier'
Maranta leuconeura var. *kerchoveana*
Pellionia pulchra
Peperomia argyreia
Peperomia caperata
Pilea cadierei
Pilea involucrata
Pilea cultivar 'Silver Tree'
Polystichum tsussimense
Pteris cretica 'Wilsonii' (Ribbon Fern)
Pteris ensiformis 'Victoriae' (Silver Lace Fern)
Sansevieria 'Hahnii'
Selaginella kraussiana (Spreading Clubmoss)
Selaginella martensii
Selaginella pallescens
Selaginella unciniata (Blue Spike moss)
Sinningia concinna
Sinningia pusilla 'White Sprite'*
Soleirolia soleirolii
Tolmiea menziesii 'Variegata'

*Sinningia pusilla A real dwarf, one of the smallest members of the *Gesneriaceae*.

PLANT LIGHT TABLES

Foliage plants, page 151
Ferns, page 154
Flowers, page 155
Bromeliads, page 155
Cacti and succulents, page 158
Orchids, page 162
Bulbs and corms, page 164

Most of the species and cultivars of plants, shrubs and trees within the Plant Light Tables are quite widely available and not difficult to obtain. However, if a species does not seem to be available locally, the best way to find a suitable source of supply is to contact your national or state horticultural society, or your regional agricultural colleges. The following are excellent sources of information:

The Royal Horticultural Society,
80 Vincent Square,
London SW1P 2PE
BRITAIN
RHS HEADQUARTERS Tel: (020) 7834 4333
RHS WEBSITE: www.rhs.org.uk

American Horticultural Society
7931 East Boulevard Drive
Alexandria
VA 22308
Tel: 703.768.5700 Toll Free: 1.800.777.7931
Fax; 703.768.8700 Publications Fax: 703.768.7533
Email: sdick@ahs.org
Website: www.ahs.org

Calgary Horticultural Society. (Their website has links to all other major Canadian Horticultural Societies or groups.)
208-50 Avenue SW
Calgary,
Alberta
T25 2S1
Phone: (403) 287-3469
Fax: (403) 287-6986
Email: office@calhort.org
Website: www.calhort.org

Australian Society of Horticultural Science - AuSHS
Mail address: The Secretary,
AuSHS, Dr Robyn McConchie
Crop Sciences
University of Sydney
NSW 2006
Email: McConchieR@agric.usyd.edu.au
Website: www.aushs.org.au

Royal New Zealand Institute of Horticulture (RNZIH)
P.O. Box 12
Lincoln University
Canterbury
New Zealand
Phone: +64 3 325 2811 Ext 8670
Email rnzih@xtra.co.nz
Website: www.aushs.org.au

Plant light requirements

See Slide C16. Exotica General View.

See Slide C19. Top left *Dracaen marginata*, top right *Calathea zebrina*, 'White Butterfly', left centre *Tradescantia zebrine*, top centre *Codiaeum variegatum*, bottom left *Adiantum raddianum*, bottom *Primula acaulis* with blue, orange and yellow flowers, right *Fittonia verschaffeltii* var. *argyroneura*, centre *Syngonium podophyllum*.

For convenience, five basic categories have been adopted for the light requirements of indoor plants under fluorescent lamps:

I.	Plants which need a very high level of light	Very High	7,500 to 15,000 lux
II.	Plants which need a high level of light	High	4,500 to 7,500 lux
III.	Plants which need a medium level of light	Medium	2,000 to 4,500 lux
IV.	Plants which tolerate a low level of light	Low	900 to 2,000 lux
V.	Plants which tolerate a very low level of light	Very Low	400 to 900 lux

Some examples of plant light requirements:

I. Plants requiring a very high light intensity for healthy growth and flowering; 7,500-15,000 lux. e.g. *Aphelandra squarrosa,* Cacti (generally), Orchids many species, *Pelargonium* species, and Tomatoes.

II. Plants requiring a high light intensity for healthy growth, and flowering 4,500-7,500 lux e.g. *Euphorbia milii,* *Fuchsia,* *Saintpaulia ionantha*, and *Solenostemon scutellarioides*, syn. *Coleus blumei.*

III. Plants needing a medium intensity of light for healthy growth and flowering 2,000-4.500 lux. e.g., *Begonia corallina, Crassula ovata, Fittonia verschaffeltii, Nephrolepis exaltata*, and *Soleirolia soleirolii.*

IV. Plants requiring a low light intensity for healthy growth and flowering; 900-2,000 Lux. This category includes many ornametal foliage plants and a few of the flowering species. *Anthurium scherzerianum, Dieffenbachia maculata, Maranta leuconeura* and *Pandanus veitchii.*

V. Plants that will tolerate a very low light for healthy growth; 400-900 lux e.g. *Aglaonema crispum,* X*Fatshedera lizei, Philodendron bipinnatifidum,* and *Syngonium podophyllum.*

Amongst the plants listed in the <u>Plant light Tables</u>, are also to be found plants, which Dr. Wolverton recommends make good air filter plants. Each of these has had an asterisk placed next to it, for easier identification by readers, when selecting species, and cultivars of plants, for indoor cultivation, e.g., **Nephrolepis obliterata.*

Foliage Plants	**Light Needs** **12 to 14 hours per day**
Abutilon pictum 'Thompsonii'	I, II
Acalypha wilkesiana	I, II
*Aglaonema (all Cultivars)	IV, V
Alocasia Xamazonica	II, III
Alocasia cuprea	II, III
Anthurium crystallinum	III, IV
Araucaria heterophylla	III, IV
Asparagus densiflorus	II, III, IV
Asparagus setaceus	II, III, IV
Aspidistra elatior	IV, V
Begonia Rex – Cultorum Hybrids	II, III
Begonia masoniana	II, III
Caladium hybrids	II,III
Calathea spp.	III, IV
*Calathea makoyana	III, IV
Callisia elegans	III, IV

Caryota mitis	III, IV
*Chamaedorea elegans	IV
Chamaedorea erumpens	IV
*Chamaedorea seifrizii	IV
*Chlorophytum comosum 'Vittatum'	III, IV
*Chrysalidocarpus lutescens	III, IV
Cissus antarctica	III, IV
Cissus discolor	III, IV
Cissus rhombifolia	IV, V
*Cissus rhombifolia 'Ellen Danica'	IV, V
X*Citrofortunella microcarpa*, (Stand outdoors May/September.)	III, IV
*Codiaeum variegatum var. *pictum*	IV
Coffea arabica	IV
Cordyline stricta	IV, V
Cordyline terminalis	IV
Ctenanthe amabilis	III, IV
Ctenanthe oppenheimiana	III, IV
Cycas revoluta (King Sago.)	III, IV
Cyperus alternifolius	III, IV
Cyperus papyrus	III, IV
Dieffenbachia maculata 'Tropic Snow'	IV
*Dieffenbachia 'Camilla'	IV
*Dieffenbachia 'Exotica Compacta'	IV
Dieffenbachia maculata 'Veerie'	IV
Dracaena deremensis 'Compacta'	IV
*Dracaena deremensis. 'Janet Craig'	IV
Dracaena deremensis. 'Lemon and Lime'	IV
* Dracaena deremensis 'Warneckii'	V
*Dracaena fragrans 'Massangeana'	IV
*Dracaena marginata	V
* Dracaena marginata 'Tricolor'	IV
Dracaena reflexa	IV
Dracaena reflexa 'Variegata'	IV
*Epipremnum aureum	IV, V
Epipremnum aureum 'Marble Queen'	IV, V
Epipremnum aureum 'Silver Queen'	IV, V
X*Fatshedera lizei*	V
Fatsia japonica	IV
*Ficus benjamina	III, IV
*Ficus elastica	IV, V
Ficus lyrata	IV

Ficus pumila	IV, V
Fittonia verschaffeltii	III, IV
Grevillea robusta	III, IV
Gynura procumbens	II, III
Hedera algeriensis 'Gloire de Marengo'	IV
*Hedera helix	IV, V
Howea forsteriana	V
Livistona chinensis	III, IV
Maranta spp.	III, IV
*Maranta leuconeura var. *kerchoveana*	III, IV
Mimosa pudica (Sensitive Plant.)	II, III
Monstera deliciosa	V
Monstera deliciosa 'Variegata'	IV, V
Nolina recurvata	III, IV
Oplismenus hirtellus	III, IV
Pandanus veitchii	IV
Pelargonium crispum 'Variegatum' (Lemon Scented geranium grown for its foliage rather than its indifferent flowers.)	I
Peperomia spp.	IV
*Philodendron bipinnatifidum	IV, V
*Philodendron domesticum	IV
*Philodendron erubescens 'Red Emerald'	IV
Philodendron melanochrysum	IV
*Philodendron scandens	V
*Phoenix roebelinii	III, IV
Pilea spp.	II, III
Piper ornatum	I, II
Pisonia unbellifera	III, IV
Plectranthus spp.	III, IV
Podocarpus macrophyllus	III, IV
Polyscias filicifolia	IV, V
Polyscias fruiticosa	IV, V
Polyscias scutellaria Balfourii.'	IV, V
*Rhapis excelsa	IV
*Sansevieria trifasciata	IV, V
Saxifraga stolonifera	II, III
*Schefflera actinophylla	IV
Schefflera arboricola	IV
Schefflera elegantissima	IV
Scindapsus pictus 'Argyraeus'	IV, V
Soleirolia soleirolii, syn. *Helxine soleirolii*	III, IV

Solenostemon scutellarioides, syn. *Coleus blumei*	II, III
Sonerila margaritaceae	I, II
Sparmannia africana	II, III
Strobilanthes dyerianus	I, II
Syagrus cocoides	IV
Syngonium podophyllum	V
Tolmiea menziesii	II, III
Trachycarpus fortunei (Stand outdoors May/September)	III, IV
Tradescantia fluminensis	III, IV
Tradescantia pallida	III, IV
Yucca elephantipes	III, IV

Some of these ornamental foliage plants are so adapted to low light intensities because they inhabit the floor of the tropical and subtropical forests and are used to dense shade. Some also have the ability to acclimatise to their new indoor environment and make good us of the available light. If these plants produce new leaves you will know that the light intensity, quality and duration are adequate. Nevertheless, you should not expect the lush, vigorous growth typical of these plants in their native habitat, which is just as well, since they would quickly outgrow the available space.

If the light intensity is not sufficient to enable the plants to produce new leaves, but the existing leaves remain healthy, the light intensity is down to the compensation point. That is the point where the processes of photosynthesis and respiration are equal. If no additional light is provided, the plants will be able to maintain themselves for some time, but when their existing leaves grow old and are shed no new leaves will be produced and the plants will die. Some of the foliage plants listed here will tolerate a very low light intensity for healthy growth; 400-900 lux, but for all these plants a brighter light, within limits, is beneficial.

Ferns

	Light Needs 12 to 14 hours per day
Adiantum raddianum	II, III
Adiantum tenerum	II, III
Asplenium bulbiferum	III, IV
Asplenium nidus	III, IV
Nephrolepis exaltata	IV, V
Nephrolepis exaltata 'Bostoniensis'	IV, V
Nephrolepis obliterata	IV, V
Polystichum tsussimense	IV, V
Pteris cretica	III, IV
Pteris tremula	III, IV

Flowering Plants	Light Needs	Hours per Day
Achimenes cultivars	I	14 to 16
*Anthurium andraeanum	II, III	14 to 16
Anthurium scherzerianum	III, IV	14 to 16
Aphelandra squarrosa	I	14 to 16
Ardisia crenata 'Coralberry' (Stand outdoors May/September.)	IV	12 to 14
Begonia corallina	III	14 to 16
*Begonia Semperflorens	I	14 to 16
Browallia speciosa	I	14 to 16
Catharanthus roseus	I	14 to 16
Crossandra infundibuliformis	I	14 to 16
Episcia spp.	I	14 to 16
Euphorbia milii	I	14 to 16
Exacum affine	I	14 to 16
Fuchsia cultivars	I, II, III	14 to 16
Genista canariensis (Stand outdoors May/September.)	I, II, III	12 to 14
Hoya carnosa	III, IV	14 to 16
Impatiens hybrids	I, II	14 to 16
Justicia brandegeana syn. *Beloperona guttata*	I	14 to 16
Pelargonium mini hybrids	I	16 to 18
Saintpaulia cultivars	II	14 to 18
Sinningia speciosa	I	15 to 16
*Spathiphyllum (all cultivars)	IV	12 to 14
Streptocarpus x*hybridus*	I	15 to 16
Thunbergia alata 'Suzie Hybrids'	I	14 to 16

Bromeliads

The term bromeliad indicates that a plant is a member of the family Bromeliaceae. This is a very large grouping of plants, consisting of 46 genera and more than 2,000 species, and their number is increasing yearly as a result of further hybridisation work.

Bromeliads are easy plants to grow, and while they can withstand a little neglect, they remain at the same time some of the most spectacular of ornamental plants to grow.

While they vary in size from the tiny *Tillandsias* to the majestic *Vrieseas*, all bromeliads share similar basic physical characteristics, and are similar in their requirements. They are either stemless or have only a short stem carrying a rosette of stiff, spiny leaves. The base of the rosette forms a reservoir that collects water. In a number of species, the leaves tend to curve outward or bend back from the centre of growth. This habit is described as "recurving". Flowers appear as terminal clusters, often on a stiff stem. A grouping of such flowering bromeliads can create the most spectacular of indoor displays.

While some bromeliads have showy flower bracts, and attractive foliage, many others have delightful foliage but their flowers are insignificant. The species selected here include those that are generally available and well adapted to indoor cultivation. All bromeliads are either tropical or sub-tropical, and most are native to tropical America, and more rarely, tropical West Africa.

Bromeliads flower only once in their lives, and then die. However, before the life cycle is completed, each plant produces one or more offsets which will replace the parent plant and follow the same life pattern. Some species may take several years to produce flowers, but their flowers will then last for several months. In most instances the flowers, are composed of coloured bracts, and the true flowers only put in a fleeting appearance.

Billbergia nutans is the easiest bromeliad to grow and flower in the garden room. Due to its pendulous character, the plant is seen at its best when placed on a pedestal, or in a hanging basket beneath a fluorescent lamp, where it will produce its arching flower heads throughout the summer.

Ananas bracteatus*, and *Ananas comosus** are both terrestrial species which will make fine ornamental pot-plant subjects for display in the garden room, either on their own, or as part of the general foliage plant displays, as will their more striking variegated forms, *Ananas bracteatus*. var. *tricolor*, and *Ananas comosus* 'Variegatus.'

*Indeed, with some bottom heat and strong direct sunlight, *Ananas bracteatus*, and *Ananas comosus* will produce fruit at about three years of age, if grown in a heated greenhouse.

Once you have selected desirable stock plants, a bromeliad collection can provide you with much pleasure over the years, if its cultural requirements are met and new plants are propagated from offsets. The general conditions and care are similar for all the species listed below.

See Slide F8. *Fascicularia bicolor.*

All enjoy bright light, but most do not like direct sunlight. While some will do well in a garden room, others will flourish more readily in the brighter illumination of your light garden. However, unless there is plenty of headroom, the taller ones will have to be removed from there when flowering spikes begin to arise. But the ideal place for them is in an illuminated tropical plant case with its controlled environment, where they can enjoy all the humidity and warmth they need. This can, in a sense, be a tropical greenhouse on casters, which can be moved easily from room to room, according to your desires. Someone handy at carpentry could make one for themselves', but others would be well advised to purchase one ready made.

Such a tropical plant case could also be the place to create a bromeliad tree to which some of the smaller species could be attached by means of fine nylon thread, so that they may be seen in a more natural setting.

Light Needs: I, II, III, in the light garden, and in the garden room, IV - 14, hours per day except in December and January, when it is reduced to 12 hours per day.

Temperature: The minimum night temperature should be 10°C (50°F) for foliage species and plants already in flower. A warm environment of 21°C (70°F) is best for inducing plants to flower. Once established indoors a range of between 16-21°C (60-70°F) is suitable for the maintenance of bromeliads.

Watering: It is important to keep the potting mix on the dry side when watering into the reservoir at the centre of each plant. Keep it filled with rainwater, which should as far as possible be freshly collected. For species without this natural reservoir, it is necessary to keep the potting mix moist at all times, but be sure to avoid flooding the roots. The plants will benefit from occasional misting during spring and summer time.

Feeding: Give a dilute liquid feed, at half the recommended strength, once a month during the spring and summer. This may be sprayed over the foliage, and will be absorbed directly by the plants.

Re-potting: Bromeliads do not tend to have very extensive root systems. Their potting mix can be freshened yearly, but you will not have to provide larger pots unless the roots seem to be filling the existing ones. A standard peat based potting mix to which has been added the same volume of sharp sand is suitable for all species. Small tillandsias can be mounted as epiphytes on cork-bark, or driftwood, with their roots wrapped in a thin layer of sphagnum moss and then secured in place with some nylon thread, Once here, they will dig their tough roots into the cork-bark, or driftwood, to gain an anchorage.

Pruning: Pruning is not necessary, except for the removal of any dead foliage.

Propagation: Young offsets should be transplanted when they are several months old, and big enough to be detached from the parent plant. Put each offset into a small pot containing the same potting mix, and stand the pots on a thin layer of potting mix inside a propagation case, with the bottom heat set at 21°C (70°F). Keep the under-layer of potting mix barely moist, and mist the foliage daily.

Bromeliads	Light Needs
	14 hrs Per Day
	I, II, III

Aechmea chantinii
*Aechmea fasciata
Aechmea fosteriana
Aechmea fulgens var. *discolor*
Ananas bracteatus

Ananas comosus 'Variegatus'
Ananas nanus
Billbergia nutans
Billbergia ×*windii*
Cryptanthus acaulis
Cryptanthus bivittatus 'Minor'
Cryptanthus bivittatus 'Pink Starlite'
Cryptanthus bivittatus 'Tricolor'
Cryptanthus zonatus.
Cryptanthus zonatus 'Zebrinus'
Guzmania lingulata
Guzmania lingulata 'Minor Orange'
Guzmania musaica
Guzmania sanguinea
Neoregelia carolinae
Neoregelia carolinae 'Tricolor'
Neoregelia 'Madame Van Durme'
Nidularium innocentii
Nidularium 'Citrina'.
Tillandsia aeranthos
Tillandsia albertiana
Tillandsia andreana
Tillandsia bergeri
Tillandsia.caput-medusae
Tillandsia crispa
Tillandsia.cyanea
Tillandsia. ionantha
Tillandsia magnusiana
Tillandsia plumose
Vriesea carinata
Vriesea guttata
Vriesea splendens

Cacti and succulents

Cacti and succulents are some of the most weird and wonderful forms of plant life. Groupings of cacti make intriguing light garden features, and cultivation of these plants can become an absorbing specialist interest.

As a result of their adaptation to semi-desert and desert regions, most cacti and succulents are highly tolerant plants particularly suited to indoor conditions. Since rain falls infrequently in their native habitats, they can store moisture in the tissues of stems or leaves, and during periods of drought release very little of the moisture in the normal process known as transpiration (see page

46). If drought lasts a long time, the plants will shrivel but will swell again when they do receive moisture.

All cacti belong to the *Cactaceae* family. There are two basic divisions of cacti-desert or terrestrial cacti, and forest or epiphytic cacti, which originate from the tropical forests of America. Except for a few shrubby species, all cacti are stem succulents, meaning that they are leafless, with greatly thickened stems.

The cactus stem assumes the function of the absent leaves and also becomes a storage organ for water. The *Cactaceae* family additionally has another unique feature, the areole; a modified cushiony side shoot from which the spines, wool, and flowers arise.

The forest cacti differ from desert cacti in appearance and in the care required. They root in decaying vegetation among tree branches, where there is considerable shade. Natural conditions are wet in some seasons and dry in others. These cacti are spineless, with extended arching stems and vivid flowers.

Succulents belong to a number of different families, having in common fleshy stems or leaves that retain vital moisture. Some species have spines that resemble rose thorns. Succulents are slightly more demanding than terrestrial cacti, but are still extremely tolerant and easy to maintain. The range of leaf shapes and colours, height and growth habits, can contribute an engaging variety to your indoor garden.

159

Because cacti and succulents are so well adapted to varying conditions - high and low temperatures, water shortages, dry atmosphere - they will tolerate some neglect. However, if you care for them properly in a light garden, they will reward you by thriving and extending their complex forms, flowering readily at the appropriate times.

Light Needs: 1 with a variable day length, which coincides with the natural day length, at the various seasons of the year. Cacti and succulents can be grown and flowered indoors with the aid of artificial light by varying the period of illumination in line with the natural day length. But they appreciate bright light, and some direct sunlight during the growing period. So move them outside to the shade of a tree or the north side of a building in summer*, once they have finished flowering, and bring them back indoors again in September, and they will flower more profusely the following year.

*Their tissues which have developed indoors under weak artificial light are likely to be scorched, if set in full sun-hence their need for some shade.

Temperature-warm: The minimum winter temperature is 4°C (40°F) for desert cacti and succulents. During winter dormancy, an unheated room is a suitable spot. Forest cacti require a minimum of around 10°C (50°F).

Watering: Let the potting mix of desert cacti dry out between waterings. Treat succulents like ordinary houseplants in spring and summer but keep the potting mix barely moist, during dormancy. Excess moisture can cause rotting and death.

Feeding: Give succulents a dilute liquid feed every 14 days during spring and summer.

Re-potting: Desert cacti and succulents require a well-drained potting mix, ideally 2 parts soil-based mix to 1 part sand.

Forest cacti need a standard peat-based potting mix.

Only re-pot cacti and succulents to a slightly larger pot when necessary.

Wrap a folded newspaper around cacti when handling them.

Pruning: Pruning is not necessary, except for the removal of any dead parts.

Propagation: Take stem cuttings or offsets from cacti, and leaf cuttings in addition from succulents. Leave small cuttings to dry for a few days before planting, and large ones for one or even two weeks.

Root formation takes several weeks to occur, so it is pointless watering rootless cacti and succulent cuttings. However, misting the stem segments daily will maintain the humidity and delay the shrivelling process, thus giving the cuttings some additional time to root successfully.

If rooting is slow to occur, a little bottom heat will encourage this and subsequent growth, but do not cover them with a plastic or glass dome.

You can also propagate cacti and succulents from seed in spring and early summer, maintaining a temperature of 21-28˚C (70-80˚F).

The Light Needs of cacti and succulent: 1 with a variable day-length that coincides with the natural day-length at the various seasons of the year.

Cacti & succulents

Terrestrial (Desert) Cacti

Astrophytum myriostigma (Bishop's Cap)
Cephalocereus senilis (Old Man Cactus)
Echinopsis chamaecereus. (Peanut Cactus)
Mammillaria zeilmanniana (Pincushion Cactus)
Opuntia brasiliensis (Tropical Tree opuntia)
Rebutia deminuta
Stenocactus multicostatus (Brain Cactus)

Epiphytic (forest or jungle) cacti

Aporocactus flagelliformis (Rats-Tail Cactus)
*Hatiora gaertneri (Easter Cactus)
Nopalxochia ackermannii 'Midnight' (Orchid Cactus)
Rhipsalis baccifera (Misletoe Cactus)
Rhipsalis paradoxa (Chain Cactus)
*Schlumbergera Xbuckleyi (Christmas Cactus.)
Schlumbergera truncata (Thanksgiving Cactus.)

Succulents

Agave americana (Century Plant)
Agave filifera (Thread Agave)
Aloe humilis (Hedgehog Aloe)
Aloe variegata (Partridge Breast)
*Aloe vera
Ceropegia linearis (Rosary Vine)
Crassula ovata (Jade Plant)
Crassula perforata (String of buttons)
Echeveria elegans (Mexican Snowball)
Echeveria nodulosa
Hylotelephium sieboldii 'Mediovariegatum' (Japanese Stonecrop)
Kalanchoe beharensis (Velvet Leaf)
Kalanchoe blossfeldiana
Kalanchoe daigremontiana
Kalanchoe pumila
Kalanchoe tomentosa (Panda Plant)
Sedum adolphii (Golden Sedum)

Sedum morganianum (Donkey's Tail)
Sedum rubrotinctum (Jelly Bean Plant)
Sempervivum arachnoideum (Cobweb Houseleek)
Sempervivum tectorum (Hens & Chickens)
Senecio herreianus – (Green marble vine)

Orchids

Orchids can be grown in the home quite successfully, with the aid of fluorescent lamps, providing that their other cultural requirements are met. Given this you can grow orchids to equal any produced in a greenhouse.

All orchids need fresh air without drafts. They cannot thrive surrounded by stale air. In winter, use an air-circulating fan (see page 31). On warm summer days you can stand your orchids outdoors during the day, in a shady spot away from direct sunlight.
Light Needs: 1, 11. - 12 to 14 hour per day.

See Slide G15. *Phalaenopsis* hybrids flowering in the light garden.

Phalaenopsis hybrids may be had in bloom throughout the year in a light garden, and *Paphiopedilums* produce the most exquisite blooms there too. Other orchids that do well under fluorescent lamps include: *Coelogyne, Cymbidium, Dendrobium, Miltonia, Odontoglossum.*and *Oncidium.*

See Slide G9. *Miltonia* 'Sherpa'.

Temperature:

Warm-growing orchids: Minimum night temperature-throughout the year 20°C (68°F).

Examples: *Paphiopedilum,* and *Phalaenopsis.*

Intermediate growing orchids: Minimum night temperature 15°C (58°F).

Examples: *Brassia, Coelogyne, Dendrobium.*

Cool-growing orchids: Minimum night temperature. 10-13°C (50-55°F).

Examples: *Cymbidium* mini hybrids, *Miltonia, Odontoglossum,* and *Oncidium.*

Watering: Use rainwater, if possible. With a spouted watering can, flood the potting mix at the rim of the pot, then let it partially dry out before watering again. Keep the potting mix barely moist during dormant periods. Over watering is a common reason for failure with orchids. Two exceptions to these guidelines are *Paphiopedilum* and *Phalaenopsis*, which should be kept moist at all times.

Orchids do require a humid atmosphere. You can achieve this most easily by standing the plants on inverted saucers on a tray filled with moist gravel or peat. Mist the foliage daily and sponge leaves regularly to keep them clean.

If you plan to grow orchids in a room where overall humidity is undesirable, because of the needs of other plants, or because the room itself is used for other purposes, you may want to buy an orchid case. This is a self-contained indoor light garden: a glass sided box complete with fluorescent lighting, electrical heating, and ventilation. It allows you to adjust the environment precisely to suit the specific needs of any orchid you may wish to grow.

Feeding: Give a dilute liquid feed every 14 days during active growth. Overfeeding can be harmful, so dilute the solution more than usual.

Re-potting: Orchids appreciate being pot bound so do not worry if a few roots grow over the side of the pot. Re-potting is necessary only when the leading (front) bulb has ventured over the lip of the pot, and there is no more room left. This normally takes about two years. Use a lightweight mix of two parts osmunda fibre and one part sphagnum moss, except with *Cymbidium* hybrids, and *Phalaenopsis*, which prefer equal parts of fibre and moss.

Pruning: Pruning is not necessary, except for the removal of dead leaves or flowers.

Propagation: Divide plants when re-potting. Stake each orchid you have divided.

Orchids   **Light Needs**
                                                    12 to 14 hours per day
                                                               I, II

Brassia maculata
Coelogyne cristata
Cymbidium mini hybrids
*Dendrobium nobile
Miltonia spectabilis
Odontoglossum crispum
Oncidium pusillum
Paphiopedilum insigne
Paphiopedilum sukhakulii
*Phalaenopsis hybrids

FLOWER FORCING WITH BULBS AND CORMS

Some bulbs already have their flower buds formed inside them and enough stored food to enable them to develop and flower without the need for any further photosynthesis, e.g., hyacinths, narcissus (daffodils), and tulips, The process of flower forcing in their case therefore only requires a modest light intensity of 2,000-4,000 lux, for 12 hours per day, to bring about their earlier flowering. This level of illumination serves merely to prevent unnatural etiolation of the flower stems and foliage and enables the flowers to colour up properly.

Hyacinths

For the earliest flower forcing it is necessary to purchase the specially prepared bulbs. But all the bulbs either specially prepared for forcing, or ordinary are started into growth outdoors in the open ground, or in a cold-frame with the light removed, where they must spend sometime in the cold. They are only brought indoors once the shoots are sufficiently advanced to enable the forcing process to commence.

Hyacinths are purchased by the size of the bulb, either as prepared or unprepared bulbs. For very early flower forcing choose the top sized 17/18cm bulbs, and for later forcing the 16/17cm bulbs.

Prepared bulbs are lifted and stored at carefully controlled temperatures for a specified period of time, and removed when the internal development of the bulbs has reached the correct stage. This procedure enables the bulbs to be forced into flower earlier than those bulbs, which have not received this type of treatment.

The bulbs are best potted individually into 10cm (4") pots or into boxes, allowing 1.25cm (½") of space between each bulb, and with three quarters of each bulb buried This way they can be potted up later, as there can be no certainty that bulbs planted initially, at one and the same time, three to a 15cm (6") pot, will all necessarily flower at the same time. This way you can avoid disappointment. They are then plunged to the rim/top of the pots or boxes in the open ground in a shady cool place. Once there they are watered and covered with a 2.5cm (1") layer of sand and then a further 15cm (6") layer of soil. This is then topped off with a covering of straw or bracken, to help keep the bulbs cool during the autumn and also offer some protection from frost.

The bulbs are lifted ready for forcing when the flower spike has pushed itself through the neck of the bulb. With specially prepared bulbs, which have been plunged in the open during August, they should be ready for lifting and force flowering some 11 weeks later in November. For later forcing unprepared bulbs may be plunged up to mid-October. It is important to keep the newly lifted bulbs cool and in the dark for the first 7 days after they have been lifted. This can be achieved by placing them in a tool shed or coalhouse, where the temperature does not rise above 10°C (50°F), after which they may be moved into somewhere else which is dark but where the temperature may rise to 16°C /20°C (60°F/ 68°F). When the shoots are about 7.5cm to 10cm (3" to 4") in height, and the flower stalks can be seen, move the pots containing the hyacinths into the light (2,000/4,000 lux for 12 hours per day), and as soon as half the flowers on the spikes are fully developed reduce the temperature to 10°C (50°F) by night and 16°C (60°F) by day, so as to retain the hyacinths in good condition for as long as possible. A cool verandah or front vestibule to the house, are ideal places. The later batches of unprepared bulbs require the same treatment.

Suitable varieties of Hyacinths include **Ann Mary** (soft rose pink), **Bluejacket** (bluebell blue), **John Bos** (rich rose red), and **L'Innocence** (pure white).

Narcissus

Narcissus (Daffs), are amongst the most popular of bulbs for flower forcing and are best planted at four or five bulbs per each 12.5cm to 15cm (5" to 6") pot, depending on the size of the bulbs, as soon as they are received. They are then plunged to the rim in the open ground in just the same manner as hyacinths. They should remain there for a minimum of 12 to 15 weeks, after which they may be placed either into a cold-frame or brought into an unheated room with a temperature of 7°C/10°C (45°F/50°F) to enable the development of the plants to continue until the flower buds are clearly in evidence. The temperature should then be allowed to rise to 16°C (60°F) and bulbs brought within the vicinity of a fluorescent lamp with a modest light intensity of 2,000-4,000 lux, for 12 hours per day to encourage their earlier flowering.

Unlike *Hyacinths, Narcissus* cannot be grown in boxes and later transferred into pots when coming into flower, neither can they be forced at the same higher temperatures as hyacinths. Narcissus also need to be staked to prevent their flowers and foliage toppling about. The pots will each need three split canes placed around their outer rim and either a loop of raffia or green horticultural twine then be placed around these, to ensure a good presentation of the pot of narcissus.

The following varieties are suitable to grow as pot-plants:

Division 1 *Trumpets daffodils*: **Golden Harvest**, (deep golden yellow colour throughout). **Dutch Master**, (rich golden yellow).

Division 2 *Large-cupped daffodils* **Carlton**, (soft yellow throughout), **Professor Einstein**, (clear white perianth, large flat orange crown).

Division 8 *Poetaz daffodils*: **Cheerfulness** (solid white perianth and fully double creamy-white centre with yellow shading), sweetly scented. **Scarlet Gem**, (deep yellow perianth, brilliant orange/red, and prettily frilled cup), scented.

Tulips

You need top sized bulbs for flower forcing. Early single tulips produce 12cm bulbs, while those of early double tulips are smaller at 10cm.

The bulbs are potted up starting in early September and plunged to their rim in the open ground as previously described for hyacinths, but the timing of this operation is dependent on when they are to be brought back indoors again, as they must not be plunged in the open ground for much longer than three months.

The following varieties are suitable grown as pot-plants:

Brilliant Star, (scarlet). **De Wet**, (golden orange, stippled orange scarlet), sweet scented. **Yokohama**, (sulphur yellow). **Christmas Dream**, (soft rose pink). **Snow Queen**, (pure white).

Iris

Bulbous irises, such as the dwarf *Iris danfordiae*, (deep lemon yellow flowers), and *Iris* reticulata Hybrids: **Cantab** (deep blue), **Professor Blaauw** (ultramarine violet blue), and **Natasha**, (flowers suffused with a bluish tinge and marked orange yellow), can be force flowered indoors, but as they are not well endowed with a store of food, further photosynthesis is necessary before they can be flowered successfully in a light garden. To achieve this requires a light intensity of 8,000/10,000 lux for 12 hours each day, for some weeks after they are brought indoors for flowering.

All the bulbs mentioned here either specially prepared for force flowering, or unprepared bulbs, are potted up six bulbs per 8.75cm (3½") pot, from mid-September onwards, watered and stood in the open garden, or in an uncovered cold-frame, but not plunged, where they must remain until such time as both their shoots and their root systems are developed enough for them to be taken indoors for flower forcing. Once indoors they are grown at a temperature of 10°C-13°C (50°F-55°F).

Crocus

These cannot be forced in any way. They are potted up in 8.75cm (3½") pots in October with four to six corms per pot according to size of the corms. The pots are then watered and plunged to their rim in the open ground where they are given a 2.5cm (1") covering of sand.

The pots of crocuses are brought indoors in December or early January, and placed in a cool place, where the temperature cannot rise much above 10°C

(50°F), and they will then flower naturally in a light intensity of 2,000/4,000 lux. If the room where they are placed is too warm their flowering will be very fleeting.

The following varieties are suitable for growing as pots plants:

Kathleen Parlow (white), **Large yellow** (yellow), **Pickwick** (white with deep lilac stripes), **Queen of the Blues** (Silvery violet blue), and **Remembrance** (deep silvery purple flowers).

Bulbs & Corms	**Light Needs** **12 hours per day**
Crocus	III
Hyacinthus orientalis (common hyacinth)	III
Iris bulbous	I
Narcissus (daffodil)	III
*Tulipa (tulip)	III

Flower Forcing

Convallaria majalis, (Lily of the valley) an herbaceous perennial, is another example of a plant which may be force flowered during the winter months without any further photosynthesis being necessary. All that is required to achieve this is a light intensity of around 2,000-3,000 lux for 12 hours per day.

The flowers are formed before flower forcing takes place and, after the crowns have been potted up and left outside to experience some cold, in a well ventilated cold-frame, they are brought indoors, into a cool room, where the available light will enable them to colour up their leaves and send forth their white flowers.

See Slide A47. *Cyas revoluta*.

Final thoughts

A better understanding of how plants grow can enhance our own personal interest and enjoyment of them. It can also lead us to look upon them with some added reverence. For when we consider that one of their smallest of components, the microscopic chloroplasts, contains the pigment chlorophyll essential to the process of photosynthesis, and the release of the life supporting oxygen, which sustains the rest of the living world, we do in deed owe them a great debt of gratitude. For we are only here ourselves, courtesy of the green leaf! We are a late addition to the planet and represent only a very tiny part of all Creation.

Some species of flora have been here many millions of years, and some such as the *Cycads*: over two hundred million years! They are very ancient plants and are deservedly called 'living fossils.' *Cycas revoluta* (Sago palm), a fine slow growing indoor foliage plant, has remained virtually un-changed within this immensity of time, and its presence fills me with a sense of awe whenever I cast my eyes upon its fronds. It is worth bearing in mind too, that the largest living organism on earth is a tree, which likewise has also been here over two hundred million year, the *Sequoiadendron giganteum* (Giant Sequoia). It attains an astounding height of 95 M (316 ft), and has a diameter of 10 M (32 ft) or more, at its base. And every day it draws up to the tips of its branches water from its roots, against the force of gravity, this is truly amazing! This giant weighs some 2,000 tons or more, a colossal weight. And to think that all its' great bulk springs initially from a 3mm to 5mm (5th inch) long seed!

We should do all in our power to stop people upsetting the balance of nature, by the wanton destruction of the rainforests and other flora that clothe our beautiful planet* We live in a fragile environment, with just a thin veneer of an Earth's atmosphere, in the midst of a hostile Universe. And we are ourselves an endangered species, which could so easily be eliminated from the scheme of things, if we do not do something to reduce the reckless pollution and destruction of our only home, "Planet Earth."

*We can start initially by making a symbolic gesture-that of improving the quality of the air in our own homes, with the introducing of some air filter plants. And we can follow this up by playing a more vocal roll whenever green issues come up, by lobbying our local councillors, members of Parliament, and members of the European Parliament. If enough people do this on a sustained basis, then these people will have to respect the wishes of their constituency voters or risk losing their seats at election time.

TOOLS AND EQUIPMENT

When there are only a few pot-plants to care for very few tools are necessary e.g., an old dinner fork will do to loosen and aerate the compost about plants and a pencil will do as a dibber to prick out the few seedlings. A larger range of tools and equipment become desirable as the indoor garden becomes more extensive, but they need not take up much space. A small kitchen-top unit will serve very nicely as a tool cupboard come compost store. The sorts of things you will need are as follows:

Scissors
Screwdriver
A sharp Pocket knife
Small Secateurs
Small Water Can with a thin spout
Small Mist-sprayer (1 pint/ 0.5 litre size)
Min/Max Thermometer
Small Dibber
Plant Labels
Note Pad and Pencil
Plastic bucket
Sellotape
Fine green plastic covered wire, and nylon thread
A small selection of bamboo canes
Green Split-canes
Green Twine
A dustpan and brush
A selection of plastic pots and containers
Seed/Potting Compost
Spare fluorescent lamps, spare starters, replacement fuses/fuse wire etc.
A Sponge
Cotton Wool
Garden trowel
Gloves
Insecticide
Leaf Shine
Liquid Fertilise
Methylated Spirit
Plastic Sheeting to protect carpets and furniture when working
Strips of artificial grass matting to hide plant-pots from view.

GLOSSARY

A commercial growing room. A room that provides the complete controlled plant environment for the commercial growing of plants. Akin to this, but more sophisticated, are the **Phytotrons,** and **Growth Chambers** used for scientific plant research at some universities and other leading agricultural/horticultural, and biological research stations, where the lighting and other growth related influences are fully controlled, both in quantity and quality, from day to day, and from moment to moment. Here the lighting may be required to provide illuminance levels up to the equivalent of summer sunlight-100'000 lux, and its spectral distribution must be adaptable to a variety of requirements.

Acclimatization. A plant's adjustment from one environment to another e.g., to cooler condition's when it is hardened off prior to being planted in the open garden during the summer months or lower light levels when it is prepared for growing as an indoor plant, e.g., some long term indoor foliage plants.

Active Growth Period. That measure of time within a twelve months period when a plant produces new shoots and leaves and increases in size. Flowers too may be in evidence, but not always. This active growth period need not necessarily coincide with the calendar year. The opposite of dormancy.

Aerial Root A root, which grows above ground level on the stem of a plant e.g. *Monstera deliciosa.*

Air Layering A method of propagation by which a plant is stimulated to form roots on stems or branches. This is particularly useful in dealing with plants that have grown too tall and leggy e.g., *Dracaena terminalis*, and *Ficus elastica.*

Annual. A plant that completes its life cycle within one year or less from germination.

Artificial Light Illumination from incandescent lamps, fluorescent lamps, and high-energy discharge lamps.

Automatic trickle irrigation An irrigation system comprising of a siphon tank, length of irrigation tubing and trickle irrigation nozzles which enables individual plants to receive just the right amount of water for their needs.

Bigeneric hybrid A hybrid plant resulting from the cross breeding between two plants of distinct genera but the same family e.g. X*Fatshedera lizei* is the result of a cross between *Fatsia japonica* and *Hedera helix*, Family *Araliaceae*. Many bigeneric hybrids are to be found in the orchid and bromelaid families.

Bolting The premature production of a flower stalk, particularly amongst some leafy vegetables e.g., lettuce.

Bract A modified leaf, which is often highly coloured, at the base of a flower e.g. *Anthurium scherzerianum*, and *Euphorbia pulcherrima* (Poinsettia).

Bulb A fleshy growth bud, consisting of a flattened and compressed base of a stem surrounded by many fleshy leaf bases containing stored food: these in turn are protected by papery outer scale leaves. In the centre of the bulb, is the main bud, containing next season's flower, and surrounded by next seasons foliage leaves e.g., narcissus, and tulip.

Cactus (plural Cacti) This is the common name that has been adopted for members of the family *Cactaceae*. All but a very few cacti are succulents, but not all succulents are cacti. While leaves appear in a few species most cacti are leafless stem succulents with the stem having taken on the function of the leaves. Many have spines and most of them are native to the desert regions of the world, where conservation of water is essential. Others are epiphytic cacti and dwell in forests.

Cambium (vascular) A thin layer of cells, between the xylem and phloem, that increases the girth of stems and roots. The existence of the cambium layer is important to vegetative propagation, as it is from this that a protective callus and then roots are formed, when stem cuttings are taken, and when root cuttings are taken, new shoots are formed.

Carbohydrate: This is an organic compound formed during the process of photosynthesis from carbon, hydrogen, and oxygen, e.g. starch and sugar.

Capillary matting. An absorbent felt matting, specifically formulated, to provide a constant supply of water to the base of pot-plants, which are stood upon its surface.

Capillary Watering A method of watering plants by placing a wick in the drainage hole of a pot whilst the other end is allowed to dangle into a container just below holding water.

Catch crop A crop which matures in a short period of time. In an indoor garden Mustard and Cress, and Radishes are good examples.

Cell The basic structure of all plant tissue, of whatever kind.

Chlorophyll A green pigment present in plants, which absorbs light in photosynthesis.

Chloroplasts Specialized microscopic components within green plant cells, which contain the chlorophyll.

Colour rendering The perceived colour of plants, people and furnishing under a particular electric lamp e.g., fluorescent lamp, incandescent lamp, etc., compared to their appearance in natural daylight.

Compensation point The light intensity at which a plant's photosynthesis and respiration are equal. The plant will be able to maintain itself for some time, and look attractive but, if more light is not provided, as the leaves grow old and are shed no new leaves will be produced, and the plant will die.

Conservatory A glass covered structure attached to a dwelling house, providing direct access from one of its rooms e.g. drawing room. The modern day variant is the home extension, which may or may not have large expanses of glass and serves as a garden room or simply provides additional living accommodation.

Corm The swollen base of a stem that acts as a storage organ, protected by a papery outer skin. A corm always has a bud at the top. Examples of these include crocus, freesia, and gladiolus.

Cortex The primary tissue of a stem or root between the vascular system and the epidermis.

Cristata. Literally of crested or cockscomb-like growth, e.g., *Celosia cristata* (flower) and *Pteris cretica cristata* (cockscomb-like leaflet tips).

Cultivar A cultivated variety of garden origin. A name used to describe a plant, which has come into being as a result of man's intervention in the plant kingdom. (See hybridization).

Cuticle The waxy impermeable outermost surface layer on the epidermis of a plant organ.

Cutting A piece of leaf, stem, or root, detached from a parent plant which is stimulated to form new roots and/or shoots and develop into a new plant.

Damping off. A pathogenic disorder causing seedlings to collapse and die shortly after germination.

Day length The number of hours of daylight in each 24 hour period.

Day-neutral plants Plants, the flowers of which are unaffected by photoperiodism, (day length) e.g., *Begonia* Semperflorens, *Browallia*, *Exacum*, and *Impatiens*.

Division An easy way of propagating clump-forming plants is by pulling or teasing their roots apart.

Dormancy This is a period of time when bulbs, corms, seeds, and tubers, are resting and there are no signs of visible activity. And a time too of inactivity during which other plants will not grow, regardless of how favourable the conditions, e.g. ornamental foliage plants. (See Rest Period**.)**

Drawn (see etiolated).

Epidermis The outermost layer of cells on plant organs e.g. stems, leaves, roots, flowers, fruit and seeds. The only area where this layer is not present is at the tips of the roots and shoots, as these are potentially involved in growth activities.

Epiphyte An air plant. A plant that grows upon another plant for support without establishing a parasitic relationship.

Etiolation A condition originating from growing plants in very poor light intensity or darkness. The resulting growth is weak, spindly, and lacking in chlorophyll.

Exotic In strict horticultural terms this word denotes a plant that is not native to the country in which it grows. But it is frequently used for unusual or showy tropical plants.

Family: In plant taxonomy, (the science dealing with the classification of plants) a major group of plants made up of one genus, or a number of genera, which have certain characteristics in common; for example, the BROMELIACEAE family.

Flower Forcing The process of encouraging a plant to grow and flower before its natural time to do so.

Fluorescent Lamp A low-pressure mercury discharge lamp, the inner surface of the glass envelope of which has a covering of phosphor. Light is generated when electricity is passed through the gas sealed within the tube.

Focal Point The position within a plantscape design, which stimulates the greatest attention. It can also be that position within the apartment, house or office, best suited to the introduction of a special feature for display e.g. a light garden, a water feature, or a fine specimen indoor tree, etc.

Foliage plants Plants grown more particularly for the colour, pattern, and texture of their foliage, than for any flowers, which they may bear.

Foot-candle (Fc) A unit of illumination equal to the light of one standard candle falling on a surface 1 foot away from the candle. 1 fc is the equivalent of 10.76 lux. (See Lux page 175).

Frond The leaf of a fern or a palm.

Fungus (plural fungi) A primitive form of plant life which lacks chlorophyll and cannot photosynthesize its' food. It therefore either lives on other plants and animals as parasites, or decaying matter as saprophytes.

Fungicide A chemical substance used to kill fungi or prevent fungus diseases of plants.

Genus (plural genera). A name which defines a group of plants with certain particular characteristics in common. (See Family page 173)

Germination Seed germination - that period when the resting embryo awakens and commences active growth and development, the first stage in the development of a seedling.

Glass substitutes Alternative transparent materials suitable for use indoors where the presence of children may require, for safety reasons, that the use of glass be avoided in the construction of propagation cases, orchid cases, etc., e.g. plastic film, polyvinyl chloride (PVC), acrylic, and polycarbonate.

Grana A series of green granules stacked up like plates within a chloroplast.

Growth The act of growing. The irreversible increase in cell size and/or cell multiplication.

Habit A word used to describe the characteristic form of growth of a plant-its physical appearance, e.g. erect, pendulous, prostrate, creeping, etc., etc.

Hardening off The gradual acclimatization of plants grown in warm equitable conditions, in the greenhouse, or garden room, in readiness for planting outdoors. This is particularly applicable to tender and half-hardy plants propagated indoors and destined for planting outside during the summer months.

Herbs. (a) Botanically any herbaceous plant. (b) Plants grown for their medicinal properties or for food seasoning.

Herbaceous. Any plant that does not develop woody stems. Such plants may be annual, biennial or perennial. Herbaceous is the opposite of shrubby.

Honeydew A sticky, sugary secretion which coats leaves and stems which is associated with sap sucking insects, such as aphids, and scale insects.

Hormone A chemical substance, synthesized in one part of a plant, which influences a growth response in another part. There are a number of different hormones present within a plant, and between them they control all aspects of growth, and development.

Houseplants Plants, which have been found adaptive to cultivation in the home or office environment. The numbers of such plants are on the increase, as more indoor gardeners turn their attention to gardening indoors with the aid of artificial light, and appreciate the potential this new technique offers them for the cultivation of plants indoors.

Humidity The amount of water vapour found in the air.

Hybridization The intentional cross between two parent plants. The resulting plant variation is a cultivar.

Hydroculture Growing plants in water containing all the mineral nutrients necessary for healthy balanced growth. This technique is also referred to as 'Hydroponics', and 'Soilless Cultivation'.

Hydroleca Lightweight expanded clay aggregate used in hydroculture as a medium for soilless cultivation. This absorbs moisture slowly when soaked, and releases it gradually.

Indigenous. Living naturally in a particular environment.

Inflorescence A term used to cover the flowering parts of plants e.g., panicle, raceme, spadix, spike, umbel, etc.

Insecticide Any chemical substance used to control insect pests.

Internode The area of stem between two nodes (leaf-joints).

Leggy Weak stemmed spindly plants with few leaves, (See Etiolation page 173).

Light Intensity Brightness of light.

Light Quality The spectral composition of light.

Liquid feed A dilute solution of fertiliser in water for feeding plants.

Long-Day Plants Plants, which flower when the days are lengthening, (nights are short) e.g., *Phlox, Rudbeckia, Scabious, Sedum.*

Lux The international unit of illumination. The amount of light impinging upon a surface one meter distant from a uniform point source of light from a candle. 1 Lux = 0.09 footcandle.

Microbe Any microscopic organism, e.g., bacteria, fungi, or virus.

Microclimate The atmospheric environmental conditions within the close vicinity of plants e.g., warmth and humidity of the air, additional to the general conditions prevailing in the room.

Mist propagation The application of water in the form of a fine mist to the leaves of cutting, to reduce transpiration, while rooting is taking place.

Morphology (plants) That branch of botany concerned with the form structure and development of plants.

Nanometre (nm) A unit of length equal to one millionth of a millimetre.

Natural Light Light from the sun.

Node The region on the stem where leaves, buds, or flowers are located.

Offset A young plantlet produced vegetatively close to the parent plant, and easily removed from this for propagation, *Bromeliads* and *Sansevieria* being good examples of such plants.

Osmunda fibre The roots of the Royal Fern *Osmunda regalis*, which are dried and chopped into pieces as a potting medium for orchids.

Parenchyma A tissue composed of thin-walled loosely packed, un-specialised cells.

Peat. Partially decayed plant material derived from vegetation in bogs, marshes, and heath-lands. Peat is a variable product depending upon its place of origin and that which is used for horticultural purposes consists of specially selected grades.

Pelleted seed. Seed coated with an inert substance to make it easier to handle when sowing.

Perlite Heat-expanded granules of volcanic rock, containing holes able to absorb air, and up to four times their own weight in water. Perlite is added to composts to increase aeration. (also to facilitate drainage.)

Petiole A leaf stalk.

Photoperiodism The response of plants to the changes in the length of the daily period of light and dark. See day neutral plants, long-day plants, and short-day plants.

Photosynthesis A process, which is unique to green plants. The manufacture of carbohydrates from carbon dioxide and water in the presence of chlorophyll and light energy, accompanied by the release of oxygen into the atmosphere.

Phylloclade A Plant whose flattened stems carry out the food manufacturing functions of leaves. They demonstrate that they are stems by bearing flowers. e.g., *Schlumbergera Xbuckleyi* (Christmas Cactus). Also sometimes known as Cladodes.

Pigment Molecules coloured by the light they absorb.

Plunging Burying a plant-pot up to it's rim, outdoors in soil, peat, or ashes.

Pot-bound A plant growing in a pot which has become too small for its' needs because its roots have completely filled the pot.

Pricking out The process of transferring seedlings from a seed tray, or seed pan, in which they were raised, into other pots or containers, so that they may have more room to grow.

Propagation The multiplication of plants by any appropriate means, e.g. seeds, cuttings, layering, air layering, division, offsets, etc.

Propagation case A special box-shaped structure, with either a glass or rigid clear plastic canopy, used for the propagation of plants from seeds and striking cuttings. They are designed for use either in a greenhouse or indoors.

Protoplasm The basis of all living matter - the essential viscous contents of plant cells, upon which all the vital functions for growth and reproduction depend. The main portion of the protoplasm is composed of <u>cytoplasm</u> a colourless liquid the other portion is the <u>nucleus</u>. Living protoplasm is an extremely complex substance both physically and chemically. It consists of 85% to 95% water, and 5% globular and fibrous proteins. And it represents something more than the sum of these substances, for therein lies the mystery of life!

Re-potting (Potting-on). The process of moving a pot-grown plant into a larger pot which will allow it to continue its' root development.

Respiration A continuous process in plants in which oxygen is absorbed from the atmosphere and used for the conversion of the carbohydrate, created by photosynthesis. Energy is released in this process and used in the synthesis of organic materials needed in plant growth. Carbon dioxide and water are given off as waste products.

Rest Period This is the period when little or no growth is to be detected and plants are said to be at rest. Even evergreen plants, shrubs, and trees, unless they come from the tropical rain forests and grow continuously, like to have a partial rest period with some reduction in watering and the withholding of liquid feed during the winter months. (See Dormancy)

Rhizome An underground stem lasting more than one season, which usually grows horizontally, and is distinguished from a root by the presence of nodes and internodes. It also bears scale-like leaves or buds capable of producing new shoots, and acts as a storage organ e.g., *Achimenes* x*hybrida* (Hot water plant, Magic flowers), and *Convallaria majalis* (Lily-of-the-valley).

Root That part of a plant usually below ground, which serves as anchorage for the plant and absorbs and conducts water, and dissolved mineral nutrients, to other parts of the plant where they are required. (See also epiphyte)

Root hair. A root hair in the vicinity of the root tip, which absorbs water, and mineral nutrients, from the soil is a single cell belonging to the epidermal cells of the root.

Sand Soil particles between 0.05mm (very fine) and 2.0mm (very coarse) in diameter, derived from rocks-useful in providing added aeration in seed and potting composts.

Setting, or **Set Fruit.** Said of flowers that have been pollinated and are starting to develop small fruit or seed pods.

Short-day plants Plants, which only produce flowers when the days are short (nights are long) e.g., *Chrysanthemum, Kalanchoe*, and *Schlumbergera*.

Spadix A fleshy spike of tiny flowers usually surrounded by a modified bract called a spathe e.g., *Anthurium, Spathyphyllum*.

Spathe A bract, sometimes highly coloured, which surrounds or encloses the spadix.

Species The fundamental unit of classification occurring below genus level used to designate groups of plants that can'be recognised as distinct kinds.

Sphagnum peat (moss peat). The dried and partially decayed remains of sphagnum moss, a very water retentive material with many uses e.g., lining hanging baskets, for making moss-poles for climbing indoor plants, used in orchid compost, etc.

Stomata (single stoma) The microscopic breathing pores in leaves by which gaseous interchanges, including water vapour, take place during the processes of photosynthesis and respiration.

Succulent A plant having fleshy leaves and/or stems for the storage of moisture in arid regions of the world e.g., *Crassula, Opuntia*.

Supplementary Lighting: Additional artificial light together with natural light to increase light intensity to that desired.

Systemic An insecticide which, when sprayed onto a plant, is absorbed and then travels to all parts of the plant, rendering it toxic to sap sucking insects. Generally longer lasting than a spray application would be

Taxonomy The science dealing with the classification of plants and animals.

Terrarium (Wardian Case) An enclosed glass case used to house a collection of indoor plants requiring high humidity.

Terrestrial Plants: Plants, which live on the ground (in the soil), as opposed to water (aquatics plants), and those growing on rocks and trees (epiphytic plants).

Translocation The movement of water, food materials, and hormones within a plant.

Transpiration The escape of water vapour from plants through the stomata of leaves, and its diffusion into the atmosphere.

Truss A compact cluster of flowers e.g. pelargonium, or fruits e.g., tomatoes arising from one centre.

Tuber An enlarged stem or root that is used by a plant as a food storage organ during a resting season e.g. *Begonia, Caladium, and Cyclamen.*

Variegated This is usually a term used in reference to the leaves of plants, where they are blotched and marked in two or more colours. It is usually confined to the presence of yellow, cream or white colorations on green leaves.

Variety A variation in a wild species that is so distinct it is given a name of its own. (See also Hybrid.)

Vascular System A system of tubes within a plant, which permit the movement of water, nutrients, manufactured foods and hormones.

SOME REVISION IN PLANT NOMENCLATURE
UNDERSTANDING PLANT NAMES (See pages 7-9)

The Latin plant names used in this book generally conform to those listed in **The New Royal Horticultural Society DICTIONARY OF GARDENING** published in the United Kingdom by THE MACMILLAN PRESS LIMITED, 1992 and published in the United States of America and Canada by THE STOCKTON PRESS, 1992.

Where some plant names of long horticultural usage have changed the following synonyms are provided to assist the reader:

Araucaria heterophylla, syn. *Araucaria excelsa*

Asparagus setaceus, syn. *Asparagus plumosus*

Brunfelsia pauciflora syn. *Brunfelsia calycina*

Caladium lindenii, syn. *Xanthosoma lindenii*

Calathea lancifolia, syn. *Calathea insignis*

Calathea rosea-picta, syn. *Maranta rosea-picta*

Callisia elegans, syn. *Setcreasea striata*

Catharanthus roseus syn. *Vinca roseus*

Ceropegia linearis syn. *Ceropegia woodii*

Cissus rhombifolia, syn. *Rhoicussus rhomboidea*

Cordyline stricta, syn. Cordyline congesta

Crassula ovata syn, *C. argentea*

Cryptanthus acaulis syn. *C. undulatus*

Ctenanthe amabilis, syn. *Stromanthe amabilis*

Dahlia hortensis syn. *Dahlia variabilis*

Dendranthema Xgrandiflorum syn. *Chrysanthemum morifolium*

Dieffenbachia maculata 'Tropic Snow', syn. *Dieffenbachia amoena* 'Tropic Snow'

Dorotheanthus bellidiformis, syn. *Mesembryanthemum criniflorum*

Dracaena reflexa, syn, *Pleomele reflexa*

Dracaena reflexa 'Variegata', syn. *Pleomele reflexa* 'Variegata')

Dracaena surculosa, syn. *Dracaena godseffiana*

Epipremnum aureum, syn, *Scindapsus aureus*

Fatsia japonica syn. *Aralia sieboldii*

Ficus elastica, syn. *F.Robusta*

Ficus sagittata, syn. *F radicans*

Geogenanthus poeppigii syn *Geogenanthus undatus*

Gynura procumbens, syn. *G. sarmentosa*

Hedera algeriensis 'Gloire de Marengo', syn. *Hedera.canariensis* 'Gloire de Marengo'

Hemigraphis alternata, syn. *Hemigraphis colorata* (Red Ivy)

Hylotelephium sieboldii 'Mediovariegatum', syn. *Sedum sieboldii* 'Mediovariegatum'

Hypoestes phyllostachya, syn. *Hypoestes, sanguinolenta*

Justicia brandegeana, syn. *Beloperona guttata*

Lobularia maritima syn. *Alyssum maritimum*

Nertera granadensis, syn. *Nertera depressa*

Nicotiana alata, syn. *Nicotiana affini*

Nolina recurvata, syn. *Beaucarnea recurvata*

Nopalxochia ackermannii 'Midnight', syn. *Epiphyllum ackermanii* 'Midnight'

Pellionia repens syn. *P daveauana*

Peperomia serpens 'Variegata', syn. *Peperomia scandens* 'Variegata'

Pericallis X*hybrida* 'Stella' syn. *Senecio cruentus* Cinareria 'Stella' (Florist's Cineraria)

Philodendron bipinnatifidum, 'German Selloum', syn. *Philodendron.selloum*

Philodendron melanochrysum, syn. *Philodendron andreanum*

Philodendron scandens, syn. *Philodendron. oxycardium*

Pisonia unbellifera, syn. *Pisonia alba*

Polyscias scutellaria "Balfourii,' syn. *P. balfouriana* (Dinner plate aralia)

Rhipsalis baccifera, syn. *Rhipsalis casssutha (Misletoe Cactus)*

Schefflera actinophylla, syn. *Brassaia actinophylla*

Schefflera elegantissima, syn. *Dizygotheca elegantissima*

Schlumbergera truncata syn. *Zygocactus truncata* (Thanksgiving Cactus)

Schlumbergera X*buckleyi*, syn. *Schlumbergera bridgesii* (Christmas Cactus)

Senecio cineraria 'Silver Dust,' syn., *Cineraria maritima*, 'Silver Dust'

Soleirolia soleirolii, syn. *Helxine soleirolii*

Solenostemon scutellarioides, syn. *Coleus blumei*

Stenocactus multicostatus syn. *Echinofossulocactus zacatecasensis* (Brain Cactus)

Syagrus cocoides, syn. *Cocos weddellii.* (Dwarf coconut palm)

Tagetes tenuifolia, syn. *Tagetes signata*, ('Signet Marigold')

Tradescantia pallida, syn. *Setcreasea purpurea.* 'Purple heart'

Tradescantia spathacea, syn. *Rhoeo discolor.*

INDEX OF POPULAR PLANT NAMES
Understanding plant names (See pages 7-9)

SOME COMMON NAMES OF EXOTIC PLANTS:
Common name - Botanical name:

Africian Violet - *Saintpaulia ionantha*.
Alpine violet – *Cyclamen persicum*
Aluminium Plant - *Pilea cadierei*
Amaryllis – *Hippeastrum*
Amazonian Zebra Plant - *Aechmea chantinii*
Angelwing begonia – *Begonia corallina*
Angel's Wings - *Caladium* hybrids
Areca palm - *Chrysalidocarpus lutescens*
Artillery Plant - *Pilea microphylla*
Asparagus Fern - *Asparagus densiflorus*
Baby's Tears- *Soleirolia soleirolii*
Bamboo palm - *Chamaedorea erumpens*
Barberton daisy - *Gerbera jamesonii*
Basket Grass - *Oplismenus hirtellus*
Beed plant – *Nertera granadensis*
Beefsteak plant, Bloodleaf – *Iresine herbstii*
Begonia Vine - *Cissus discolor*
Bird-Catcher Tree - *Pisonia unbellifera*
Bird of Paradise – *Strelitzia reginae*
Bird's Nest Fern - *Asplenium nidus*
Bird's Nest Bromeliad - *Nidularium innocentii*
Bishop's Cap - *Astrophytum myriostigma*
Black-eyed Suzie - *Thunbergia alata*
Black-Leaf Panamica - *Pilea repens*
Blue Flower Torch - *Tillandsia lindenii*
Blue Gum – *Eucalyptus globulus*
Blushing Bromeliad - *Neoregelia carolinae* 'Tricolor'
Blushing cup – *Nidularium fulgens*
Boat Lily – *Tradescantia spathacea*
Boston Fern - *Nephrolepis exaltata* 'Bostoniensis'
Brain Cactus - *Stenocactus multicostatus*
Broom - *Genista canariensis*
Bush Violet - *Browallia speciosa*
Busy Lizzie- *Impatiens* hybrids
Button fern – *Pellaea rotundifolia*
Cabbage Tree - *Cordyline australis*
Calamondin orange - X*Citrofortunella microcarpa*

Canary date palm - *Phoenix canariensis*
Cape Grape - *Rhoicissus capensis*
Cape Primrose – *Streptocarpus* X*hybridus*
Cast-Iron Plant - *Aspidistra elatior*
Celebes Pepper - *Piper ornatum*
Century Plant - *Agave americana*
Chain Cactus - *Rhipsalis paradoxa*
Chernille plant - *Acalypha hispida*
Chestnut Vine - *Tetrastigma voinierianum*
Chinese Evergreen - *Aglaonema species*
Chinese Fan Palm - *Livistona chinensis*
Christmas Cactus - *Schlumbergera* x*buckleyi*
Christmas Pepper – *Capsicum Annuum*
Climbing fig. Creeping fig - *Ficus pumila*
Cobweb Houseleek - *Sempervivum arachnoideum*
Coffee - *Coffea arabica*
Copper Leaf - *Acalypha wilkesiana*
Coralberry - *Ardisia crenata*
Coral Berry - *Aechmea fulgens* var. *discolor*
Corn Palm - *Dracaena fragrans*
Cotton Palm, Desert Fan Palm – *Washingtonia filifera*
Creeping Charlie - *Pilea nummularifolia*
Croton, Joseph's Coat - *Codiaeum variegatum* var. *pictum*
'Crown of Thorns' - *Euphorbia milii*
Crystal Anthurium - *Anthurium crystallinum*
Cupid's Bower, Hot Water Plant - *Achimenes*
Delta Maidenhair - *Adiantum raddianum*
Desert Privet - *Peperomia magnoliaefolia*
Devil's backbone - *Kalanchoe daigremontiana*
Devil' Ivy - *Epipremnum aureum*
Dinner plate aralia - *Polyscias scutellaria* 'Balfourii'
Donkey's Tail - *Sedum morganianum*
Dragon Tree – *Dracaena draco*
Dumb cane - *Dieffenbachia*
Dwarf coconut palm - *Syagrus cocoides*
Dwarf date palm - *Phoenix roebelinii*
Easter Cactus - *Hatiora gaertneri*
Elephant's-Ear Plant - *Alocasia* X*amazonica*
Emerald Ripple Pepper - *Peperomia caperata*
English Ivy - *Hedera helix*
Eyelash Begonia - *Begonia bowerae*
False aralia - *Schefflera elegantissima*
Fan Palm – *Trachycarpus fortunei*

Feather Fern - *Nephrolepis exaltata* 'Fluffy Ruffles'
Fern-leaf aralia - *Polyscias filicifolia*
Fiddle Leaf Fig - *Ficus lyrata*
Firecracker-flower – *Crossandra infundibuliformis*
Fishtail Palm - *Caryota mitis*
Flame Nettle - *Solenostemon scutellarioides*, syn. *Coleus blumei*
Flame Violet - *Episcia cupreata*
Flaming Katy – *Kalanchoe blossfeldiana*
Flaming Sword - *Vriesea splendens*
Flamingo Flower, Flamingo Plant - *Anthurium scherzerianum*
Florists Chrysanthemum - *Dendranthema Xgrandiflorum*
Florist's Cineraria- *Pericallis Xhybrida*
Florist's Gloxinia - *Sinningia species*
Flowering tobacco - *Nicotiana alata*
Friendship Plant - *Pilea involucrata*
Frosted Sonerila - *Sonerila margaritaceae*
Giant caladium - *Alocasia cuprea*
Glory of the Snow – *Chionodoxa luciliae*
Gold-dust dracaena – *Dracaena surculosa*
Goldfish vine - *Columnea microphylla*
Golden Sedum - *Sedum adolphii*
Goose Foot Plant - *Syngonium podophyllum*
Grape Ivy - *Cissus rhombifolia*
Green Marble Vine - *Senecio herreianus*
Heart-Leaf Philodendron - *Philodendron melanochrysum*
Hedgehog Aloe - *Aloe humilis*
Hens & Chickens - *Sempervivum tectorom*
House Lime - *Sparmannia africana*
Iron Cross - Begonia - *Begonia masoniana*
Ivy Tree - X*Fatshedera lizei*
Ivy-leaved Geranium - *Pelargonium peltatum*
Ivory Pineapple - *Ananas comosus* 'Variegatus'
Jade Plant - *Crassula ovata*
Japanese aralia - *Fatsia japonica*
Japanese Stonecrop - *Hylotelephium sieboldii* 'Mediovariegatum'
Japanese yew - *Podocarpus macrophyllus*
Jelly Bean Plant - *Sedum rubrotinctum*
Kaffir Lily - *Clivia miniata*
Kangaroo Vine - *Cissus antarctica*
Kentia palm - *Howea forsteriana*
Kimberley queen fern – *Nephrolepis obliterata*
King Sago - *Cycas revolute*
Lacy Tree Philodendron - *Philodendron bipinnatifidum*

Lady's eardrops - *Fuchsia*
Lady Palm - *Rhapis excelsa*
Lemon-scented Geranium - *Pelargonium crispum* 'Variegatum'
Lily of the Valley - *Convallaria majalis*
Lipstick Vine – *Aeschynanthus lobbianus* italics
Livingstone Daisies - *Dorotheanthus bellidiformis*
Madagascar Dragon Tree – *Dracaena marginata*
Madagascar Periwinkle - *Catharanthus roseus*
Maidenhair Fern - *Adiantum tenerum*
Medicine plant - *Aloe vera*
Mexican Snowball - *Echeveria elegans*
Ming aralia - *Polyscias fruticosa*
Mistletoe fig - *Ficus deltoidea*
Mock Orange – *Pittosporum tobira*
Monkey Plant – *Ruellia makoyana*
Moses-in-the-cradle - *Tradescantia spathacea*
Mother-in-law's Tongue - *Sansevieria trifasciata*
Mother of Thousands - *Saxifraga stolonifera*
Mother Spleenwort - *Asplenium bulbiferum*
Never - Never - Plant - *Ctenanthe oppenheimiana*
Norfolk Island pine - *Araucaria heterophylla*
Oakleaf Ivy – *Cissus rhombifolia* 'Ellen Danica'
Old Man Cactus - *Cephalocereus senilis*
Orange Star - *Guzmania lingulata* 'Minor Orange'
Painted Net Leaf - *Fittonia verschaffeltii*
Painted Tongue - *Salpiglossis sinuata*
Painter's Palette - *Anthurium andraeanum*
Panda plant - *Kalanchoe tomentosa*
Pansy Orchid – *Miltonia*
Parasol Plant - *Schefflera arboricola*
Parlour Maple - *Abutilon pictum* 'Thompsonii'
Parlour palm - *Chamaedorea elegans*
Partridge Breast Aloe - *Aloe variegata*
Peanut Cactus - *Echinopsis chamaecereus*
Peace Lily - *Spathiphyllum* cultivars
Peacock Plant - *Calathea makoyana*
Persian Sheild - *Strobilanthes dyerianus*
Persian Violet - *Exacum affine*
Piggyback Plant - *Tolmiea menziesii*
Pincushion Cactus - *Mammillaria zeilmanniana*
Pink Quill - *Tillandsia. cyanea*
Plume Asparagus – *Asparagus densiflorus* 'Myers'
Poinsettia – *Euphorbia pulcherrima*

Polka dot plant; Freckle face - *Hypoestes phyllostachya*
Pony Tail - *Nolina recurvata*
Poor Man's Orchid, Butterfly Flower - *Schizanthus*
Prayer Plant - *Maranta leuconeura* var. *kerchoveana*
Purple Heart - *Tradescantia pallida*
Purple Passion Vine - *Gynura procumbens*
Queen's Tears – *Billbergia nutans*
Rats-Tail Cactus - Aporocactus flagelliformis
Rattlesnake Plant – *Calathea lancifolia*
Rex Begonia - *Begonia* Rex – Cultorum Hybrids
Rex Begonia Vine – *Cissus discolor*
Red Ivy - *Hemigraphis alternata*
Red-Leaf Philodendron - *Philodendron erubescens* 'Red Emerald'
Reed palm - *Chamaedorea seifrizii*
Ribbon Fern - *Pteris cretica*
Ribbon plant - *Dracaena sanderiana*
Rosary Vine - *Ceropegia linearis*
Rose of China – *Hibiscus rosa-sinensis*
Rosy Maidenhair Fern - *Adiantum hispidulum*
Rubber Plant - *Ficus elastica*
Satin Potho - *Scindapsus pictus* 'Argyraeus'
Scarlet-sage - *Salvia splendens*
Screw Pine - *Pandanus veitchii*
Sensitive Plant - *Mimosa pudica*
Seersucker plant – *Geogenanthus poeppigii*
Shrimp Plant - *Justicia brandegeana*
Sicklethorn - *Asparagus falcatus*
Signet Marigold - *Tagetes tenuifolia*
Silk Oak - *Grevillea robusta*
Silver Lace Fern - *Pteris ensiformis* 'Victoriae'
Slipper Flower – *Calceolaria herbeohybrida*
Slipper Orchid – *Paphiopedilum*
Snapdragon - *Antirrhinum majus*
Song of India - *Dracaena reflexa*
Spade-Leaf Philodendron - *Philodendron domesticum*
Spanish Bayonet - *Yucca aloifolia*
Spider plant - *Chlorophytum comosum* 'Vittatum'
Spineless Yucca - *Yucca elephantipes*
Stag's Horn Fern - *Platycerium bifurcatum*
String of Beads – *Senecio rowleyanus*
String of buttons - *Crassula perforata*
Striped Inch Plant - *Callisia elegans*
Sweet Alyssum – *Lobularia maritima*

Sweat Plant – *Selaginella pallescens*
Sweetheart Plant - *Philodendron scandens*
Swiss Cheese Plant - *Monstera deliciosa*
Sword Fern - *Nephrolepis exaltata*
Teddy Bear Vine - *Cyanotis kewensis*
Thanksgiving Cactus - *Schlumbergera truncata*
Thread Agave - *Agave filifera*
Tiger Orchid - *Odontoglossum*
Ti plant - *Cordyline terminalis*
Trailing Fig - *Ficus sagittata*
Trailing Watermelon Begonia – *Pellionia repens*
Trembling Fern - *Pteris tremula*
Tropical Tree opuntia - *Opuntia brasiliensis*
Trout Begonia - *Begonia* X*argenteo-guttata*
Tsusina Holly Fern - *Polystichum tsussimense*
Umbrella Plant - *Cyperus alternifolius*
Umbrella Tree - *Schefflera actinophylla*
Urn plant - *Aechmea fasciata*
Velvet Leaf - *Kalanchoe beharensis*
Wandering Jew - *Tradescantia fluminensis*
Watermelon pepper - *Peperomia argyreia*
Wax Begonia - *Begonia* Semperflorens-Cultorum Hybrids
Wax Flower – *Stephanotis floribunda*
Wax plant - *Hoya carnosa*
Wax Vine – *Senecio macroglossus*
Weeping fig - *Ficus benjamina*
White edged Swedish ivy - *Plectranthus forsteri* 'Marginatus'
Windmill Palm – *Trachycarpus fortunei*
Winter Aconite – *Eranthis hyemalis*
Winter Cherry – *Solanum capsicastrum*
Yesterday - Today - and - Tomorrow – *Brunfelsia pauciflora*
Zebra Plant - *Aphelandra squarrosa*
Zebra Plant - *Cryptanthus zonatus*

THE MIRACLE OF THE GREEN LEAF

Photosynthesis and the flourishing Earth

Plant life on the Earth is crucial to the survival of all animal life, as we know it today. It is entirely dependent upon the miracle of the green leaf or more precisely, the green pigment chlorophyll within the leaves and in some green-stemmed plants. This is the vital link between the Sun and life on Earth. This is what maintains the thin veneer of an Earth's atmosphere in the midst of a hostile universe. (See page 12).

The leaves of plants act as the sole channel for the reception and trapping of the sunlight energy (particles of light called **photons**) that powers the Earth; and the magnitude of all this photosynthetic process each year is stupendous! It is estimated to create some 243 billion metric tons of dry plant matter, to release 238 billion metric tons of oxygen into the atmosphere and to remove 3 billion metric tons of carbon dioxide. The total of all the industrial productive capacity of the Earth each year is as nothing, when it is compared to that of the sheer enormity of this photosynthetic process.

Plants convert the Sun's energy into food, fuel and shelter for the rest of creation. They provide us with cotton, dyes, fabric, fodder, food, fuel, oils, paper, wood and timber products, and a great many other commodities too.

Plants are an important source of many of our medicines, drugs and pesticides*, and every time a plant species is lost forever through the destruction of the rain forests, we put our health at risk.

Plants cleanse the Earth of the increasing quantities of man-made pollutants in the air, in the soil and in the water.

Plants both interact with the weather and have some influence upon the weather patterns and climate.

To survive on Earth we have to work with nature-we have to protect our natural environment. The consequences for mankind if we fail to do this will be disastrous.

The old adage that "All flesh is grass," is well-founded, provided that the word 'grass' is taken as meaning green plants; for while many animals ourselves included do not eat 'grass' they do feed on animals that do e.g. cattle and sheep.

* Some examples of plants important as sources of medicines, drugs and pesticides:

Aspirin is derived from the bark of the willow and is used for the relief of pain and the reduction of fever.

Atropine is an alkaloid derived from *Atropa belladonna*. This relaxes the gastro-intestinal tract-affects parasympathetic nervous system.

Cocaine is an alkaloid extracted from the leaves of *Erythroxydon coca (the coca plant)*

Colchicine is an alkaloid derived from *Colchicum autumnale,* (the autumn crocus). This induces chromosome doubling and relieves gout symptoms.

Derris is an insecticide derived from the swollen roots of *Derris elliptica*

Digitalis is derived from the dried leaves of *Digitalis purpurea* (the purple foxglove) and is used in the treatment of certain heart conditions.

Hydrasine is derived from *Hydrastis canadensis* – antihemorrhagic.

Nicotine is an insecticide derived from *Nicotiana tabacum.*

The latex of the opium poppy *Papaver somniferum* contains the drug opium, and its alkaloids morphine, codeine and heroin.

Quinine is an alkaloid derived from the *Chinchona succirubra*. This is an antimalarial medicine also a cardiac depressant.

Reserpine is an alkaloid derived from *Rauwolf serpentia* used as a tranquillizer, and for the treatment of high blood pressure.

Strychnine is an alkaloid obtained from the wood and bark of *Strychnos nux-vomica*. Poison, stimulates the central nervous system.

Taxol an alkaloid derived from *Taxus brevifolia* (The Pacific Yew) and it is used for the treatment of ovarian, colon and skin cancer.

Vinblastine and Vincristine are alkaloids derived from *Catharathus roseus* used to retard leukaemia.